D0206277

NATIVE LITERATURE

N CANADA

om the Oral Tradition
the Present

PENNY PETRONE

NATIVE LITERATURE IN CANADA
From the Oral Tradition to the Present

NATIVE LITERATURE IN CANADA

From the Oral Tradition to the Present

PENNY PETRONE

Toronto OXFORD UNIVERSITY PRESS 1990

Oxford University Press, 70 Wynford Drive, Don Mills, Ontario, M3C 1J9

Toronto   Oxford   New York   Delhi   Bombay   Calcutta   Madras   Karachi
Petaling Jaya   Singapore   Hong Kong   Tokyo   Nairobi   Dar es Salaam
Cape Town   Melbourne   Auckland

and associated companies in
Berlin   Ibadan

PM
238
P4
1990

ROBERT MANNING
STROZIER LIBRARY,

OCT 25 1991

Tallahassee, Florida

CANADIAN CATALOGUING IN PUBLICATION DATA
Petrone, Penny.
Native literature in Canada
Includes bibliographical references.
ISBN 0-19-540796-2
1. Canadian literature (English) — Indian authors — History and criticism.*
2. Canadian literature (English) — Métis authors — History and criticism.*   I. Title.
PS8089.5.I5P4 1990   C810.9'897   C90-094762-4
PR9188.2.I5P4 1990

Copyright © Oxford University Press Canada 1990
OXFORD is a trademark of Oxford University Press
1 2 3 4 – 3 2 1 0
Printed in Canada by Metrolitho Inc.

Contents

THE

ILLUSTRATIONS

APPEAR

BETWEEN

PAGES

70 AND 71

AND BETWEEN

PAGES

136 AND 137

Preface

Over the past two decades the trickle of writing by native Canadians has become a flood as more and more natives have found their voice and achieved publication of fiction, drama, poetry, memoirs, and journalism, recording the multitude of problems that have affected them in their place and time and revealing a distinct Indian aesthetic in drawing on the narrative and lyrical traditions of their past. As a literature grounded in the political and social realities of life on Canada's reserves and in its urban centres, while also being rooted in oral tribal traditions, it reveals a continuum of the ancient and the modern that is complex because it is coloured by several stages in the development of writing in English. But it exemplifies a rich tradition, and the time has come to study it in a historical perspective—examining all that preceded it—and to discern significant patterns and directions.

This book traces the long development of Indian and Métis literature in Canada and attempts to interpret the aesthetic dimensions of native sensibilities. Some works do not conform to Western structural conventions and notions of what is literary, but all forms of verbal expression discussed are important because, among other things, they put us in touch with a tradition that prized eloquence and that offers intimate glimpses into suffering and protest, aspirations and visions—universalities that have been particularized within a native consciousness. Over many years of teaching, my native students have made me realize the need for such a book, and to a large degree have influenced my choice of works to feature.

I wish to acknowledge gratefully the assistance provided by Lakehead University in helping to defray the research and typing costs, and to thank Sheila Wilson, my typist, who worked far beyond the call of duty. I should also like to thank all the writers who gave me permission to use their works in my discussions, and Daniel David Moses, Lenore Keeshig-Tobias, Cat Cayuga, Duke Redbird, Marie Annharte Baker, and Tom King, who, in my conversations with them, helped me sharpen my thinking. To William Toye, my editor, I am particularly indebted.

Thunder Bay, Ont.   PENNY PETRONE
July 1990

Introduction

The study of the vast and rich body of the literature of the native people of Canada has been too long neglected and ignored. Whether it has been the oral literature that transcends the European concepts of genre, or the written literature that spans a wide range of genres— speeches, letters, sermons, reports, petitions, diary entries, essays, history, journals, autobiography, poetry, short stories, and novels— very few literary scholars are familiar with it. There are at least five reasons for this neglect: European cultural arrogance, and attitudes of cultural imperialism and paternalism that initiated and fostered patronizing stereotypes of the Indian; European antipathy and prejudice towards the oral literatures of so-called primitive peoples; the European belief that the Indian was a vanishing race; the purist attitude of Western literary critics towards literature that does not conform totally to their aesthetic criteria; and, finally, the difficult problems of translating native literature.

The inhabitants of the New World—whom Columbus had called Indians, on the false assumption that he had reached India—puzzled the Europeans. The natives posed serious challenges to traditional authority: that of Aristotle and the ancients, the Bible, and the Church fathers. These people of the New World seemed to have no definite place in the Renaissance world picture. The popes, however, issued many bulls declaring that Indians were truly men and condemning their enslavement or ill-treatment. For example, Pope Paul III issued a *Pastorale Officium*, dated 29 May 1537, which declared 'that it was heresy to say that they were irrational and incapable of conversion.'[1] But this did not impress the early European arrivals in North America, who carried their old ethnocentric prejudices with

1

them. Europeans of the Renaissance—the age of Individualism—were not concerned with distinguishing one Indian from another. Indians were comprehended either in the negative and unflattering image of 'sauvage', or in the romanticized image of primeval innocence—the 'bon sauvage', a Rousseauesque pure being. Both were self-serving images—ideological weapons in the Indians' subjugation that obscured their true identity. Sixteenth-century Englishmen assumed that Indians were wild and animal-like, as they appeared in Edmund Spenser; it was this view that produced Shakespeare's Caliban. Throughout the Renaissance (the age of a new belief in the dignity and worth of the human being), the ages of Reason and Enlightenment, and the Victorian age, the age of Evangelical Protestantism, Europeans over the centuries exploited a progression of stereotypes to define the native people of the New World in order to explain and excuse their own vested purposes. (Even the new and overwhelming spirits of the Revolutions—Industrial, French, and American—could not alter the disparaging and demeaning stereotypes.) During the nineteenth century the Indian was seen as the simple silent child of nature just a little above the anthropoids, whom the blessings of civilization and Christianity could raise to a respectable level. When these 'blessings' did not prove too successful, the Indians were seen as a social nuisance, blocking progress and impossible to civilize. More recently the stereotypes have settled either on the welfare bum or on the tragic victim debased by the alcohol, disease, and treatment of the whites.

As late as the 1930s it was assumed that Canada's Indians would become extinct. In his *Indians of Canada* (1932) Diamond Jenness wrote: 'Doubtless all the tribes will disappear. Some will endure only a few years longer; others, like the Eskimo, may last several centuries.'[2] Indeed, some native religions, languages, and even whole tribal cultures were forgotten, or disappeared altogether. The theme 'Lo, the poor Indian' was expressed by poets, historians, and politicians alike. And the Indians stoically accepted their fate. From the mid-nineteenth century onward, Canadian politicians regarded the Indians in the settlement areas as 'foreigners', to be civilized. Civilization was possible only through Christianity and assimilation eventually into the dominant white mainstream. (There were even some Canadians who believed that the Indians were a degraded and hopeless race, incapable of any mental progress, and possessed of so little that was human that even compassion was wasted on them.) Elements of Spenserian and Darwinian theory, moreover, explained and excused the phenomenon whereby one civilization could subjugate another. The notion of manifest destiny, furthermore, strengthened the concept of white dominion.

The 'doomed culture theory' of the nineteenth century—the belief that the race would disappear, die out, or become assimilated—prevailed until the middle of the twentieth century. Instead of disappearing, however, Canada's Indians are now increasing at a faster rate than the general population. Since the 1950s Canadians have been becoming more and more aware of contemporary native concerns, with changes in public attitudes and a policy of multiculturalism. In 1982 the native peoples of Canada won formal recognition in Canada's new constitution. Young educated Indians are leading their peoples to demand hard-earned and much-needed reforms.

The 'purist' attitudes of literary critics in North America have hampered serious critical study of native literatures. Indeed, the history of native literatures has been plagued by this cultural chauvinism. In the days of first contact the literature was simply ignored; later, brief excerpts were randomly recorded in bits and pieces as art objects, novelties to illustrate the Indians' amazing use of pathos, irony, or wit; still later it was collected merely for antiquarian reasons or as quaint relics of a dying race. Paternalistic and/or romantic attitudes towards the literary accomplishments of simple children have prevailed. In the early years of the twentieth century and onward, the Hollywood image of the silent Indian occasionally expressing himself in grunts, in monosyllabic sounds of an alien tongue, or in simple utterances in English, only helped to entrench these attitudes.

Although the stereotypes of the past are fading now, they are so deeply rooted that they continue to haunt us still. They have perpetuated, through the centuries, a negative psychological orientation that has erected a barrier to giving the intelligence of Indians, their culture, and their spiritual and aesthetic values the respect and understanding they deserve.

As Canada's native peoples were originally not literate, their literature was, perforce, oral. Historically the oral literature of aboriginal peoples everywhere has been deemed inferior by literate western societies not only because it was unwritten, but also because it was not understood properly. The highly developed and extensive body of native Canadian oral literature was no exception.

It was misunderstood because, although it did not conform to the conventions of Western literary criticism, scholars still treated it as Western literature. The oral literature of Canada's native peoples embraces formal narrative, informal storytelling as well as political discourse, song, and prayer. Much of this literary expression was didactic in nature, communicating the respective histories and rules of belief and behaviour of the diverse tribes, and perpetuating their specific world views that gave the cosmos its origin, order, and meaning. It bound 'the sacred and the profane, the individual and the tribal, the past, present, and future, and it encompasse[d] the teller, the listener, the tribe, and the land, and the universe.'[3] By transmitting specific cultural knowledge, with its specific meanings and messages, it helped strengthen tribal identity and provided for its continuity.

Western readers are prone to view non-Western literatures in terms with which they are familiar, however irrelevant those may be to them, and have therefore called traditional North American Indian literatures 'primitive', 'pagan', 'savage', and 'childlike'. At best they were relegated to folklore studies or specialized ethnographies. Such has been the fate of the oral traditions of Canadian Indians, which have been studied by scholars under the rubric of anthropology, ethnology, folklore, or linguistics. Their concern was largely the information or data that Indians, as subjects of observation, yielded for their particular thematic studies and narrow focus. And although such distinguished specialists as Franz Boas (1858-1942), Diamond Jenness (1886-1969), and Marius Barbeau (1883-1969), collected and recorded a considerable body of Indian oral material that might have been lost forever without their efforts, they evaluated it from the point of view of their own academic disciplines. Deemed unimportant and inappropriate for literary scholarship, Canadian Indian literature has gone largely unrecognized and neglected until recently, when white prejudice and ignorance regarding oral literature and the Indian people respectively have undergone a drastic alteration.

The term oral literature was once considered to be a contradiction in terms, in the belief that literature applied only to material that could be read, that belonged to a condition of literacy. In recent years much work has been done by American scholars to recognize traditional oral material as literature. Karl Kroeber, Dell Hymes, Jarold W. Ramsey, Alan Dundes, and Dennis Tedlock have shown, each from his particular perspective, that the oral traditions of North American Indians are as intricate and meaningful as written tradition, and that they are not simply a less-polished, more haphazard or cruder form of literature. According to Karl Kroeber, 'one should begin by assuming that an Indian oral narrative may be a first rate work of art. One must abandon the misconception that this literature is "primitive". It is not.'[4] He admits, however, that it is difficult, that it raises troubling problems, and that it needs sophisticated critical attention—but that an intense analysis will be worth the trouble.

The primary role of oral literature was utilitarian and functional rather than aesthetic. And according to the native critic George L. Cornell, 'the complicated cultural complex of indigenous ideas, socio-political thought and action, celebration, and spirituality is consequently subordinated to formulated treatment.'[5] Yet its aim was to communicate to one another, and/or to powerful spirits. To this end it was necessary to communicate effectively. Thus one finds a number of literary devices—including figurative language, analogy, parallelism, symbolism, and allegory—to clarify understanding and enrich appreciation. However, this craft, or artful manipulation, was considered secondary to the content or text of the oral expression. Indian oral literature was not art for art's sake. As a result, the study of indigenous oral literature posed a problem for Western scholars who, trained in European critical traditions, worked in accordance with different aesthetic assumptions and narrative structures.

In the growing movement today among American scholars to treat Indian oral traditions as literature, and the recent debate regarding their interpretation and literary treatment, American native critics such as Paula Gunn Allen and George Cornell object to the imposition of the structures and criticism of Western literature upon native oral traditions.

It is frequently contended that Indian writings do not fit the criteria that govern the literary genres of the Western tradition. As a consequence they appear confused and quaint, or obscure and turgid, and unworthy of serious critical attention. However, context is important to understanding Indian stories, and for Indian writers that context is both ritualistic and historical, contemporary and ancient. The various genres as non-natives perceive them may seem to be violated by Indian narratives that combine myth with personal and communal experiences and even 'how to' essays. As Paula Gunn Allen explains: 'What has been experienced over the ages mystically and communally—with individual experiences fitting within that overarching pattern . . . forms the basis for tribal aesthetics and therefore of tribal literatures.'[6] It becomes clear, therefore, that oral literatures must be approached from the religious, social, and literary traditions that influence them.

The foremost Ojibway translator and short-story writer Basil H. Johnston objects to the translations by white anthropologists and ethnologists unless they have learned the particular language exceedingly well. For instance, he disapproves of the universal translation of the Ojibway word 'Manitou' as 'the Great Spirit' when it really means 'the Great Mystery'. The word is rich in connotative meanings: 'Manitou' also suggests 'substance', 'essence', potentiality', even 'talent', each meaning determined by the specific context. Canada's native languages contain many problems of meaning, sometimes arising from their agglutinative and holophrastic nature; the great differences of style, syntax, structure, and function; and the inappropriateness of European turns of phrase. Finally the subtleties—rhythm, nuance, and ambiguity—are difficult to capture, as they are in any foreign language. Each linguistic native group has acquired, over a long history, its own peculiar way of expressing itself, and this diversity has complex origins in climatic and geographical differences, cultural environment, group configuration, and individual disposition. As Jeffrey F. Huntsman writes:

> The inherent differences between languages, combined with symbolism, figurative or metaphoric bendings of ordinary language, secret or esoteric linguistic formulations, and fossils of an earlier, now-archaic diction, all contribute to a maddening Arabesque of many varieties of meaning that only the most perceptive and careful translator should confront.[7]

Since oral confrontation created divisiveness that was detrimental to the welfare of the tribe, native orators rarely put their speeches to this use. The purpose of their orations was agreement, persuasion, and devices such as allegory, symbolism, and figurative language were frequently employed to facilitate this end by creating a distance between orator and listener. By addressing concerns in abstract terms and in analogy, personal insult or injury could be alleviated. Native listeners understood this style of oral communication, but non-natives frequently missed the important connotations.

Ironically, those very literary qualities—the use of figurative language, of symbol and allegory—at which the Indians excelled were often the sources of difficulties. In the late seventeenth century Father Chrestien Le Clercq recognized this problem:

> Metaphor is largely in use among these Peoples; unless you accustom yourself to it, you will understand nothing in their councils where they speak almost entirely in metaphors.[8]

The well-meaning interpretations of non-natives led to words and phrases being mistranslated, lost, substituted, or deliberately distorted to fit some preconceived image or the ethos of the times. For instance French missionaries exaggerated the Christian piety of the natives, and the French soldier-iconoclast, Baron de La Hontan, conveyed an anti-clerical bias. Nineteenth-century pioneers in Indian studies from Henry Rowe Schoolcraft to Silas Rand reshaped the stories and songs they recorded to suit the sentimental and romantic style popular in their day.

Although any lexical or literal translation—strict word-for-word translation in interlinear style often found in the renditions of social scientists—is unsatisfactory, too much intervention of freedom, while it may achieve a certain literary flavour, may also seriously impair the meaning and significance of the original. There is no doubt that a certain creative element has to enter the translation process, for if translation is not in some respects creative, it is then merely recreative work, with meaning and significance becoming blunted, obscured, or lost. In translating a narrative or song, for example, the translator must consider not only linguistic fidelity but also the connotative and denotative meanings of words and the cultural matrix informed by the attitudes, beliefs, and customs of the tribe of which the original is an organic part. Quite apart from the abilities of the translator and his or her degree of familiarity with Indian languages and cultures, a translation can be coloured by personality, taste, purpose, and bias. There is no doubt that the reader is at the mercy of the translator.

Can the translator ever accurately reproduce on the printed page an oral literature that depends so much on performance? Is it possible for the translated song/poem, chant or prayer, for example, to hold the same power that it was supposed to have for the original singer? Probably not. The translation risks are so many that one is apt to question not only the accuracy and quality of translation but also the validity of the entire translation process. One can only guess what subtleties of thought and style have been lost through translation.

What are needed today are gifted and trained scholar/poet/translators who are not only completely bilingual in English and an Indian language but are also familiar with specific cultural contexts for the retranslation of texts from the *Jesuit Relations* to the present and for the translation of a large body of manuscript texts that lie buried in repositories across Canada. One can only imagine what would then be made available in quantity and in linguistic accuracy as well as sensitivity to style and aesthetic form. The task is great. But significant new discoveries await their efforts.

This book is a history of the literary achievements of Canada's native peoples excluding the Inuit, and (with a few exceptions) Indians writing in French, because an adequate study of their tradition and writings would require books of their own. (I have included all Indians, whether status or non-status or Métis—a reference to any mixed bloods, whether or not their background is part French.) I have tried to show how their literature fits into a historical context, how it reflects the times in which it was spoken or written, and something of the beliefs, the spiritual elements, and imagination that created it. My focus is therefore historical and cultural rather than purely aesthetic, though I have offered critical commentary on a number of works that deserve attention because of their subject matter, thought, form, or their use of language, imagery, and symbolism. I present the literature not as quaint relics or ethnic curiosities but as a significant cultural manifestation that is both unique and universal. In tracing a continuity through its various historical stages beginning with the traditional, through its transitional and modern stages, I have endeavoured to reveal a richness and complexity that are worthy of serious and enlightening examination. As an attempt to correct the neglect that has plagued the literature of Canada's native peoples, this study—the first of its kind—is exploratory and tentative; it would be presumptuous to consider it definitive or exhaustive. A great deal remains to be done in the study of native literature in Canada. I sincerely hope that this pioneering work will be followed by others, written by natives and non-natives alike who, with a sensitive awareness of native texts, will bring to a new level of scholarship the study and appreciation of native Canadian literature.

I

Oral Literatures

Long before Europeans came to Canada, even long after their arrival, the natives of Canada had an oral literature that had been transmitted by word of mouth from generation to generation through story-telling, song, and public ceremony, which itself involves oration and song.

Canada's Indian peoples, however, do not share a common literary heritage. Tribal literatures are culturally specific to each of the five cultural groups in Canada—Eastern Woodlands, Plains, Plateau, sub-Arctic, and Northwest Coast, where over fifty languages, derived from ten basic language families, are spoken. Their oral cultures reflect this great diversity in their histories and literatures.

The culture inherited by any group of people is more accurately determined by its language than by any other media known. No society can be more advanced or complex than its members have language to express. Indian languages are remarkable for their complexity of structure and the precision with which they can be used.

The nineteenth-century Ojibway, George Copway, the first Canadian Indian to publish a book in English, wrote: 'I cannot express fully the beauty of the language, I can only refer to those who have studied it as well as other languages, and quote their own writing in saying, "every word has its appropriate meaning, and with additional syllables give additional force to the meanest of most words." '[1]

Central to the ancient oral traditions was the power of the *word*, spoken, intoned, or sung. Whether Cree or Ojibway, Iroquois or Mic-mac, Haida, Tlinglit, or Hare, Loucheux or Montagnais, each in story, speech, or song made the *word* sacrosanct—of far greater importance than people in literate cultures were generally aware of. The *word* carried the power to create, to make things happen—medicine to heal, plants to grow, animals to be caught, and human beings to enter the spiritual world. Through this sacred power of the *word*, aboriginals sought to shape and control the cosmic forces that governed their lives. Such power is not attributed to the spoken word in literate societies, where attempts to change the physical world through language are regarded as magic, as 'hocus-pocus'.

Words did not merely represent meaning. They possessed the power to change reality itself. They were 'life, substance, reality. The word lived before earth, sun, or moon came into existence.'[2] For a people who carried their history in the spoken word and incorporated their values in story and song, it was only natural for them to invest words with power and reverence. They relied on the ability to use and manipulate language—the fluent and artful use of words—to influence not only other people but also spirits. Indeed, these skills were as vital to success as a hunter's skill and strength. Although they employed a few mnemonic devices—wampum belts and strings, board plates or bundles of notched sticks—these were no substitute for words. Europeans who had contact with the Indians marvelled that a people who knew neither the wheel nor writing knew well the power of the word.

NARRATIVE

Canada's native people have created a vast and remarkably diversified body of oral narratives. Each linguistic group has its own particular set that accords with its own regional ecologies, its own values, customs, and tastes, embodying its own religious and philosophical beliefs. As a consequence, tribal literatures are unique and culturally specific.

The importance of these early narratives was noted as early as 1830, when the acculturated Ojibway, George Copway, wrote in *The Traditional History and Characteristic Sketches of the Ojibway Nation*:

The Ojibwas have a great number of legends, stories, and historical tales, the relating and hearing of which, form a vast fund of winter evening instruction and amusement. . . .

Some of these stories are most exciting and so intensely interesting that I have seen children during their relation, whose tears would flow most plentifully, and their breasts heave with thoughts too big for utterance.

Night after night for weeks have I sat and eagerly listened to these stories. The days following, the characters would haunt me at every step, and every moving leaf would seem to be a voice of a spirit. . . .

These legends have an important bearing on the character of the children of our nation. The fire-blaze is endeared to them in after years by a thousand happy recollections. By mingling thus, social habits are formed and strengthened.[3]

Many narratives were considered private property in some tribes, or in societies within the tribe (for example, the Midewewin Society of the Ojibway), and were owned by a particular person or family. This secrecy meant that only a limited few—certain initiated elders—had knowledge of them. Only they had the right to tell or hear them, or to perform the associated rituals. Restricted access to certain kinds of knowledge helped to ensure their power and authority. Unfortunately many stories did not survive and were lost forever when no successors were left to remember them.

Not all traditional narratives belonged to this restricted category. There were many stories for everyone to hear, and those for secular hearing were not necessarily steeped in ritual and ceremony. They were ordinary stories told for entertainment or instruction.

To the non-Indian mind, Indian tales are baffling in their intricacies, inconsistencies, and leaps of logic, creating difficulties and frustrations in trying to understand them. For example, the Reverend Silas Rand (1810-89), a Baptist missionary among the Micmacs of Nova Scotia, for forty years collected, recorded, and translated narratives, but in one of his lectures he dismissed them with the casual comment: 'Now what sense or meaning there may be at the bottom of all this nonsense, I leave it to the speculation of others.'[4] However, he did praise the Micmac language, calling it 'copious, flexible, and expressive. Its declension of Nouns, and conjugation of Verbs, are as regular as the Greek, and twenty times as copious.'[5]

The world-view of aboriginal people produced mythologies as means of understanding the world about them. Essentially religious in character, it contains the spiritual beliefs, traditions, laws, morals, and history of the culture-group transmitted by the elders of the tribe in order to explain the mysteries of the universe. The many aboriginal cultures of Canada all have a variety of narratives to formulate their understanding of the world. Their basic assumptions about the universe and their place in it are alien to non-Indian thought and the European tradition. Early non-native readers, therefore—with their different conceptions of time, space, material possessions, phenomena of nature, the supernatural, and their different sense of humour and language—regarded Indian narratives as quaint and childish fairy tales, as superstition or primitive folklore. (It is very easy to get a false idea about aboriginal narratives from present-day versions of the literature written for children, which simply recount stories about culture heroes, the animal kingdom, and natural phenomena that are unrelated to the social, economic, and religious life of the tribes.) Contemporary critics argue that in order to appreciate the significance of these narratives in the lives of the native people, it is important to read the stories not as isolated literary narratives, but as part of the socio-cultural and historical contexts of the culture groups in which they developed, since they become relatively meaningless— though entertaining as stories—if they are removed from their cultural settings. Several recent collections—for example, Catherine McClellan's *The Girl Who Married the Bear* (1970), and *Clothed-in-Fur and Other Tales* (1982) by Thomas W. Overholt and J. Baird Callicott— provide philosophical, cultural, and historical contextualizations for narratives that are seen as products of a particular aboriginal culture and convey the interrelationship of humans with the planet. The American native critic Paula Gunn Allen tells us that 'the unifying structures that make the oral tradition coherent are less a matter of character, time, and setting than the coherence of common understanding derived from the ritual tradition that members of a tribal unit share.'[6]

George Copway put oral narratives into three distinct classes: the Amusing, the Historical, and the Moral. Most scholars since his time have loosely used the terms 'myths and legends' as labels to categorize them. In order to provide convenient frameworks for understanding, others have classified them in the contexts of themes, motifs, linguistic families, geographical regions, and culture groups, or by a number of labels like 'sacred and secular', 'news and tidings', 'folklore and fables'. But terms such as myths and legends, folklore and fables, are European and have specific literary meanings. Myth, for instance, in the mind-set of a non-native reader, is considered as fiction. But the traditional narratives that whites have categorized as myth are not regarded by natives as untrue. All Indian traditions are valid guides to reality. Conversely, 'because Indian oral tradition blends the material, spiritual and philosophical together into one historically entity, it would be a clear violation of the culture from which it is derived if well-meaning scholars were to try to demythologize it, in order to give it greater validity in the Western sense of historiography.'[7]

As a result, Indian oral narratives defy simple categorization, and European classifications are inadequate. In the absence of suitable terminology, the terms 'traditional narrative' or 'oral narrative' or 'story' will be used in this book instead of 'myth' or 'legend'.

We must remember that traditional stories were not told to be read. They were performed by gifted and respected storytellers— entertainers whose use of body and voice was determined by the context of the story. Certain liberties might be taken according to particular interests, but the fundamental actions, characters, and theme always remained the same. Listeners did not expect to hear all the details since they already knew them, but there were times when they participated directly by prompting the narrator. Each telling was a unique event.

One of the most popular stories of the southern Yukon Indians is about a girl who was abducted by a bear after she had insulted it. There are many versions of this story. In *The Girl Who Married the Bear*, McClellan includes eleven of them. One variation was told by John Fraser, who was born in 1883:

This is a story my grandmother told me. It happened at Dalton Post. Four young girls were out in the woods berrying. They saw some bear droppings. The last girl slipped on the droppings, and she said bad words to it. They went home.

Soon they went way up the hill a long ways from camp hunting wild rhubarb. They got lots of rhubarb, and they were packing it down to the old people in the camp. The last girl had such a big pack that she couldn't keep up with the other three, and she was left far behind. The other three returned to camp safely.

The fourth girl soon saw a handsome young man. He talked to her, and she talked to him. She was out of her mind. That man was really a bear, but she thought he was a handsome young man. They went along together for a long time.

Pretty soon they got married. It was getting late. It was October, and it was time for the bear to make his den. He dug a den. She marked it by hanging blackberry and willow branches real high.

The bear said, 'Why did you make those marks?'

She said, 'I didn't make any marks.'

But he said, 'You did!' [John Fraser commented: 'I don't know how he knew. He just knew.']

All the time the bear looked like a man. But one night the girl woke up and saw that it was really a bear sleeping beside her. She couldn't do anything about it.

They went to sleep. In January he heard a dog. His wife was sitting beside him. He wanted to go after the dog. He said to his wife: 'I'm going to get that dog!'

He rushed out. He threw the dog back into the cave, and he said,

'You kill this. I want to go outside!'

There were four men outside around the den. They were all ready to kill him with their bows and arrows. The arrows had long detachable copper heads. In the old days they got the copper from the Copper River Indians.

They killed the bear. They sent the youngest brother up to get the copper arrowheads.

The girl was in the cave, and she called out to him.

'Are you my brother?'

He was afraid. So she called him by his own name. Then he was sure she was his sister. She told her brother to tell her mother to bring her clothes. She was all hairy now—all over her body and limbs—like a bear. And all up her front and up her back.

The boy went way back down where they had taken the bear and told his brothers about her. When they heard, they didn't want to eat the bear. They went home. They told the villagers about her. Some of the people wanted to kill her, but two of her brothers said, 'No!'

They decided to go out and bring her back to the village. So they took her clothes up to her. They brought her in. She had trouble getting used to the smell of humans. She didn't like their smell. When she first came down, she could hardly come close to camp, because the smell of humans was so strong.

Later when she would look high up on the hillside, she would see something that looked like a fire burning. She would tell them that they would find a bear there, and they would. That's the end of my story.[8]

Another version was given by Sam Williams, who was in his mid-fifties at the time.

This happened around Klukshu. Some women were out picking berries, and there was a pretty young girl, maybe she was a chief's daughter. You know, where the bear passes, he leaves droppings. Well, it's *duli* [tabu] to step over it, for everybody, not just girls. You must walk around it.

So this girl jumped over it and said, 'Why do you leave that stuff around?'

After a while, after about half an hour, she upset her berries. So she had to stop to pick them up. . . .

The other women went on ahead without her. And right there she saw a handsome, good-looking young man. And he must have hypnotized her. He told her,

'Come with me!' And she did. That's the story.

He just seemed like a young man. She seemed to forget her family.

So they went together. And then in the night when they were sleeping, she woke up, and she could see that she was with a bear. That's the story. I guess he wanted her to know.

So she just had to stay with him. She didn't like to leave him. Sometimes he looked like a bear; sometimes he looked like a man.

Then, after a while, it was time to go to sleep for the winter. I guess it was late fall. The man said,

'Where shall we make our house?'

The girl's brothers used to go hunting all of the time, and she knew where their trail was. So she said, 'Let's put our house here.' It was near where she knew her brothers would come.

So they went in and went to sleep. And—it's the story—he used to take out his teeth and hang them up. [Indicates teeth hanging on the wall behind him.] And towards spring the bear woke up and told his wife he wanted his teeth. He knew that her brothers were coming.

The girl said, 'Oh don't go out there and hurt them!'

Then he said he had to go out, but he knew that he would be killed. And then he told his wife just how they were to fix him after he was dead, to put the skull up high—just what we do today. That's why we know. . . . No, you don't have to face the skull any special way.

Then those brothers had some little dogs to help in the hunting. And they barked, and the bear came out. And the brothers killed him.

Then—I guess this happened before they had guns—the brothers used bows and arrows and spears. So the girl took the broken arrowheads and tied them together in a bundle and attached them to a little dog. She knew the dog would go back to her brothers.

Then her brothers knew she was up there.

And she told them, 'Go tell my mother I'm up here. And tell her to bring me some clothes.'

So her mother brought her some clothes, and they took her back home. They didn't take her right into camp, but they made her a place near it, about a hundred feet away I guess. She was still kind of wild. She stayed there.

Then—this is kind of funny—but it's the story. She had two younger brothers. And they kept asking her to act as if she were a bear so they could pretend to shoot at her. She didn't want to do it. They kept asking her mother to make her do it. She didn't want to, but they just kept after her.

So, after a while she did it. She went out on the hillside. And she has two little ones, you know.

And then—she can't help it. She just turned to a bear, and she killed all her brothers. It's the story. She just had to, because she had become a real bear.

And she went up in the hills then.[9]

Though the versions differ in the amount of detail and dialogue, and in the asides of the narrator, the plots are basically the same, and both versions have for the non-native the same matter-of-fact 'voice'. Non-natives would be intrigued by the marriage and transformations, whereas native listeners would accept them and be entertained, as well as instructed, by the taboos and rituals relating to the bear and what can happen when they are broken.

Trickster/transformer/culture-hero stories were very important. The trickster is one of the most widespread mythological figures in North America. On the Pacific coast in British Columbia he is known as Raven; on the plains he is Old Man; among the Ojibway he is called Nanabozho; among the Micmacs of Nova Scotia he is called Glooscap; the Cree and Saulteaux call him Wisakedjak; among the Tagish he is known as Crow. Across the country he is also known as Mink, Coyote, Bluejay, and Badger. Trickster stories are all variations on the same theme; only names and locales change. The trickster's adventures, as he wanders from place to place, always take place in well-known localities within the territory of the group among whom the story is told. In his trickster role he behaves in a most anti-social manner, systematically violating all accepted human values, and relies on cunning deceptions and mean tricks to reach his goals, which are usually food, or the possession of women. According to Tomson Highway: 'The Trickster was a very sensual character—making love, eating—all those bodily functions he celebrated them, he lived for them.'[10] In his heroic role as culture hero he is identified with creative powers and is benevolent to man, bringing him fire and food. He performs his altruism, however, first to satisfy his own ends and only incidentally for man. Daniel David Moses has called the trickster a baffling figure, 'half-hero, half fool, an every man and a no one'.[11] He is at once like each one of us and like none of us.

The trickster has intrigued a number of scholars who have contributed significantly to our understanding of so elusive a figure in American Indian mythology. In the view of Paul Radin (1883-1959), a student of Boas and probably the best known of all the trickster/transformer critics, the trickster represents man's coming to consciousness. Another critic, Barbara Babcock-Abrams, focuses on the trickster as an expression of the ambiguous and paradoxical power derived 'from [his] ability to live interstitially, to confuse, and to escape the structures of society and the order of cultural things.'[12] She rejects as reductionist Carl Jung's view, shared by Paul Radin, that the trickster myth reflects an earlier, rudimentary stage of consciousness. Other critics have taken a number of interesting positions, but there is little agreement in their efforts to make the trickster intelligible and meaningful. This disagreement notwithstanding, Indians and non-Indians alike still laugh at the trickster's escapades, and 'his creative cleverness amazes us and keeps alive the possibility of transcending the social restrictions we regularly encounter.'[13]

Origin, Creation, and Migration tales are also widespread. An important origin tale among a number of tribes is that of the Earth Diver, the story of water creatures who take turns diving for a piece of solid land. The muskrat dives so deep that by the time he returns he is half-drowned or dead; in his claws, however, he holds a bit of mud that increases in size until it becomes the earth. The theft of fire—in which a culture hero obtains fire from a distant source, often through trickery, and carries it home—is also widespread.

Traditional narratives include a number of recurrent patterns and motifs that transcend geographical and linguistic barriers: heroic encounters with supernatural powers; animal-wives,-husbands,-parents,-divinities; guardian-spirit powers; a world flood; journeys to other worlds; animal totems; vision quests (requiring fasting, prayer, deprivation, and ceremonial purity); powerful magicians; belief in the significance of dreams, in a spirit world and the indwelling spirit of every created thing, inanimate and animate. And plots may use ancient tribal rituals (those of the shaking tent, sweat lodge, bear walk, sun, rain, and ghost dances, the potlatch), purification and expiation ceremonies, as well as initiation, puberty, and mortuary rites.

Oral traditions have not been static. Their strength lies in their ability to survive through the power of tribal memory and to renew themselves by incorporating new elements. 'When contact with the white man is established, a new set of problems arises and requires a logical cultural explanation to restore the world to order. Hence old myths are altered or new ones are generated to explain the process of cultural change.'[14] As a consequence, narratives of more recent origin have adapted and absorbed European folktales, Christian legends, historical accounts, contemporary reserve and urban stories and jokes.

In recent years there has been a resurgence of native pride in oral storytelling. A number of young writers—including Lenore Keeshig-Tobias and John McLeod—consider themselves to be oral storytellers. Moreover, along with Daniel David Moses and Tomson Highway, they have founded the Committee to Re-Establish the Trickster, a Toronto-based native writers' group to reclaim the native voice.

The printed collection of Canadian oral narratives began in the seventeenth century when the Jesuit missionaries recorded the oral traditions of the natives east of Georgian Bay and published them in the *Jesuit Relations*; later, explorers and traders, missionaries and government officials, and an assortment of interested laymen included Indian tales in a piecemeal fashion in their books. But it was the publication of *Algic Researches* (1839) by Henry Rowe Schoolcraft (1793-1864), Indian agent among the Ojibway of the Great Lakes between 1822 and 1842, that first aroused excitement in Indian narratives.

Schoolcraft expressed his elation at having discovered the rich narrative tradition of the Chippewa (Ojibway) in his diary entry for 31 July 1822:

> Who would have imagined that these wandering foresters should have possessed such a resource? What have all the voyageurs and re-markers from the days of Cabot and Raleigh been about, not to have discovered this curious trait, which lifts up indeed a curtain, as it were, upon the Indian mind, and exhibits it in an entirely new character?[15]

In the same entry Schoolcraft had an insight that informs present-day scholarship when he wrote: 'Some of these tales, which I have heard, are quite fanciful, and the wildest of them are very characteristic of their notions and customs. They often take the form of allegory, and in this shape appear designed to teach some truth or illustrate some maxim.'[16]

In Nova Scotia, Silas Rand published *Legends of the Micmacs* in 1894. The Reverand Adrien G. Morice (1859-1938) worked among the Déné. Both were pioneers in recording examples of the oral literature, with Rand attempting a literary and Morice a literal translation.

At the end of the nineteenth century collecting began in earnest when the doomed-culture theory prompted ethnologists, anthropologists, and folklorists to rescue the oral literatures from oblivion. The basic pattern was for scholars from the United States to work on research projects in Canada (chiefly British Columbia, since the natives there were the least touched by European contact) and then publish most of their results in the United States. The pioneer was the German-American anthropologist Franz Boas, who worked among the coastal tribes of British Columbia with native informants Henry Tate, George Hunt, and Louis Shortage. A number of other anthropologists and linguists—Alexander Francis Chamberlain, John Reed Swanton, and Edward Sapir—produced their impressive studies in the Boas tradition of field work. Marius Barbeau, with his Tsimshian informant William Beynon, and Diamond Jenness with Old Pierre— both working for the National Museum of Canada—also made valuable contributions. The early twentieth century saw more anthropological studies by George Laidlaw, William Mechling, James Teit, Charles Hill-Tout, Frank Speck, and Edward Curtis. From 1903 to 1905 William Jones, an American Indian who was a highly skilled ethnographer, translated into English Ojibway narratives that he had collected west and north of Lake Superior under the auspices of the Carnegie Foundation.

SONG

Song/music/dance have occupied an essential place in Canadian

Indian cultures because they played a vital role in everyday life. In 1634 Father Paul Le Jeune recorded the importance of song:

> As for their superstitious songs, they use them for a thousand purposes, for which the sorcerer and that old man, of whom I have spoken, have given me the reason. Two Savages, they told me, being once in great distress, seeing themselves within two finger-lengths of death for want of food, were advised to sing, and they would be relieved; and so it happened, for when they had sung, they found something to eat. As to who gave them this advice, and how it was given, they know nothing; however, since that time, all their religion consists mainly in singing. . . .[17]

Every experience in life—every occasion—was celebrated with song. There was no act of life that did not possess its fitting song, from those experiences that completely transcended the ordinary to those that were commonplace. These were usually humorous, soothing, entertaining or instructive—lullabies, jokes, corn-grinding and work songs, dance songs. Ceremonial songs that were considered sacred and had power concerned healing, initiation, hunting, planting, harvesting, blessing new houses, journeys, and undertakings. There were also dream-related songs: war songs, personal-power songs, purification and vision-seeking songs.

Songs had a purpose, a function—'to get hold of the sources of supernatural power, to trap the universal mystery in a net of magical words.'[18] Their words held this potential for power and magic. For example, songs not only increased the hunter's ability to hunt, they were also thought to influence the animals who freely gave themselves to him. The strongest weapon in the hunt was the word. During the whale hunt, the greatest event in the life of the West Coast Nootka, songs were sung to the whale. The following Whaling Song suggests that the whale desires to be captured and looks forward to being respected on his death.

Whale, I have given you what you are wishing to get—my good harpoon. And now you have it. Please hold it with your strong hands and do not let go. Whale, turn toward the beach of Yahksis, and you will be proud to see the young men come down on the fine sandy beach of my village at Yahksis to see you; and the young men will say to one another: 'What a great whale he is! What a fat whale he is! What a strong whale he is!' And you, whale, will be proud of all that you will hear them say of your greatness. Whale, do not turn outward, but hug the shore, and tow me to the beach of my village at Yahksis, for when you come ashore there, young men will cover your great body with bluegill duck feathers and with the down of the great eagle, the chief of all birds; for this is what you are wishing, and this is what you are trying to find from one end of the world to the other, every day you are travelling and spouting.[19]

The killing of an animal was a religious act. The Indians' environmental ethics assumed that all beings must be respected, and ceremoniously and courteously treated.

This prayer to the beaver after it has been killed reveals the hunter's admiration and respect:

'Welcome, friend, Throwing-down-in-One-Day, you Tree-Feller, for you have agreed to come to me. The reason why I wished to catch you is that you may give me your ability to work that I may be like you; for nothing is impossible for you to work at, friend, you, Throwing-down-in-One-Day, Tree-Feller, you Owner-of-the-Weather. And also that nothing evil may befall me in what I am doing, friend.' says he.[20]

Because the word has supernatural power, the Indian sang to ward off evil, to cure the sick, to kill the enemy. This is an Ojibway song of Healing:

You will recover; you will walk again.
It is I who say it; my power is great
Through our white shell I will enable
You to walk again.[21]

The Sekani Indians of northern British Columbia sang this medicine song to the caribou to obtain healing powers:

I need your help, O caribou
Come swiftly to me.
You see I have laid my hands on the sufferer.
Come and lay your hoofs where I have laid my hands,
I need your help.
Without your help there is no healing in my hands today.
Come so quickly that your tail stands erect.[22]

This request is perfectly natural for a people who believe in a dynamic universe in which all things are related, where each creature is part of a living whole.

The following Iroquoian song was probably sung during sowing time when the rain deities are addressed and offerings are made:

RAINMAKING
I want you to take care
of the Indians,
Your own people.
My family here,
I want rain.
Things won't grow,
too dry,
we must have corn,
so here is some tobacco
for you
so you know we are here
and want rain.[23]

Here is another Iroquoian prayer:

INVOCATION
May the scent of the tobacco
I have thrown on the fire
reach Thee to let Thee know
we are still good,
and that Thou mayest give us
all that we have asked.[24]

Songs presented on the printed page are lacking several dimensions: the singer and his or her vocal style, the audience, many of whom danced, and the accompaniment of drums, whistles, rattles etc. Music as it is usually appreciated is composed of three elements: rhythm, melody, and harmony. According to Natalie Curtis, harmony is not found in Indian music; consequently rhythm and melody, especially rhythm, are highly developed. Since harmony is absent, Indian music depends on variety of rhythm for variety of musical effect. The words may vary widely in different versions; the melody, too, may differ; but the rhythm remains paramount. No Western music 'has such complex, elaborate and changing rhythm as has the music of the American Indian'.[25]

Although Indian tribes vary as widely in their music and in their manner of singing as in their life and customs, there is 'one characteristic peculiarity of Indian song that is almost universal. This is a rhythmic pulsation of the voice on sustained notes.'[26] Notation can record the actual melody with its rhythmic accompaniment. But it cannot record the rendering of the song—'the vocal embellishment, the strange gutterals, slurs and accents that make Indian singing so distinctive.'[27] Nevertheless, the Indian song, as preserved on the printed page, can be appreciated for its highly poetic qualities. For it is distinguished by its rich use of metaphor and other figurative language, qualities usually associated with poetry.

This brief lament sung by an Ojibway maiden when she realizes her lover is leaving is tersely suggestive. But it is full of overtones and hints of things unsaid. And the metaphorical compression of the first verse bears a strong resemblance to Japanese haiku. In the second verse she is more open and direct.

> A loon
> I thought it was
> But it was
> My love's
> Splashing oar
>
> To Sault Ste Marie
> He has departed
> My love
> Has gone on before me
> Never again
> Can I see him[28]

This love song, recorded in the nineteenth century by Schoolcraft, was sung at night by the lover of a Chippewa girl who becomes bolder and more decisive as he approaches her lodge. Each verse was repeated several times, in the hope that the girl would accept the singer in her home:

> I will walk into someone's dwelling,
> I will walk into someone's home.
>
> My sweetheart, into thy home,
> I will walk, in the night.
>
> My sweetheart, in the winter,
> I shall walk into your abode.
>
> This night I will walk into your lodge,[29]

The outstanding feature of traditional Indian verse construction is repetition, which conveys the accumulation of power. Refrains, reiteration of phrases in part or in whole, meaningless vocables, and parallel phrasing all give the effect of rhyming thoughts and incremental repetition. For the Indian this effect is hypnotic and magical (though it strikes the ear of non-Indians as dull and monotonous). The constant repetition of a phrase or two may evoke an image in the mind of the singer and his audience. This Kwakiutl cradle-song is highly dependent on repetition:

> When I am a man, then I shall be a hunter, O father!
>> Ya ha ha ha.
> When I am a man, then I shall be a harpooner, O father!
>> Ya ha ha ha.
> When I am a man, then I shall be a canoe builder, O father!
>> Ya ha ha ha.
> When I am a man, then I shall be a carpenter, O father!
>> Ya ha ha ha.
> When I am a man, then I shall be an artisan, O father!
>> Ya ha ha ha.
> That we may not be in want, O father!
>> Ya ha ha ha.[30]

The following Micmac vengeance song evokes a magical coercive quality in the incremental repetition, punctuated by meaningless rhythmic vocables:

> Death I make, singing
> Heh-yeh! heh-yeh! hey-yeh! heh-yeh!
> Bones I hack, singing
> Heh-yeh! heh-yeh! heh-yeh! heh-yeh!
> Death I make, singing
> Heh-yeh! heh-yeh! heh-yeh! heh![31]

A repeated refrain is also common. For example, in this mourning song a West Coast Chief who has lost his child sings, and the mourning tribe responds:

MOURNING SONG

CHIEF: Don't mourn any more, don't mourn.
CHORUS: We do not mourn any more.
CHIEF: He went up to play with his brethren the stars.
Don't mourn any more.
CHORUS: We do not mourn any more.
CHIEF: There he is hunting with the hunters the nimble deer.
Don't mourn any more.
CHORUS: We do not mourn any more.
CHIEF: We will see his beloved face in the new moon.
Don't mourn any more.
CHORUS: We do not mourn any more.[32]

Aside from repetition, stylistic devices such as contrast, metonymy, synecdoche, apostrophe, personification, euphony, and onomatopoeia are also common.

In the view of Dell Hymes, an eminent American anthropologist and linguist, the oral tradition in North America was basically verse drama. On the strength of this proposition the Sepass Poems or the 'Songs of Y-Ail-Mihth'—recited by Chief Khalserten Sepass (1841-1943) of Chilliwack, British Columbia, to Eloise Street and translated by her mother into English from 1911 to 1915—are interesting. Mother and daughter were very much aware of the difficulties of translation. As Eloise commented, 'Setting thought on paper is to the Indian a new art, difficult to acquire.'[33] Street explains that the Chief's songs were his own and known only to himself, but he wanted them published because he believed that otherwise they would be lost. In explaining the method of translation, Street noted that the Chief insisted that the translation be in verse, 'correct in meaning, and that each line had the same syllable length as his original, and had the same stresses.'[34] 'The Beginning of the World' is the first of a cycle of fifteen long songs and gives the history of the Chilliwacks, as handed down from medicine man to medicine man. It tells of the creation of the world through a love-match of the sun and moon, and begins:

> Long, long ago,
> Before anything was,
> Saving only the heavens,
> From the seat of his golden throne,
> The Sun-god looked out on the Moon-goddess
> And found her beautiful.
>
> Hour after hour,
> With hopeless love,
> He watched the spot where, at evening,
> She would sometimes come out to wander
> Through her silver garden
> In the cool of the dusk.
>
> Far he sent his gaze across the heavens
> Until the time came, one day,
> When she returned his look of love
> And she, too, sat lonely,
> Turning eyes of wistful longing
> Toward her distant lover.

> Then their thoughts of love and longing,
> Seeking each other,
> Met halfway,
> Mingled,
> Hung suspended in space . . .
> Thus: the beginning of the world.[35]

The translation, as Street herself acknowledges, is in the 'slightly Victorian English of a person of her mother's education and time'.[36]

Literature relating to ceremonials was vital to Indian societies across Canada. For example, when the Mohawks of the League of Six Nations came to Canada during the American Revolution they brought with them rituals based on ancient prescribed forms of lengthy set speeches having considerable metaphorical content, interspersed with chants, prayers, hymns, and formulaic expressions. The Mohawks were led to the Grand River and the Bay of Quinte respectively by Joseph Brant (Thayendanegea, 1742-1807) and John Deserontyon (Odeserundiye, c. 1742-1811). Both were interested in the preservation of their oral traditions, much of which still survive partly thanks to them. Deserontyon—whom Daniel Claus, the Deputy Superintendent of Indian Affairs, called 'the clearest & best speaker of the 6 Nations according to the old ways'—recorded the form of ritual condolence, 'The Rite of the Condoling Council', which was not only a public lamentation for the death of a chief but also an induction ceremony for the new chief. It began with a long prose address that included the following hymn:

> To the great Peace bring we greeting!
> To the dead chief's kindred, greeting!
> To the warriors round him, greeting!
> To the mourning women, greeting!
> These our grandsires' words repeating,
> Graciously, O Grandsires, hear us![37]

We are to imagine that in the singing each line is repeated twice and is followed by many ejaculations of Haih-haih! (All hail!).

ORATIONS

Oratory played an extremely important role in Indian life. Tribes across Canada varied in their form of governance and in the degree of power they gave to their chiefs: chiefs were leaders only insofar as they were able to persuade their kinsmen to follow them. Eloquence was held in high esteem, probably in equal or even in higher honour than skill and courage in hunting and in war. The seventeenth-century Jesuit missionary, Paul Le Jeune, stated: 'There is no place in the world where Rhetoric is more powerful than in Canada . . . as the Captain [chief] is elected for his eloquence alone, and is obeyed in proportion to his use of it for they have no other law than his word.'[38] George Copway wrote:

Our orators have filled the forest with the music of their voices, loud as the roar of a waterfall, yet soft and wooing as the gentle murmur of a mountain stream. We have had warriors who have stood on the banks of lakes and rivers, and addressed with words of irresistible and persuasive eloquence their companions in arms.[39]

The early French missionaries who had learned the Indian languages were invariably amazed that natives 'so pagan and barbaric' were capable of expressing themselves in beautiful language. In his report of 1633 Father Le Jeune praised a Montagnais chief for a 'keenness and delicacy of rhetoric that might have come out of the schools of Aristotle or Cicero.'[40] To be compared to such writers of classical antiquity was the very highest praise indeed. A century later the first Superintendent of Indian Affairs, Sir William Johnson, was also impressed by the 'Attic elegance' of diction and the compelling rhythm of the orators of the Five Nations, and the American historian Cadwallader Colden, in his *History of the Five Nations* (1747), stated that their greatest speakers attained a certain 'Urbanitas or Atticism'.[41] He too expressed his amazement that the untrained Indian mind was capable of eloquence: 'The Speakers whom I have heard, had all a great Fluency of Words, and much more Grace in their Manner, than any man could expect, among a people intirely ignorant of all the liberal Arts and Sciences.'[42]

There is no doubt that the natives' oratorical skills had been developed long before contact with Europeans. Their reverence for the word and inherent love of drama, their organizational and reasoning powers and retentive memory, all helped to make the Canadian Indian an artist with words. Young men of the tribe were highly trained in the art of oratory: a mastery of the language and rhetoric in which Indian diplomacy was expressed, and the skills of dramatic presentation and memorization. To speak for them on important occasions each tribe appointed the most eloquent of its members, someone who could combine his talent for persuasive speech with knowledge of the history and traditions of his people. Oratory was more than talk, it was a source of power; the ultimate purpose was to persuade. Formal occasions were governed strictly by ritual and tradition, called for considerable speaking, and were democratic in their proceedings. When we remember that having no *written* language,

Indian orators had to speak without recourse to notes or manuscripts, without books of reference and libraries, their oratorical skills and powers of recall become even more impressive.

After the arrival of Europeans, Indian oratory played a significant role in Indian-white relations in the various encounters with government agencies, in council meetings, and in treaty sessions. To the exasperation of the whites, Indian spokesmen sometimes spent whole days reciting tribal history, recalling ancient traditions, reviewing the history of the whites on this continent, the history of contacts between whites and a particular tribe, and speculating about the future. For example, it is said that on 18 July 1812 Chief Blackbird (Assikinack), noted warrior and orator of the Ottawas, spoke continuously without stopping from sunrise to sunset, a span of fourteen hours, to a large group of Ottawas and Chippewas at Michilimackinac, urging their support of the British cause in the War of 1812.[43]

Indian assemblies usually lasted for days because Indians not only deliberate slowly and are rarely in a hurry, but the ritual ceremonial formalities were time-consuming: the lighting of the council fires, the smoking of the ceremonial peace pipes, and the presenting or throwing of the wampum belts after each particularly important point—a ritual that attested to the honour, integrity, and sincerity of the speaker—as well as the deliberate pause for audience approval after a stylistically polished phrase was uttered or an important point was made.

The white government officials and politicians with whom the Indians had dealings were not interested in trying to comprehend Indian oratory involving complex figures of speech such as metaphor, metononymy, synecdoche, and oxymoron—figurative language one usually associates with poetry—to evoke multiple meanings. The Recollet priest Chrestien Le Clercq, who worked for many years among the Micmacs, admired this predilection in his *Nouvelle Relation de la Gaspésie* (1691):

> They [the Indians] are very eloquent and persuasive among those of their own nation, using metaphors and very pleasing circumlocutions in their speeches, which are very eloquent, especially when . . . these are pronounced in the councils and the public and general assemblies.[44]

But the eighteenth-century English fur trader Alexander Henry viewed the Indian's use of figurative language as a problem: 'The Indian manner of speech is so extravagantly figurative, that it is only for a very perfect master to follow and comprehend it entirely.'[45]

The Indians made use of extended metaphors and analogies because they associated an idea with an object and had a highly developed visual memory. For example the Flemish Bastard, a leader of a band of Mohawks in an attack on Trois-Rivières who delivered two French hostages to Quebec in July 1654, complained that the Jesuit priest Simon Le Moyne had been sent on an embassy to the Onondagas instead of to the Mohawks, who were closer neighbours to the French. The Mohawk Chief based his logically reasoned argument on a clever analogy to shame the French missionaries:

Ought not one. . . to enter a house by the door, and not by the chimney or roof of the cabin, unless he be a thief, and wish to take the inmates by surprise? We, the five Iroquois Nations, compose but one cabin; we maintain but one fire; and we have, from time immemorial, dwelt under one and the same roof. . . Well, then, . . . will you not enter the cabin by the door, which is at the ground floor of the house? It is with us Anniehronnons [Mohawks] that you should begin; whereas you, by beginning with the Onnoontaehronnons [Onandagas], try to enter by the roof and through the chimney. Have you no fear that the smoke may blind you, our fire not being extinguished, and that you may fall from the top to the bottom, having nothing solid on which to plant your feet?[46]

This power of arousing emotion by means of telling metaphorical comparisons constituted one of the strengths of Indian oratory.

Whereas the Europeans viewed such goods as the *wampum belt*, *calumet*, *hatchet* or *kettle* in materialistic terms, the Indians attached special meanings to them, viewing them as symbols. Also, the implications or suggested meanings of the word, the connotative as opposed to the specific or denotative meaning, were highly significant. Hence words like *road*, *tree*, *fire*, *chain*, *mat*, *sun* and *pipe* were loaded with emotional and abstract meanings that lifted them to the realm of symbolism.

Otreouti (fl. 1659-88), also known as Garangula or La Grande Gueule, 'Big Mouth'—so called by the French because of his abilities as an orator—was an Onondaga chief who often acted as ambassador to the French in peace negotiations that periodically occurred during the French-Iroquois wars. At a parley in September 1664 at La Famine on the south shore of Lake Ontario, where the French governor Joseph-Antoine Le Febvre de la Barre had set up camp, he attempted to intimidate Otreouti with threats the chief knew could not be executed. Otreouti rose, strode several times around the council fire, and delivered the following discourse:

Yonondio! I honour you, and the warriors that are with me all likewise honour you. Your interpreter has finished your speech; I now begin mine. My words make haste to reach your ears. Hearken to them.

Yonondio! You must have believed when you left Quebec, that the sun had burnt up all the forests, which render our country inaccessible to the French, or that the lakes had so far overflown the banks, that they had surrounded our castles, and that it was impossible for us to get out of them. Yes, surely you must have dreamed so, and the curiosity of seeing so great a wonder, has brought you so far. *Now* you are undeceived. I and the warriors here present, are come to assure you, that the Senecas, Cayugas, Onondagas, Oneidas and Mohawks [the Five Nations of the Iroquois Confederacy] are yet alive. I thank you in their name, for bringing back into their country the calumet, which your predecessor received from their hands. It was happy for you, that you left under ground that murdering hatchet, so often dyed in the blood of the French.

Hear, Yonondio! I do not sleep. I have my eyes open. The sun, which enlightens me, discovers to me a great captain at the head of a company of soldiers, who speaks as if he were dreaming. He says, that he only came to the lake to smoke on the great calumet with the Onondagas. But *Garangula* says, that he sees the contrary; that it was to knock them on the head, if sickness had not weakened the arms of the French. I see Yonondio raving in a camp of sick men, whose lives the Great Spirit has saved by inflicting this sickness on them.

Hear, Yonondio! Our women had taken their clubs, our children and old men had carried their bows and arrows into the heart of your camp, if our warriors had not disarmed them, and kept them back, when your messenger came to our castles. It is done and I have said it.

Hear, Yonondio! We plundered none of the French, but those that carried guns, powder and balls to the Twightwies and Chictaghicks, because those arms might have cost us our lives. Herein we follow the example of the Jesuits, who break all the kegs of rum brought to our castles, lest the drunken Indians should knock them on the head. Our warriors have not beaver enough to pay for all the arms they have taken, and our old men are not afraid of the war. This belt preserves my words.

We carried the English into our lakes, to trade there with the Utawawas and Quatoghies, as the Adirondacks brought the French to our castles, to carry on a trade, which the English say is theirs. We are born free. We neither depend on Yonondio or Corlear [the English governors of New York]. We may go where we please, and carry with us whom we please, and buy and sell what we please. If your allies be your slaves, use them as such, command them to receive no other but your people. . . .

Hear, Yonondio! Take care for the future that so great a number of soldiers as appear there, do not choke the tree of peace planted in so small a fort. It will be a great loss, if, after it had so easily taken root, you should stop its growth, and prevent its covering your country and ours with its branches. I assure you, in the name of the Five Nations, that our warriors shall dance to the calumet of peace under its leaves. They shall remain quiet on their mats, and shall never dig up the hatchet, till their brother Yonondio, or Corlear, shall either jointly or separately endeavor to attack the country, which the Great Spirit has given to our ancestors . . .[47]

Otreouti's address—recorded in French by Baron de La Hontan, who was an eyewitness—is a masterpiece of forcible declaration and demonstrates the formality and the literary devices of the declamatory style that characterized such speeches: apostrophe, rhetorical question, balance, antithesis, as well as repetition of both idea and expression. In the event, La Barre retreated to Montreal.

Speeches such as Otreouti's cast a strong light on the remarkable depth and dignity of Indian thought. For if the occasion warranted it, the Indian could be effusive in feeling and bountiful in language. He had the ability to think in logical and convincing terms on all the major issues that faced him—whether they dealt with war or peace, religion or trade—and to express himself forcefully with such emotions as pride or defiance.

Minweweh (c. 1710-70), 'The one with the silver tongue'—also known as Minavavana, or Le Grand Saulteux because of his six-foot height—was a chief of the Ojibways on Mackinac Island. During the Seven Years' War he was allied with the French, and after their defeat refused to accept English sovereignty. However, when the English trader Alexander Henry arrived at Fort Michilimackinac in 1761 Minweweh made the following declaration (after which he allowed Henry to trade unmolested):

Englishman, it is to you that I speak, and I demand your attention!

Englishman, you know that the French King is our father. He promised to be such; and we, in return, promised to be his children.—This promise we have kept.

Englishman, it is you that have made war with this our father. You are his enemy; and how, then, could you have the boldness to venture among us, his children?—You know that his enemies are ours.

Englishman, we are informed, that our father, the King of France [Louis XIV], is old and infirm; and that being fatigued, with making war upon your nation, he is fallen asleep. During his sleep, you have taken advantage of him and possessed yourselves of Canada. But, his nap is almost at an end. I think I hear him already stirring, and enquiring for his children, the Indians:—and, when he does awake, what must become of you? He will destroy you utterly!

Englishman, although you have conquered the French, you have not yet conquered us! We are not your slaves. These lakes, these woods and mountains, were left to us by our ancestors. They are our inheritance; and we will part with them to none. Your nation supposes that we like you ought to know, that He, the Great Spirit and master of Life, has provided food for us, in these spacious lakes, and on these woody mountains.

Englishman, our father, the King of France, employed our young men to make war upon your nation. In this warfare many of them have been killed, and it is our custom to retaliate, until such time as the spirits of the slain are satisfied. But, the spirits of the slain are to be satisfied in either of two ways; the first is by the spilling of the blood of the nation by which they fell; the other, by covering the bodies of the dead, and thus allaying the resentment of their relations. This is done by making presents.

Englishman, your king has never sent us any presents, nor entered into any treaty with us; therefore he and we are still at war; and until he does these things, we must consider that we have no other father, nor friend, among the white men, than the King of France; but, for you, we have taken into consideration, that you have ventured your life among us in the expectation that we should not molest you. You do not come armed, with an intention to make war; you come in peace, to trade with us, and supply us with necessities, of which we are much in want. We shall regard you, therefore, as a brother; and you may sleep tranquilly, without fear of the Chipeways. As a token of our friendship, we present you with this pipe, to smoke.[48]

From its opening coercive expression, typical of Indian oratory, to its conciliatory invitation to friendship, Minweweh's proud and frank speech is noteworthy not only for its content but also for its style, at times reaching grandiloquent logic.

Two of the most important speeches made after the Conquest were by Pontiac and Tecumseh.

Pontiac (c. 1720-69), or 'He who unites or joins together', chief of the Ottawas, was an unwavering ally of the French. He resented and feared British expansion into the interior, and successfully united an armed resistance from more than a dozen tribes in the Ohio Valley and the Great Lakes to drive the British from his country. He tried to take Fort Detroit, but when it became apparent that he would receive no help from the French, he was forced to raise the siege. In a formal council-of-war at Detroit on 23 May 1763, uninformed of the Treaty of Paris by which Great Britain had acquired a vast empire in North America from the French, Pontiac denounced his French friends and allies as traitors to his cause:

My Brothers! . . . I have no doubt but this war is very troublesome to you, and that my warriors, who are continually passing and re-passing through your settlements, frequently kill your cattle, and injure your property. I am sorry for it, and hope you do not think I am pleased with this conduct of my young men. And as a proof of my friendship, recollect the war you had seventeen years ago [1746], and the part I took in it. The Northern nations combined together, and came to destroy you. Who defended you? Was it not myself and my young men? The great Chief, Mackinac [the Turtle], said in Council that he would carry to his native village the head of your chief warrior, and that he would eat his heart and drink his blood. Did I not then join you, and go to his camp and say to him, if he wished to kill the French, he must pass over my body, and the bodies of my young men? Did I not take hold of the tomahawk with you, and aid you in fighting your battles with Mackinac, and driving him home to his country? Why do you think I would turn my arms against you? Am I not the same French Pontiac, who assisted you seventeen years ago? I am a Frenchman, and I wish to die a Frenchman . . .[49]

Here are shrewd reasoning, cruel truth, poetic imagery, leadership, past history, loyalty, determination, and dignity—Indian oratory at its best. But Pontiac's eloquent indictment was in vain. The Royal Proclamation of 1763 gave Britain the sole right to alienate lands from the Indians and initiated the procedure of signing land-surrender treaties between the British and Indians in North America.

Tecumseh (1768-1813)—whose name means 'Shooting Star', and in Shawnese imagery is a panther in the sky springing on its prey—was one of the greatest of all Indian chiefs and one of the leading opponents of American expansion on the frontier. 'A more sagacious or more gallant warrior does not exist,' Sir Isaac Brock wrote of Tecumseh, who supported the British in the War of 1812, in which he was given the regular commission of Brigadier-General in command of more than 2,000 Indian warriors. Tecumseh was killed in action in that war at the battle of Moraviantown on 5 October 1813.

When Colonel Henry Procter, the British commander, began to withdraw his forces from Fort Malden before the advancing American army, Tecmuseh objected to the retreat, delivering this celebrated appeal at Amherstburg on 18 September 1813:

Father— . . . listen to your children. You see them now all before you. The war before this, our British father gave the hatchet to his red children when our old chiefs were alive. They are now all dead. In that war, our father was thrown on his back by the Americans, and our father took them by the hand without our knowledge, and we are afraid our father will do so again at this time.

Summer before last, when I came forward with my red brethren and was ready to take up the hatchet in favor of our British father, we were told not to be in a hurry—that he had not yet determined to fight the Americans.

Listen! When war was declared, our father stood up and gave us the tomahawk, and told us that he was now ready to strike the Americans—that he wanted our assistance; and that he would certainly get us our lands back, which the Americans had taken from us.

Listen! You told us at that time to bring forward our families to this place—we did so, and you promised to take care of them, and that they should want for nothing, while the men would go to fight the enemy—that we were not to trouble ourselves with the enemy's garrisons—that we knew nothing about them, and that our father would attend to that part of the business. You also told your red children that you would take care of your garrison here, which made our hearts glad.

Listen! When we last went to the Rapids, it is true we gave you little assistance. It is hard to fight people who live like ground-hogs.

Father—Listen! Our fleet has gone out, we know they have fought; we have heard the great guns; but know nothing of what has happened to our father with one arm. Our ships have gone one way, and we are much astonished to see our father tying up everything and preparing to run away the other, without letting his red children know what his intentions are. You always told us to remain here and take care of our lands; it made our hearts glad to hear that was your wish. Our great father, the king, is the head, and you represent him. You always told us you would never draw your foot off British ground; but now, father, we see you are drawing back, and we are sorry to see our father doing so without seeing the enemy. We must compare our father's conduct to a fat animal, that carries its tail upon its back, but when affrighted, it drops it between its legs and runs off.

Listen, father! The Americans have not yet defeated us by land; neither are we sure that they have done so by water; we therefore wish to remain here, and fight our enemy, should they make their appearance. If they defeat us, we will then retreat with our father.

At the battle of the Rapids, last war, the Americans certainly defeated us; and when we retreated to our fathers fort at that place, the gates were shut against us. We were afraid that it would now be the case; but instead of that we now see our British father preparing to march out of his garrison.

Father! You have got the arms and ammunition which our great Father sent for his red children. If you have any idea of going away, give them to us, and you may go in welcome, for us. Our lives are in the hands of the Great Spirit. We are determined to defend our lands, and if it is his will, we wish to leave our bones upon them.[50]

Tecumseh's convincing speech, translated into English, is still Indian in style: coercive, dignified, formulaic, repetitive, metaphorical, and allegorical. Like all the brilliant warrior-orators of his time and previous times, Tecumseh must have shamed those who had to speak against him in formal debate.

If Tecumseh allied himself with the British, there were Minweweh and Pontiac who sided with the French. Contrary to popular opinion, the Indians were as contradictory and complex as peoples anywhere. They presented no monolithic viewpoint but many diverse and frequently opposing positions. If there were Indians who stood in awe of European technology and their writing systems, there were others who blamed the Europeans for bringing pestilence and death. If some adopted Christianity, others had serious doubts about the new beliefs.

Whether these early orators spoke in the contexts of war, the fur trade, or missionary activity, they spoke as free men. Pitted between two great rival European powers in their struggles for a continent, Canada's natives held the balance of power. In this state of dynamic equilibrium, they kept even the scales between the English and the French. If deep in their hearts was the bitter knowledge that under British rule their supremacy was over, at least they did not relinquish this without debate.

There are those who have challenged the authenticity of many of these Indian speeches and who claim that generalizing about their content and style is problematic at best. Though the Canadian Indian was unable to communicate directly with the Europeans in their own tongue but had to rely on the translations and interpretations of his conquerors, both the content and style of all reported speeches—even when they are merely short extracts—are wholly consistent, and demonstrate convincingly the unmistakable resonances, the formal gravity and deep conviction, that lend distinction to Indian oratorical expression.

II

1820-1850

With the peace that followed the War of 1812, and the failure of Tecumseh's heroic attempts to unite the Indians into a defensive confederacy, large-scale white settlement from the British Isles began to flow into the Credit River and the Bay of Quinte areas. Missionaries arrived, not only to look after settlers but also to Christianize the Indians in a program the British government supported. One of the results of their proselytising was that by the mid-nineteenth century Canadian Indians were writing and publishing in English.

The Six Nations who came to the Grand River and Bay of Quinte areas in Upper Canada after the American Revolution enjoyed a history of literacy through their affiliation with the Anglican Church. But in the rest of Upper Canada it was the Wesleyan Methodists who were most influential in educating Indians. In the mid-1820s the Wesleyan Methodist Missionary Society began a vigorous campaign to train a number of young Ojibway in Upper Canada to become teachers, interpreters, and missionaries. They found many remarkable young men for this purpose, and some of them—Peter Jones, George Copway, George Henry, Peter Jacobs, John Sunday, Allen Salt, and Henry Steinhauer—became highly successful missionaries with both Indians and whites. Generating literary enthusiasm among themselves, they formed the first literary coterie of Indians in Canada. They worked indefatigably for their church and their people, preaching and lecturing at home and abroad to win souls and help raise money for their growing missions. And they wrote: many of their journals and diaries, autobiographies, histories, reports, letters, travelogues, and sermons in English were published and widely circulated through newspapers and missionary publications, and in books.

The acknowledged leader of the group was the Mississauga Ojibway chief—member of the Eagle totem, farmer, Methodist minister, author, and translator—the Reverend Peter Jones (1802-56), who was the first Indian in Canada to be ordained a Methodist minister. The second son of a white land surveyor and an Ojibway Indian woman, Peter Jones (Kahkewaquonaby or Sacred Waving Feathers) was born on New Year's Day at the Heights of Burlington Bay (Hamilton, Ontario). Until he was fourteen he lived with his mother's band in the vicinity of the Credit River, where he learned the skills and traditions of the Mississauga Indians. For the next seven years he lived on his father's farm on the Grand River. Here, with his father's Mohawk wife and their family, he farmed, went to school, and worked in a brickyard to obtain money for his school fees. At a Methodist camp meeting near Ancaster in 1823 he was converted to Christianity, and nearly two years later began his missionary career as an itinerant Methodist preacher among the Indians of Upper Canada. He travelled extensively, on foot and horseback, by canoe or sleigh, teaching and preaching, founding missions and visiting scattered bands around Rice Lake, Lake Simcoe, and Lake Huron. In addition he taught the Indians how to farm, all the while converting them and helping them to conform to more agrarian habits and adjust to the growing European presence. Jones also preached to many white congregations, the first time an Indian had been known to entreat the white man to godly ways.

So successful was his mission work that Jones became a fully ordained minister in 1833 and a sought-after speaker. He was invited to attend missionary meetings in Ontario, Quebec, and the United States, where thousands were thrilled with the wonderful story of his conversion. He also toured Great Britain three times to raise money for the rapidly growing Canadian missions. The presence of an Indian chief in his native costume created great excitement in British towns and cities, and Jones was so eloquent that he won the hearts of his audiences wherever he went. On his first visit alone, in 1831-2, he delivered over 150 addresses and sermons, was widely fêted, and on 5 April 1832 had an audience with King William IV. On his second trip in 1837-8 he had an audience with the young Queen Victoria, presenting her with a petition in the interests of native land claims. (The government of the Province of Canada had refused to grant the Indians title deeds to the reserves on the Credit.) He made his third British tour in 1845, when he again attracted huge crowds.

Jones devoted his life to the political, religious, and educational welfare of his own Mississauga. Scores of extant letters to government officials, sermons, lectures, reports, briefs and speeches attest to the vigorous role he played in the religious and secular life of his people. His published works are extensive. Numerous sermons and speeches given during his tours of Britain went into print in pamphlet form in Methodist periodicals and local newspapers. Besides his writing in English, Jones translated into Ojibway *Part of the Discipline of the Wesleyan Methodist Church in Canada* (1835) and *The Book of Moses Called Genesis* (1835); and (with his brother John) translated the Gospels of St Matthew (1828) and St John (1831) into Ojibway. He also translated St Luke into Mohawk and prepared a *Spelling Book* (1828), a small dictionary, and a book of hymns (1828) in Ojibway.

Jones's two most interesting books were published after his death. *Life and Journals of Kah-Ke-Wa-Quo-na-By (Rev. Peter Jones) Wesleyan Minister* (1860) was assembled by his wife, Eliza Field—an Englishwoman of culture and breeding whom Jones met on his first trip to England—and edited by the Reverend Enoch Wood, the Methodist missionary superintendent of the time. It stresses the physical hardships and the spiritual desolation of pre-Christian Ojibway life and contains much of the standard content of missionary journals—conversions, relapses into sin, and the proselytizer's hopes. There is also a first-person account of Jones's conversion to Christianity. Jones's *History of the Ojibwa Indians with Special Reference to Their Conversion to Christianity* (1861) deals straightforwardly with such topics as the Ojibway's origins, their religion, councils, amusements, languages, way of life, and their capacity for receiving instruction in the Methodist faith.

While Jones rejected the spiritual way of his people, he also criticized the new culture he had adopted. He decried the contradictions between the whites' behaviour and their religion, as well as the whites' use of alcohol, which he saw as the most important cause of the rapid decrease in population of the Indian tribes.

Oh, what an awful account at the day of judgment must the unprincipled white man give, who has been an agent of Satan in the extermination of the original proprietors of the American soil! Will not the blood of the red man be required at *his* hands, who, for paltry gain, has impaired the minds, corrupted the morals, and ruined the constitutions of a once hardy and numerous race?[1]

Jones's *History* is an interesting work by a preacher who keenly felt the plight of his people. Just how much help he received from his English wife will never be known. Suffice it to say that Jones mastered the English language. His prose is marked by a dry, quiet sense of humour and an unpretentious style. Besides his two books, a number of his letters, journals, and sermons are extant and reveal his competence in a number of literary genres. A letter he wrote in England to his brother John gives the first impressions we have of the English from a native point of view.

London, December 30th, 1831

The English, in general, are a noble, generous-minded people—free to act and free to think; they very much pride themselves on their civil and religious privileges; in their learning, generosity, manufactures, and commerce; and they think that no other nation is equal to them.

I have found them very open and friendly, always ready to relieve the wants of the poor and needy when properly brought before them. No nation, I think, can be more fond of novelties than the English; they will gaze upon a foreigner as if he had just dropped down from the moon; and I have often been amused in seeing what a large number of people a *monkey riding* upon a *dog* will collect, where such things may be seen almost every day. When my Indian name, *Kahkewaquonaby*, is announced to attend any public meeting, so great is the curiosity, the place is sure to be filled. They are truly industrious, and in general very honest and upright. Their close attention to business produces, I think, too much worldly-mindedness, and hence they forget to think enough about their souls and their God; their motto seems to be 'Money, money; get money, get rich, and be a gentleman.' With this sentiment they fly about in every direction, like a swarm of bees, in search of the treasure which lies so near their hearts. These remarks refer to the men of the world, and of such there are not a few.

The English are very fond of good living, and many who live on roast beef, plum pudding, and turtle soup, get very fat, and round as a toad. They eat four times in a day. Breakfast at eight or nine, which consists of coffee or tea, bread and butter, and sometimes a little fried bacon, fish, or eggs. Dinner at about two, P.M., when every thing that is good is spread before the eater; which winds up with fruit, nuts, and a few glasses of wine. Tea at six, with bread and butter, toast, and sometimes sweet cake. Supper about nine or ten, when the leavings of the dinner again make their appearance, upon which John Bull makes a hearty meal to go to bed upon at midnight.

The fashion in dress varies so much, I am unable to describe it. I will only say, that the ladies of fashion wear very curious bonnets, which look something like a farmer's scoop shovel; and when they walk in the tiptoe style they put me in mind of the little snipes that run along the shores of the lakes in Canada. They also wear sleeves as big as bushel bags, which make them appear as if they had three bodies with one head. Yet, with all their big bonnets and sleeves, the English ladies, I think, are the best of women . . .[2]

P. Jones

Jones was falling in love with Eliza Field—the accomplished daughter of an eminent London merchant who was also a prominent Methodist—which can account for his favourable judgement of Englishwomen, and his interest in their fashions. The letter is important not only for its content but also for its style. It is rich in detail and shrewd observations. Jones had a gift for the witty image and the amusing anecdote.

There are a number of letters extant written by Jones to Eliza in a two-year transatlantic courtship. This excerpt from a letter dated 'River Credit, 11 May 1833' reveals the difficulties inherent in their blooming relationship and the balanced view of Peter Jones:

It is pleasing to have the concurrence of our friends in our undertakings, but we very well know with the present diversity of feelings and sentiments among men on almost all subjects, that some will view things in spite of all reason & argument in the very opposite light. Why should we then wonder if some of our friends, perhaps out of the finest motive should feel infavourable to our designs. I regret to say that some of my white friends in this country who have heard of my attachment to an English lady have expressed their fears as to the result of such an union. My heart has been much grieved at some of [these] insinuations in supposing that I had not been candid in telling you my actual state & etc. Surely I told you that I was indebted to the Lord for what influence I had, & the success of my missionary labors. All acknowledge friends and enemies that the Lord has signally made use of me in christianizing and civilizing many of my perishing countrymen. To God be all the Glory! But the fact is my beloved Eliza, it is that *feeling of prejudice* which is so prevalent among the *old American Settlers* (not Indians) in this country. They think it is not right for the whites to intermarry with Indians. Now if this doctrine be true, what must we poor fellows do who in the order of God's providence are brought to be united in heart to those of a whiter hue? However I am happy to state there are some who take a right view of the origin of nations, & their relationship one to another. In my opinion character alone ought to be the distinguishing mark in all countries, and among all people.[3]

Despite much opposition, Eliza sailed to New York in 1833 to marry Jones and settle on the Grand River.

Jones was popular as a public speaker on topics dealing with the customs and traditions of the Indians. In an article entitled

'Kahkewaquonaby, the Red Indian Chief and Missionary', *The Ladies Own Journal and Miscellany* (Edinburgh) for 2 August 1845 reported that 'his oratory is varied. Now it partakes of the European, with lucid reasoning and elaborate sentences, but for the most part it abounds with the Indian characteristics of the figurative, the imaginative, and of instinctive feeling. There is often a mixture of the gravely and the humorously true which has all the effect of wit.' It cited as an example an extract from a speech Jones gave on the progress of the civilization of Indian women:

The women among us prepare their meals now as you do. They spread the white tablecloth, and place in order the spoons, the knives, and forks. Then the head man of the house lifts up his heart and his voice to the white man's God, and invokes his blessing on the bounties of which they are about to share. After they have done, the women boil the water to cleanse the dishes that have been used, and place them when cleansed in regular rows, the pride of the kitchen. Some of them have new looking glasses, by which to set off their charms. One point of civilization attained by you . . . they have not reached: they have not yet attained *curls*;—the *crowning* point of female civilization.[4]

The sermon was an important literary genre at the time. Native converts were well trained in its composition, a typical blend of straightforward exposition and practical admonition, a mixture of spirituality and practicality expressed in balanced prose. Peter Jones soon gained a reputation for his sermons. According to the *Buffalo Christian Advocate* of 10 July 1856, they 'were commonly strong and practical, sometimes enlivened with a vein of sly humour or kindly irony as he dealt with the strange inconsistencies of his white brethren, and occasionally irradiated by some grand and striking thought, or beautified by a graceful metaphor, some wild flower fresh and fragrant from the field of Nature.'[5] Reviewing his preaching in Edinburgh in 1845, the *Witness* (26 July) wrote: . . . as a preacher of the gospel, he shows a full and living comprehension of its doctrines.'[6]

A more original and colourful approach to preaching was taken by a colleague of Peter Jones, the Reverend John Sunday (1795-1875, Shawundais—'Sultry Heat'), a Mississauga Ojibway born in New York State who spent his boyhood in the traditional migratory manner around the shores of Lake Ontario. Through the efforts of Peter Jones, Sunday was converted in May 1826 and became involved in the Methodist mission at Grape Island on the Bay of Quinte, where the Ojibway were encouraged to pursue a religious life, raise crops, and acquire rudimentary academic and farming skills. Sunday was accepted as a ministerial candidate in 1832 and was the first native preacher among the Grape Island Ojibway. After a short period with them he became an itinerant missionary, travelling extensively for several years, particularly among the Ojibway in the Lake Superior region, on Manitoulin Island, at Sault Ste Marie and Fort William, and along the south shore of Lake Superior, where Methodist evangelism had spread. He was ordained in 1836. In the same year he visited England to stimulate interest in the Canadian missions and was presented to Queen Victoria. In Canada he laboured untiringly on several mission stations—Rice Lake, Mud Lake, Mount Elgin, Muncey, and Alderville—for the spiritual and temporal welfare of his people, serving in negotiations with the government on matters relating to timber and land.

Sunday was a popular preacher. Huge crowds, native and non-native alike, were always thrilled and astonished by the ingenuity and power of his appeals. It was not uncommon for congregations on Saturdays and Sundays to number 4,000. John Sunday was not entirely fluent in English, but his droll wit, irresistible humour and gift for apt illustration, whether in his own tongue or in English, delighted his audiences.

The following extract, from a sermon Sunday preached in 1835 to the Indians of Grape Island, is a specimen of his unique preaching and demonstrates his penchant for animal analogies:

. . . And I told my brethren and sisters this—When any man awake early in the morning, and then before noon he begin want to sleep again; and he sleep by and by, and so with the backslider. But let us try that we may not sleep again, but work all day long; that is, I mean man to be Christian all day to the end of his life. And we must be like bees; they all work in the summertime all day long for their provisions. They know the winter coming in the six months, so they all work for their victuals. If they do not work they shall surely die; and so with us all, if we do not work for that great provision from heaven for our souls. We must work long as we live. Let us think one thing more. In Proverbs, in 6th chapter and in the 6th verse: 'Go to the ant, thou sluggard; consider her ways, and be wise.' They all work in the summer time for making ant hills. If, then enemies come to them, they will go in the ant hill, so the enemy will not destroy them. And so, all good Christians, and watch and pray. When Christian man his enemy come near in his heart, he cry out for help from God. Brothers and sisters, we ought to be wiser than they are because ant they very small. But we are larger than they are as much as moose, he bigger than man. Devil he watch for us. Brethren and sisters, be wise. Devil he watch for us, just as wolf he try catch deer. We must watch and not sleep. Deer never does sleep, always watch for fear of enemy; deer do not like to be killed. We ought to be more careful for our souls, because devil want to destroy our souls. Animal had no soul, but animal wiser than man. But, I think man ought to be wiser than animal because man has soul. Brethren and sisters, let us be wise. It we do not be faithful to serving God, we shall be lost for ever and ever. One thing more I want to mention to you, that is about squirrel. Squirrel do not like to be suffer in the winter time. Squirrel knows winter come by and by; so in the fall work all the time; get acorns out of the trees, and carry into the hollow logs for winter. And all the good people, they know Jesus Christ come by and by, so Christians they pray every day. As squirrel do carry acorns into the hollow logs, so the good man he want to get great deal religion in his heart, so his soul might be saved. Look to the wild geese, while they feeding, one always watch for fear the enemies will catch them; wild geese do not like to be killed. I think man ought to be wiser than they are. We must watch and pray every day because devil want to kill our souls every day . . .[7]

So popular were John Sunday's sermons that they were identified as 'his Beaver speech, his Pike and Pickerel speech, his account of Mr Gold, etc.'[8] His quaint 'gold speech' always won over his listeners, as it did at the Metropolitan Methodist Church in Toronto:

There is a gentleman, I suppose, now in this house; he is a very *fine* gentleman, but he is very *modest.* He does not like to show himself. I do not know how long it is now since I saw him, he comes out so little. I very much afraid he sleeps a great deal of his time, when he ought to be going about doing good. His name is *Mr Gold.* Mr Gold, are you here to-night? or are you sleeping in your iron chest? Come out, Mr Gold: come out, and help us to do this great work, to preach the Gospel to every creature: Ah, Mr Gold, you ought to be ashamed of yourself, to sleep so much in your iron chest: Look at your white brother, *Mr Silver:* he does a great deal of good in the world while you are sleeping. Come out, Mr Gold: Look, too, at your *little* brown brother, *Master Copper.* He *everywhere!* Your little brother, running about all the time, doing all he can. Why don't you *come out*, Mr Gold? Well, if you *won't* come out, and give us *yourself*, send us your shirt, that is, a BANK NOTE.[9]

While many of the native preachers delivered stodgy, matter-of-fact sermons that displayed their learning, Sunday's sermons were unorthodox, peppered with earthy and personal anecdotes and amusing allusions. In a sermon to the congregation in Plymouth, England, in 1837, he said:

I understand that many of you are disappointed because I have not brought my Indian dress with me. Perhaps if I had it on you would be afraid of me. Do you wish to know how I was dressed when I was a pagan

Indian? I will tell you—my face was covered with red paint, I stuck feathers in my hair, I wore leggings and a blanket,I had silver ornaments on my breast, a rifle on my shoulder and a tomahawk and scalping knife in my belt—that was my dress then. Now do you wish to know why I wear it no longer? You will find the cause in 2 Corinthians 5:17—'Therefore if any man be in Christ he is a new creature: old things have passed away; behold all things are become new.' When I became a Christian, feathers and paint passed away. I gave my silver ornaments to the mission cause.' [Holding up a copy of the Ten Commandments in the Ojibway language, he said:] 'That my tomahawk now: Blanket done away: Behold all things are become new.'[10]

The most popular native writer of this period was George Copway (Kah-ge-ga-gah-bowh, 'Firm Standing'), who was the first Canadian Indian to write a book in English. Within the first year of its publication his autobiography, *The Life, History, and Travels of Kah-ge-ga-gah-bowh (George Copway)* (1847), became such a success that it was reprinted six times. It was praised by several leading literary figures, including Henry Wadsworth Longfellow—who befriended Copway —and James Fenimore Cooper. Three years later Copway published *The Traditional History and Characteristics Sketches of the Ojibwa Nation*, the first tribal history written in English by a North American Indian. In 1851 he published a travelogue on his British and European travels in *Running Sketches of Men and Places in England, France, Germany, Belgium and Scotland* and launched a brief weekly newspaper from New York, *Copway's American Indian*.[11]

Copway (1818-69) was one of the first North American Indians to have his works widely circulated and read by whites. This extraordinary Ojibway was born in an Indian camp near the mouth of the Trent River in Upper Canada. Nine years later his parents became members of the Methodist church, which had built a mission station for the Rice Lake Indian band. George joined the church in 1830 and attended the Methodist school, which at the time was taught by James Evans. He was so highly regarded that in 1834, at the age of sixteen, he was selected to accompany a missionary party, which included John Sunday, to the Lake Superior region. Working as an interpreter and teacher, Copway spent three winters in the area. During the winter of 1836, at La Pointe (Wisconsin), he helped the Reverend Sherman Hall translate the Acts of the Apostles and the Gospel of St Luke into Ojibway.

In 1838 Copway's superiors sent him to the Ebenezer Manual Labor School at Jacksonville, Illinois, where he studied until the fall of 1839. He then returned to Canada. At the Credit River Mission, Copway fell in love with Elizabeth Howell, a well-educated young

Yorkshire woman, daughter of Captain Henry Howell who had settled near Toronto. He married her six months later, in the summer of
1840, against her family's wishes. They spent two years in the Upper
Mississippi missions, in the Sioux and the Ojibway war zone, which
forced them to move the mission several times. They finally settled at
Fond-du-lac at the head of Lake Superior.

They returned to Canada in late 1842, and early in 1843 they were
sent on a three-month missionary fund-raising tour of Upper Canada
with the Reverend William Ryerson. For the next two years Copway
worked at the Saugeen and Rice Lake missions. In the summer of
1845 he reached the high point of his missionary career when he was
elected vice-president of the Grand Council of the Methodist Ojibways of Canada West. Less than a year later the Saugeen and Rice
Lake bands accused Copway of embezzlement, and during the summer of 1846 he was imprisoned for several weeks and expelled from
the Canadian Conference of the Wesleyan Methodist Church. Upon
his release the Copways moved back to the United States, where his
publications made him a literary celebrity and popular lecturer.

Copway's training as a Methodist preacher had equipped him for
extensive lecturing and fund-raising tours. His popularity as a public
speaker was unmatched. He delivered addresses on such topics as
'The Influence of Christianity on the Untutored Children of the
West', 'The Romance and Poetry of the Indians', and 'Temperance'.
His style was so striking that on hearing Copway's lecture on temperance, the editor of the *Charleston Courier* was reduced to describing it by a rather breathless list of descriptive phrases:

> Biting satire—pungent anecdote . . . strokes of wit and humour—
> touches of pathos . . . bursts of vehement declamation after the manner
> now of a Forest, or a Cooper, and now of a zealous Western preacher—
> slip-shod conversational talk—most poetical descriptions of nature,
> fearless statement, off-hand, calm, Indian independence, altogether
> formed a compound of a rather rare and inimitable nature.[12]

Copway became a major spokesman for native American rights,
touring the United States and delivering addresses from South Caro-
lina to Massachusetts, championing the cause of his people and requesting support for his scheme for a large tract of land on the east
bank of the Missouri River to be set aside as a country for Indians in
present-day South Dakota to be known as Kahgega ('Ever to be').[13]
Although Copway's vision appealed to many prominent Americans
who did not approve of their country's unfair treatment of the Indian, it was not fulfilled. The American government was deeply committed to its official Indian-removal policy.

If Copway saw this dream fail, his publications did not. His

Traditional History of 1850 was widely publicized and brought him international recognition, with invitations to speak in Europe and at the third General World Peace Congress in Frankfurt in August of that year.

On his return to the United States in 1851 he wrote about his experience abroad in his *Running Sketches* and launched his weekly newspaper to secure support for the implementation of his scheme for an Indian homeland. But the paper survived for only three months (10 July to 4 October 1851)—even though it had the support of the ethnologist Henry Rowe Schoolcraft, the novelists James Fenimore Cooper and Washington Irving, and the historian Francis Parkman (who nevertheless took a dim view of Copway's 'flash-in-the-pan' scheme). Many of Copway's admirers deserted and distrusted him. He had become a confused individual, torn by conflicting loyalties. He wanted to be accepted into the world of the white man, and yet he was bound by a pride in his own people's heritage.

After 1851 Copway fell into obscurity and poverty, trying to make a living in the United States as an American army recruiter and herbal doctor. In the summer of 1868 he appeared at the Algonkin-Iroquois mission of Lac-des-Deux Montagnes northwest of Montreal. He became involved in the quarrel between the Sulpicians, who claimed ownership of the reserve, and the Iroquois who were threatening to convert to Methodism in protest. He alienated the Iroquois when a Methodist preacher arrived and he persuaded most of the Algonkins not to attend the service. Copway was preparing for his own conversion to Roman Catholicism and was baptized on 17 January 1869. A few days later, on the night before his first communion, the former Methodist missionary, and Canada's first Indian author in English, unexpectedly died.

Copway's 1847 autobiography, which was later published in London as *Recollections of a Forest Life* (1850)—the first ever written by a Canadian Indian—provides a unique picture of what it was like to grow up as a nineteenth-century woodlands Ojibway. It is a memoir of a happy childhood spent in the traditional migratory way, hunting, trapping, fishing, and picking wild rice. But besides his happy recollections, Copway also remembers the hardships. He tells of one winter when he and his family nearly starved to death. So much snow had fallen that it was impossible to shoot or trap any game and the family was forced to eat their beaver skins and old moccasins. Only on the tenth day of their ordeal did they manage to kill two beaver, just before they became too weak to move.

The book stresses Copway's commitment to Christianity as the Indians' salvation: 'In the days of our ignorance we used to dance around the fire. I shudder when I think of those days of our darkness. I thought the Spirit would be kind to me if I danced before the old men; and day after day, or night after night, I have been employed with others in this way. I thank God that those days will never return.'[14] And when he describes his birth and youth, he waxes poetic with a romantically idealistic pride:

I was born in *Nature's wide domain*! The trees were all that sheltered my infant limbs—the blue heavens all that covered me. I am one of Nature's children; I have always admired her; she shall be my glory; her features—her robes, and the wreath about her brow—the seasons—her stately oaks, and the evergreen—her hair, ringlets over the earth—all contribute to my enduring love of her; and wherever I see her, emotions of pleasure roll in my breast, and swell and burst like waves on the shores of the ocean, in prayer and praise to Him who has placed me in her hand. It is thought great to be born in palaces, surrounded with wealth—but to be born in Nature's wide domain is greater still . . .

I remember the tall trees, and the dark woods—the swamp just by, where the little wren sang so melodiously after the going down of the sun in the west—the current of the broad river Trent—the skipping of the fish, and the noise of the rapids a little above. It was here I first saw the light; a little fallen down shelter, made of evergreens, and a few dead embers, the remains of the last fire that shed its genial warmth around, were all that marked the spot. When I last visited it, nothing but fur poles stuck in the ground, and they were leaning on account of decay. Is this dear spot, made green by tears of memory, any less enticing and hallowed than the palaces where princes are born? I would much more glory in this birthplace, with the broad canopy of heaven above me, and the giant arms of the forest trees for my shelter, than to be born in palaces of marble, studded with pillars of gold! Nature will be Nature still, while palaces shall decay and fall in ruins. Yes, Niagara will be Niagara a thousand years hence! The rainbow, a wreath over her brow, shall continue as long as the sun, and the flowing of the river—while the work of art, however impregnable, shall in atoms fall![15]

With Copway's *Traditional History*, a famous publication of the time, he hoped 'to awaken in the American heart a deeper feeling for the race of red men, and induce the pale face to use greater effort to effect an improvement in their social and political relations.'[16] Written in a rambling style, the book traces his people's migrations as described in their legends and discusses their wars with their historic enemies, the Iroquois and Sioux. His tribe's religious beliefs, forms of government, language, pictograph writings, modes of hunting and games, are also discussed, and a number of important legends are recorded, including the tale of the great Thunder Bird that lived in a time 'when no wars existed among men, and the only thing they feared was a great bird.'[17]

Copway proudly wrote of the Ojibway language: 'A person might have travelled nearly one thousand miles from the head of Lake Superior, and yet not journey from the sound of this dialect.'[18] He praised its musical qualities and its rich abundance of words.

After reading the English language, I found words in the Indian combining more expressiveness. There are many Indian words which when translated into English lose their force, and do not convey so much meaning in one sentence as the original does in one word.

It would require an almost infinitude of English words to describe a thunder-storm, and after all you would have but a feeble idea of it. In the Ojibwa language, we say 'Be-wah-sam-moog'. In this we convey the idea of a continual glare of lightning, noise, confusion—an awful whirl of clouds, and much more . . .

It is a natural language. The pronunciation of the names of animals, birds and trees are the very sounds they produce; for instance, hoot owl, o-o-me-seh; owl, koo-koo-ko-ooh; river, see-be; rapids, *sah se-je-won*. 'See' is the sound of the waters on the rocks,—'*Sah-see*' the commotion of waters, and from its sound occurs its name.

The softness of the language is caused . . . by the peculiar sounding of all the vowels; though there is but little poetic precision in the formation of verse, owing to the want of a fine discriminating taste by those who speak it.

A language, derived, as this is, from the peculiarities of the country in which it is spoken, must, necessarily, partake of its nature. Our orators have filled the forest with the music of their voices, loud as the roar of a water fall, yet soft and wooing as the gentle murmur of a mountain stream. We have had warriors who have stood on the banks of lakes and rivers, and addressed with words of irresistible and persuasive eloquence their companions in arms . . .[19]

(Mrs Anna Jameson, in her *Winter Studies and Summer Rambles in Canada* (1838), also paid tribute to the Ojibway language: 'It is not only very sweet and musical to the ear, with its soft inflections and lengthened vowels, but very complex and artificial in its construction and subject to strict grammatical rules.')[20]

Copway's *Running Sketches* contains his impressions of his travels throughout the British Isles and continental Europe as well as his experiences as a Native American delegate to the Peace Congress at Frankfurt. His divided loyalties made it possible for him to say that 'Art, Science, Literature[,] like a thousand streams[,] roll on their mighty tide, to purify and refine the Indian mind,'[21] and also to blame the white man for 'all the many aggravated wrongs which my poor brethren have received from the hands of the Pale Face.'[22] Whether his educated English wife, Elizabeth, collaborated in the writing of his books no one can be certain;[23] but in his *Traditional History*, written for a purpose, his passionate sincerity in the cause of his people shines through his colourful and sometimes flamboyant language.

Another Ojibway who wrote about his travels was George Henry (Maungwudaus), son of Mesquacosy and Tubenahneeguay, who was Peter Jones's half-brother through their mother. He was born at Forty Mile Creek in 1811, and raised in the traditional migratory manner until he converted to Christianity in 1824 and showed himself to be a promising native candidate for the Methodist ministry. He taught at the Credit Mission Sunday School, accompanied a missionary touring party to Sault Ste Marie, and acted as interpreter at the Munceytown mission. In the later 1830s he helped James Evans write an Ojibway hymn book and worked as the Indian-language preacher for the Reverend John Douse at the St Clair and Walpole Island missions. He was respected by his own people and also by the white missionaries, who had high hopes for the young native convert. From his mission station at St Clair, Henry regularly sent letters to the *Christian Guardian*, the Methodist newspaper published in York (Toronto). His letters reveal the extent of his assimilation:

> Yes, Mr Papermaker, if you had seen these Indians a few years ago, you would think they were the animals you called Ourang Outangs, for they appeared more like them than human beings; but since the Great Spirit has blessed them, they have good clothes; plates and dishes; window and bed curtains, knives and forks; chairs and tables; and one of the chiefs has saved plenty of duck and partridge feathers, and has a good feather bed,—but what is better than all these things they have the religion of Jesus Christ in their hearts'.[24]

At this stage in his life Henry seemed glad to have conformed to the customs of the white Christians. The Reverend Benjamin Slight praised him as 'a clever, respectable looking young man, and a good speaker, said to be a good divine, a tolerable poet and an excellent translator'.[25] Along with Peter Jones, John Sunday, and Peter Jacobs, Henry was considered one of the foremost pioneers of the Methodist Church in Canada.

In 1840, however, disillusioned by the factionalism that was breaking up the Church, Henry left the ministry. For the next three years he was employed as the government interpreter at the St Clair mission. In 1844, to his half-brother's horror, Henry helped organize a dance troupe, consisting of family members and several Walpole Island Ojibway, to tour England. They performed in a number of American cities on the way and on 1 March 1845 sailed from New York to Portsmouth. Henry was entertained and honoured as a celebrity by royalty and high society alike.

The following year George Catlin, the famous American artist, sponsored Henry's tour in France. King Louis Philippe invited the troupe to perform at St Cloud, just outside Paris. Four thousand people, including the King and Queen of France and the King and Queen of Belgium, watched the exotic performers. From Paris they went to Brussels and then to Britain, where they spent the next year touring England, Scotland, and Ireland. In 1848 they set sail for home. Once back in North America, Henry disappeared from the documentary record, though he wrote three travelogues about his experiences abroad. *Remarks Concerning the Ojibway Indians, By One of Themselves, Called Maungwudaus* (1847) includes a short account of the overseas tour as well as a few particulars regarding Indian religion and customs and a few testimonials. *An Account of the North American Indians* (1848) contains a very short description of their overseas tour. *An Account of the Chippewa Indians, Who Have Been Travelling Among the Whites, in the United States, England, Ireland, Scotland, France and Belgium* (1848) is by far his most detailed literary effort. Recording his impressions of London, Paris, Dublin, Edinburgh, and Glasgow, it contains quick thumbnail sketches of persons and places, shrewd comments on the contemporary scene, lively anecdotes, and touches of humour.

. . . Like musketoes in America in the summer season, so are the people in this city [London], in their numbers, and biting one another to get a living . . .

Mr Harris took us into the Queen's house. She is a small woman but handsome. There are many handsomer woman than she is. Prince Albert is a handsome and a well built man. Her house is large, quiet country inside of it. We got tired before we went through all the rooms in it. Great many warriors with their swords and guns stands outside watching for the enemy. We have been told that she has three or four other houses in other places as large. The one we saw they say is too small for her, and they are building a much larger one on one side of it.

When she goes out she has a great many warriors before and behind, guarding her; most of them seven feet tall. Their coats and caps are of steel; long white horse-hair waves on their heads. They wear long boots, long gloves, and white buckskin breeches. Their swords, guns, and everything about them are kept very clean and bright. Their horses are all black, and much silver and gold about them. They do not shave the upper part of their mouths, but let the beards grow long, and this makes them look fierce and savage like our American dogs when carrying black squirrels in their mouths . . .

The English officers invited us to eat with them in the barracks in our native costume. When the tea got ready, the ladies were brought to the table like sick women; it took us about two hours in eating. The ladies were very talkative while eating; like ravens when feasting on venison. . . . They are very handsome; their waists, hands and feet are very small; their necks are rather longer than those of our women. They carry their heads on one side of the shoulder; they hold the knife and fork with the two fore-fingers and the thumb of each hand; the two last ones are of no use to them, only sticking out like our fish-spears, while eating.

The English officers are fine, noble, and dignified looking fellows. The voice of them when coming out of the mouth, sounds like the voice of a bull-frog. The only fault we saw of them, are their too many unnecessary ceremonies while eating, such as allow me Sir, or Mrs to put this into your plate. If you please Sir, thank you, you are very kind Sir, or Mrs can I have the pleasure of helping you?

Many of the Englishmen have very big stomachs, caused by drinking too much ale and porter. Those who drink wine and brandy, their noses look like ripe strawberries.

When we got ready to leave, one of the officers said to us, our ladies would be glad to shake hands with you, and we shook hands with them. Then they were talking amongst themselves; then another officer said to us, 'Friends, our ladies think that you do not pay enough respects to them, they desire you to kiss them; then we kissed them according to our custom on both cheeks. 'Why! they have kissed us on our cheeks; what a curious way of kissing this is.' Then another officer said to us, 'Gentlemen, our pretty squaws are not yet satisfied; they want to be kissed on their mouths. Then we kissed them on their mouths; then there was a great shout amongst the English war-chiefs. Say-say-gon, our war-chief, then said in our language to the ladies: 'That is all you are good for; as for wives, you are good for nothing.' The ladies wanted me to tell them what the war-chief said to them. I told them that he said he was wishing the officers would invite him very often, that he might again kiss the handsome ladies. They said, 'Did he? then we will tell our men to invite you again, for we like to be kissed very often; tell him so.' They put gold rings on our fingers and gold pins on our breasts, and when we had thanked them for their kindness, we got in our carriage and we went to our apartments. . . .[26]

Peter Jacobs (Pahtahsega—'He who comes shining') was another early convert. Born at Rice Lake, Upper Canada, Jacobs (1809-90) was educated by the Methodists and trained by William Case (1788-1855), the former American circuit-rider who was the leader of the Methodists in Upper Canada, and by James Evans, who was very impressed by the young native convert's intelligence. While still a youth Jacobs was sent to be a missionary among the Indians in the Northwest, stationed at the Hudson's Bay Company fort, Norway House. In 1844 the Company sent Jacobs to an International Conference of Methodist missionaries in England. He was the first native to address the monster assembly in Exeter Hall, and his impassioned appeals for the Northwest missions were highly successful. During his stay in Britain he had an audience with the Queen, and was accorded the same honour thirteen years later. By 1862, after many years as a missionary among the Indians of the Northwest and in the Lake Superior region, he was posted to Rama, Upper Canada. About this time he was read out of the Methodist Church because of his heavy drinking. He then eked out a precarious livelihood and died in destitution.

When Jacobs died the Orillia *Daily Times* (4 September 1890) wrote that 'at one time Peter Jacobs was probably the best-known Indian on the continent'. He had lectured throughout Canada and the United States on the manners and customs of the Indians, and his letters, reports, and addresses had been printed in a number of Western Methodist publications. In 1858 he had published his journal, which included a brief review of his life and a sketch of the Wesleyan missions in the Hudson's Bay Company Territories, with interesting references to Jones, Evans, William Mason, Henry Steinhauer, Thomas Hurlburt, and other missionaries to native tribes. His *Journal of the Reverend Peter Jacobs, Indian Wesleyan Missionary, from Rice Lake to the Hudson's Bay Territory, and Returning. Commencing May, 1852 . . .* (1853) begins with a brief first-person narrative that focuses on his conversion. His love of nature is evidenced throughout. When he saw Niagara Falls for the first time he wrote:

. . . I went down to see the greatest fall in the world. The cataract is indeed awfully grand; and it appeared to me as if an angry God was dwelling beneath it, for my whole frame shook as a leaf while I was viewing these mighty angry Falls. Now 'tis no wonder that my forefathers, in bygone days, should offer up sacrifices at the foot of these Falls; they used to come and pray to the God of the fall to bless them in their hunt and to prolong their life and that of their children; for every Indian believed that a God dwelt under this mighty sheet of water . . .[27]

Jacobs was a magnetic speaker, and whether at home or abroad he attracted vast crowds. His gift for oratory and his sense of humour are seen in this address delivered to the annual meeting of the Wesleyan Missionary Society, held at Exeter Hall, London, in 1851:

Mr Chairman, I expect that a good many of my friends here are accustomed to hear of my long speeches; but I know that an Englishman always looks about four or five o'clock for his dinner, and as it is now past four,I do not intend to keep you from your dinner this afternoon. (Laughter.) However, I shall occupy your attention for a few moments, while I endeavour to impress on your minds some very important truths. Poor North America has very small say in this great assemblage, although you know, that North America would put your England into one of her inland seas, Lake-Huron, Lake-Superior, or Lake-Ontario. I only tell you this, to show what a tremendous large country it is. I am only twenty years of age,—in Christianity, I mean. (Cheers.) Twenty years ago, or thereabouts, I was, with my countrymen, a worshipper of the sun and the moon. When your Missionaries came to us, and preached Christ, and Him crucified,I was led, by the preaching of the Missionaries, to come and pray to God through Christ. Formerly, my prayers were something like this [the speaker, having repeated the prayer in his native language, translated it as follows:]—'O god, the moon,—O god, the sun,—direct my steps through the woods in the direction where the deer are feeding, that I may kill him, and have something to eat.' This was all the prayer we could utter; and then we were all very wicked. We had no Lawyers, and there were no law-suits; we settled all our affairs by the force of the tomahawk; and, as regards to our women, we did not use them with that civility that we now use them.

In all Heathen countries, women stand in a very low class. Now, never send a Missionary into a Heathen country without his wife. If you send a Missionary who is a single man, he is only a half a Missionary. When you send him back with his wife, he is a whole Missionary. (Laughter and cheering.) We men look to the Missionaries and respect them; but how are our females to be advanced, unless you send Missionaries' wives? Now, then, the Missionary is respected by the men, and the Missionary's wife is respected by our females; and that excellent woman, the Missionary's wife, teaches our females not to be tramped down as we did tramp them down when we were Heathens. They teach them to be respected more. They say, 'Come up, come up', and they are up. (Cheers.) Why, there was a time when a poor woman could not say any thing against her lord, for fear of the tomahawk. Now, I expect, we have been so much Christianized and civilized, that I shall when I go home, hear at my ear a voice telling me that I have been very many months away. But I shall be very deaf, that is all. (Cheering and laughter.) I have told you in what state we were. Now, at Alderville, there are beautiful buildings; there is an academy, and a large house where the whole of these young men go; and there is a house for the Missionaries, erected partly by the industry of the Indians, partly by your aid, and partly by the aid of Government. In that academy, fifty young men were educated for Missions, and also forty young women. Why, in my early day, the cry of the war-whoop was given on the birth of a boy. But what was the case, on the other hand, when a girl was born? Why, it was said, 'Another good-for-nothing girl is born'; but Christianity has taught the heart of a father to rejoice now as much in the birth of a girl as in the birth of a boy. (Cheers.) The Rev. Dr Ryerson knew the time when we did not raise a grain of wheat; we raised nothing but our Indian corn and potatoes; but now, through all Canada, what do the Indians raise?. They raise fields of wheat, fields of rye, fields of oats, and fields of Indian corn. There are Indians with fine houses, their horses, their oxen, their cows, their sheep, and their pigs; all this you have done, you, the supporters of the Mission cause. (Loud cheers.)[28]

Jacobs proceeded to review the improvements that had been made at the St Clair mission, as well as the Norway House and Oxford House missions in the Hudson's Bay Company Territories, and then pleaded for more missionaries and financial aid—very much in the style of white missionaries to India and China:

Why, Mr Chairman, when I go back to the Hudson's Bay Territory they will ask, 'Where is the Missionary you were to bring with you? You have not,' they will say, 'told the people of England anything.' I shall say, 'My dear brethren, I did plead the cause, every day and every night, in all parts of the country, while I was in England; I told the Christian people of England, we want two more Missionaries, and, if we cannot get two, we must be content with one.' Now, I join with my countrymen in praying for you, in praying that God will reward you for what you have done: he will reward you, and does reward you. I know that what you have given, year after year, towards this good cause, will not grieve you in the hour of death. On the contrary it will be a source of great joy to you, especially when you know, as I have seen many times, poor Johnny Curlyhead, in the Hudson's Bay Territories, who was a very faithful man. By and by poor John got very sick, and I went to see John. I say 'John, I see you are dying; how do you feel now in the dreadful hour of death? How is thy faith in Christ?' 'My faith in Christ,' he says, 'is as firm as a rock; I am immovable; I have nothing here on earth but Christ; I have nothing in heaven but Christ'; and he says, in closing his eyes, 'O Jesus! sweet Saviour! come now, take me away to those mansions above.' John closed his eyes in death; and he has gone to heaven. What did I feel? Pressing my hand to my heart, I said, 'My heavenly Father, help me, by the assistance of thy Holy Spirit, to walk in the right way, in that narrow path, during life; so that, when I die, I may join the spirit of poor John, which has gone to sing praises with the Redeemer at the right hand of the Father!' (Great cheering)[29]

Jacobs, like all his missionary colleagues, was a prolific letter-writer. The following extract from a letter he wrote to the Methodist Missionary Society, dated Fort Frances, 15 January 1848, shows the difficulties the missionaries encountered in their attempts to convert the Indians, as well as the scale of the competitive missionary enterprises of the nineteenth century. It also reveals Jacobs' frankness, his gift for amusing anecdote, and his ability to weave Biblical references into his writing.

Grace be to you, and peace, from God our Father, and from the Lord Jesus Christ. In speaking of my Mission among the Lac-la-Pluie Indians, I am sorry to say that they are like the Jews of old, 'Behold, this people is a stiff-necked people'; they are wholly given to idolatry in opposition to Christianity. They have in the past year erected about fifty temporary temples, wherein they assemble all their followers, and there worship their Heathen gods (idols). The glory of idolatrous worship among these people has never been so high with them since the days of the first Adam; and I think, and indeed I may hope, that these Indians are now on the summit of their Heathen glory, and from there the Heathen glory must, sooner or later, fall to the ground, and be trodden under foot by the messengers of the cross of Christ. Concerning these Lac-la-Pluie Indians I may say with St Paul, 'Woe is unto me' if I have not faithfully preached to them the Gospel of our Lord and Saviour Jesus Christ. I have done everything to promote the kingdom of God among these people; but it appears to be like the 'bread' that was 'cast upon the waters' which was found after many days. When we first came amongst these Indians, they all considered us (the Wesleyan Missionaries) their enemies; but now they all consider us their best friends. . . .[30]

Allen Salt (1818-1911) was born near Alderville, Northumberland County, Upper Canada, of an Ojibway mother and a white father. His mother died while he was young, and he was adopted and educated by the Reverend William Case. Salt excelled under Case's care and graduated from the Toronto Normal School in 1848. After he taught for several years at the Alderville Industrial School, he entered the ministry of the Wesleyan Methodist Conference in 1853. He was ordained the following year and began a ministry that was to last fifty-eight years, until his death at the age of ninety-three. He served in the Northwest Territories for four years, and in Ontario he ministered to his people at the St Clair, Garden River, Muncey, Christian Island, and Parry Island missions. His biographer stated that 'His ministry . . . parallels the welding together of isolated colonies by the railroad, the birth of Canada as a nation, and takes us on an adventure to the wilds of the frontier.'[31]

Salt was one of the best-educated Indians of his day and his writing exhibits a high degree of competence. His Journals are full of interesting entries, such as this one from the Muncey mission dated Thursday, 21 January 1875:

I buried at Colbourne Peter Simon aged about 93 years. Died in the faith. Fought with the British in 1812. He was present when Tecumseh fell.[32]

The following extract from his Annual Report on the state of the church at St Clair gives us an idea of what missionary reports were like at the time:

With feelings of gratitude to God I write to say that in the past Conference year the means of grace have been well attended. Very few families absented themselves for a little time from the Reserve. Meeting the classes personally has given me much comfort and encouragement. In this means of grace I have met some, though unlettered, yet for about 38 years have adorned the power of grace. Also a few months ago, William Kachenoding, who used to get drunk and abuse his associates, the work of God has brought to his right state of mind, and he now rejoices in God his Saviour. He assists in leading a class. A blackslider for many years, Charles Madwayah by name, joined with us a few weeks before he died. His wife, faithful to the end, followed two weeks after, saying that she was not afraid to die. An aged sick woman, about 104 years of age, requested to be baptized by your Missionary. After answering the questions she was baptized in the Christian faith. She died a few days afterwards. She was the mother of old Mr Rodd, a member of the English Church on the Reserve. One class leader, Wazah-Wahnequa, died in the enjoyment of peace. I visited and administered the Sacrament of the Lord's Supper to him. Asking him if he was happy, he said, 'Yes! and that I might be so, I have laboured while I was in health.' He looked up so happy that I said to him, 'It may be that you will recover.' He said 'Just as the Lord sees best', and he died the next morning.

The old chief, Joshua Wawanosh, has also passed away. It will be remembered that he was one of the first converts of the Methodist Missionaries on this Mission, and that a few years since had joined the English Church. I consider him a Methodist at heart . . .

His son William [Wawanosh] told me, that when his father prayed it was according to his first way, and when he sang it was the Methodist hymns. Father Waldron and I visited the Chief in his sickness. The day before he died I and his family sang and prayed in his room. In consciousness he said that his trust was in Jesus.

The membership now, after deducting deaths, is 190, there being a small increase of 5. The day-school has been well kept, and attended by about 40 scholars. The band furnishes the school books and the greater part of the teacher's salary. The Sabbath-school has also been kept up, but is in want of catechisms and singing books.

Our Indians, with their own hands, have put up a neat frame Church, 30 by 50 feet, with a coat of paint and a tower for a bell, and the floor laid; what it needs is lath and plastering, pews and pulpit, paint and a bell. A tea-making was furnished by Wm. Wawanosh, which brought $23.71, and this is all the money we have at present. Another Indian is to furnish a tea-meeting next Thursday, the proceeds to be applied to the new Church. May the Lord send help. With the work that our people can do I think $200 would finish it. ...

Allen Salt[33]

An Ojibway named Sowengisik, who later became the Reverend Henry Bird Steinhauer (1804-85), was born on the eastern shore of Lake Couchiching near Rama in Upper Canada. He was brought into the Methodist Church by William Case, who sent him to the Grape Island school to be educated. Possessing a very musical voice, he was selected by Case to be one of a little group of native children to tour various parts of the United States to sing Indian hymns, give addresses, and display samples of their work in order to show their audiences the Indians' capabilities. During a visit to Philadelphia a gentleman named Henry Steinhauer was so impressed by the young Indian boys that he asked William Case to select a promising lad whom he would educate at his own expense. Case chose Sowengisik, who took his benefactor's name.

Steinhauer was sent to the Grape Island school (1829-32) and to the Cazanovia Seminary in New York (1832-5), and then began working as a school-teacher at the Credit River mission on Lake Ontario. After a year there Egerton Ryerson sent him to the Upper Canada Academy, Cobourg (later known as Victoria College). A year later he went to Alderville to teach school and then returned for another year to the Academy, where he was a first-class student and a proficient Greek and Hebrew scholar. Having finished his course, he returned to Alderville and taught school there until 1840, when he was sent with James Evans to a mission near Norway House in Canada's Northwest and worked with Evans on the Cree syllabic characters, translating into Cree large sections of the Old and New Testaments. In 1851 he established a Methodist mission at Oxford House (Manitoba), and in 1855, after a trip to England with the Reverend John Ryerson, he was ordained into the Wesleyan Methodist Church. He was posted to what is now Alberta, and in 1860 established a mission at Whitefish Lake, where he died in 1885.

Many of the Indians converted by the Wesleyan missionaries in Upper Canada and who became missionaries themselves, isolated as they were from each other, kept in contact through letters, which were often published in the *Christian Guardian*. For example, Steinhauer wrote to Peter Jacobs from the Wesleyan mission station at Jackson's Bay, Oxford Lake:

To the Rev. P. Jacobs,   *3rd Dec., 1853*

Rev. and Dear Friend,—Again the usual season for writing to friends at a distance has come about, and as such seasons in this country are like Angels' visits 'few and far between', I therefore avail myself of it, in tendering you my grateful acknowledgements for the very kind and welcome favour of May last, the contents of which as containing sentiments of the kindest regard for my poor self,—personal welfare,—and for the prosperity of the good cause among the people belonging to the Station with which I am connected; and for which, please accept my best and sincerest thanks.

You may be sure we are very much disappointed after anxiously waiting your arrival, the summer at last ended and you did not come.—How is this?—There must certainly 'be something wrong in the state of Denmark', and now all hope of your coming to this country in '53 must be given up altogether, and are we to bless ourselves with the idea the great ones of the great world have given us up and forgotten us, buried as we are amid the snows of the inhospitable region? Be that as it may. I feel thankful to Almighty God, that through his good providence myself and family are in the enjoyment of good health, and endeavouring to our humble way to press forward in the good way, and are still trying by feeble efforts to induce others to do the same. And we are encouraged to persevere in this work of faith and labour of love, from the manifest tokens of God answering prayer, and blessing the feeble means made use of to make His name and love to this benighted people. My heart's desire and prayer to God for this people, is, that they may be saved from sin—truly converted. I have some hopes for the male part of those who are now with us, inasmuch as they appear to be orderly in their deportment, and seriously concerned about their soul's salvation, and dare very regular (when at home) in their attendance to the means of grace.

There are only four families and three widows remaining and spending the winter with us, and all snug and comfortable in their houses, and all I think, pretty well supplied with fish, and rabbits are quite numerous; so that we, by the good providence of God, are freed, at least for the present, from the fearful apprehension of starving for want of those things which God provides and places within our reach.

My school this winter numbers twenty scholars of boys and girls, and four adults. They are very regular in their attendance, and quite anxious to learn. Our only drawback in this department, is the want of school-books. We shall be glad when your box of books comes, which you have promised to the Hudson's Bay Missions, and gladder still will we be should we have the happiness of seeing you again in this country.—I must also thank you for your kindness which you have exerted in my behalf with the great folk in Canada, and also for the kind manner in which you have communicated their opinion, which is, for me to remain in this country; and I suppose I must, not as a matter of choice, but of necessity. I must conclude by requesting an interest in your prayers, and with hoping to see you here or hear from you the next summer; and till then Adieu.

I remain, as ever,

Yours most truly,
Henry B. Steinhauer[34]

Letters such as Steinhauer's reveal the fluency with which the early preachers—with little formal education, but a thorough knowledge of the Bible—wrote in English.

Cross-cultural marriages resulted in the spread of literacy and of writing. Children from these marriages were sometimes sent abroad to complete their education, and the home often had good libraries. This was true, for example, in the frontier society around Sault Ste Marie, where there was a surprising amount of literary activity among the Indian, French, and English families. Though it took place mainly in the Michigan settlement of that name, rather than in the Canadian one across the St Mary's River, the border was disregarded and there was exchange between those who were loyal to the British Crown and those who remained on the American side, by reason of both trade and affection.

Henry Rowe Schoolcraft—the Indian agent at Sault Ste Marie, Michigan, from 1822 to 1833—began to produce, in the context of the local society of readers, the first magazine in Michigan and one of the first ethnological magazines in North America, *The Literary Voyager or Muzzeniegun*, published irregularly between December 1826 and April 1827. Schoolcraft's Indian wife Jane (1800-42) contributed to the journal under the pen-name Rosa. Jane was the daughter of Susan, a well-known storyteller, herself the daughter of a Chippewa chief (Waubojeeg, c. 1747-93), who was also a distinguished storyteller. Jane's father was John Johnston, a British trader at Sault Ste Marie.

Jane Schoolcraft and Mrs Anna Jameson became close and dear friends while Mrs Jameson was in the region in the summer of 1837. A poem by Jane illustrates the evangelical sentimental romanticism of her circle:

TO SISTERS ON A WALK IN THE GARDEN, AFTER A SHOWER
Come, sisters come! the shower's past,
The garden walks are drying fast,
The Sun's bright beams are seen again,
And nought within, can now detain.
The rain drops tremble on the leaves,
Or drip expiring, from the eaves:
But soon the cool and balmy air,
Shall dry the gems that sparkle there,
With whisp'ring breath shake ev'ry spray,
And scatter every cloud away.

Thus sisters! shall the breeze of hope,
Through sorrow's clouds a vista ope;
Thus, shall affliction's surly blast,
By faith's bright calm be still'd at last;
Thus, pain and care,—the tear and sigh,
Be chased from every dewy eye;
And life's mix'd scene itself, but cease,
To show us realms of light and peace.
—*Rosa*[35]

While the Methodists were active in Upper Canada—after 1828, under the leadership of William Case, who had become superintendent of the Upper Canada Conference—the Church Missionary Society (Anglican) was asked to enter the Red River Settlement to minister to the white settlers and evangelize and civilize the Indians. The Reverend James West, who was appointed the first chaplain at the Hudson's Bay Company fort, selected promising native youths from York Factory to be educated as interpreters, teachers, and possibly missionaries. There was scarcely anything that could be called a literary movement and there was no such central figure as Peter Jones in the Red River area. But there were several individual writers of some significance, such as Henry Budd. West named Budd (c. 1810-75) after his former rector in England and helped defray the costs of his education.

Budd proved to be an exceptional student, learning to speak English perfectly. He worked for a short period as a Hudson's Bay clerk and then became a teacher in several Anglican parish schools in the Northwest. His unusual talents for interpreting, translating, and speaking were recognized, and on 22 December 1850 Budd was named a Deacon. Three years later he became the first North American Indian to be ordained an Anglican minister. Budd then worked at a number of mission stations in the Northwest, including

Nepowewin, The Pas, and Cumberland House, teaching children and adults alike, in both English and Cree, and giving instruction in farm techniques and the care of livestock to a people who traditionally survived, and sometimes starved, on a hunting and trapping economy.

Budd's *Diary* for the years 1870 to 1875 (published in 1974, edited by Katherine Pettipas) records useful information on the weather and the spiritual and secular everyday activities of the members of his congregation. The methodical recording of routine events tends to make the journal monotonous reading, but here is a vivid extract:

August 26, Wednesday [1874]. The long expected Steamer 'North Cote', came puffing up in sight, they blew the whistle so loud that they made the very cattle reel up their heels, and took to full gallop with their tails up in the air in full speed for the woods. But, not only the cattle but the people of all ages and both sexes were no less excited at the sight of the boat, the first boat of the kind to be seen by them all their life; in fact, the first Steam boat going in this river since the Creation. But what concerned [me] most was, knowing that my dear daughter and her husband was in the boat. I thanked God when I met with them. To me, it was the highest gratification I could enjoy on earth. To see my dear daughter with her Sister the youngest of my children once more in the flesh, I could almost cry out in the words of Old Simeon 'Now Lord lettest thou thy Servant depart in peace for, my eyes have seen thy salvation.' In an hour the captain said he would start and Mr Cochrane had to go then, and leave his wife here for the winter. She is not overstrong, neither has the fits of fainting left her.[36]

THE BEGINNING OF WRITTEN DISSENT

In addition to their histories, journals, travelogues, religious writings, and letters, many of the early native preachers took part in the political activities of their time. By 1820 the government of Upper Canada had confined the Indians to reserves through a series of land surrenders. With the loss of the land they had always thought of as their own, they soon discovered that they had also lost the source of their very identity. Their lives became increasingly regulated, and previously stable village communities were gradually destroyed by dislocation, poverty, liquor, and disease. As a result there emerged a new genre of Indian literature that would continue to this day: a protest literature, official in nature, taking the forms of letters, petitions, and reports, written to a variety of government agencies, British and American. The overriding theme is a sense of loss—loss of land, loss of hunting and fishing rights, loss of self-sufficiency and dignity, loss of nationhood.

Although Peter Jones encouraged civilization as a blessing of progress, he identified most strongly with his native heritage and appreciated the difficult process of changing a free and independent hunting and gathering culture based on sharing to a hierarchical, acquisitive agricultural society. As a consequence he, along with his colleagues, wrote much protest literature to government authorities reporting the grievances of diverse Indian tribes of Upper Canada. In the following official letter Jones voices the objections of the St Clair Indians to conversion to Christianity:

River Credit June 14th, 1830

Sir, For the information of His Excellency Sir John Colborne, I beg leave to say that I have lately returned from a tour to the River St Clair, and have seen and conversed with the Chiefs belonging to that place—I am sorry to state that they are at present much opposed to the introduction of Christianity and civilization among their people. They requested me to inform their Father Sir John Colborne, that in contrary to their desire to remove from the Reserve on Walpole Island: in as much, as the graves of their fathers were placed here and that it was their wish to lay down by the side of them—They also said that it was not their wish to live in houses or villages like white People, to have schools among them. I informed those Chiefs that I had nothing to do with the affairs of the Indian Dept. that I had merely paid them a friendly visit and to shake hands with them, but as they requested me I should inform their Father the Governor all that they had said.

I saw Mr Ironsides at Muncy Town, and consulted with him as to what course to take for the religious instruction of the St Clair Indians—It was his opinion that it would not be prudent at present to broach the subject of Christianity to them, on account of the strong prejudices they have against it. I concurred with him in this opinion, and therefore I did not attempt to preach to them, for fear of increasing their opposition to religion etc.

The prospects at Muncey Town are very encouraging; but will require time and hard labour to accomplish their civilization.

I leave the Credit to day for Lake Simcoe, and will probably return in the course of eight ten days, at which time I hope to have the pleasure of waiting upon His Excellency—

To Mudge Esqr)	I am your most
Secretary)	Humble Servant
York)	*Peter Jones*[37]

Besides addressing their literature of protest to local officials, Canada's Indians even appealed to the English. Here is 'An Address of the Chiefs of Lake Huron to the Christians of England', 17 February 1831, written to elicit their sympathy, and with the hope of influencing the Colonial Office to redress Indian grievances. (This tradition of appealing abroad is maintained today.)

To our Fathers and Brothers across the great waters in England—We the principal Chiefs of the Chippeway Indian Nation residing on the waters of Lake Huron in Upper Canada, desire to tell you what is in our hearts.—

A great while ago, our white brothers came over to this country and found us in our Wigewamms.—We took them by their hands and called them brothers.— They then asked for our Lands, & we gave them as much as they wanted; for which they gave us presents & the fire waters. (Rum)—

When the Fire-waters came among us, it made us very poor and very sickly, & many of our Fathers died off, & left us very small in number to what we used to be once.—

While we were in this miserable state, the Great Spirit sent good white people among us, & told us about the Great Saviour of the World dying for poor Indians as well as for the white people.—

Our hearts were affected with these great words, & we began to pray to the great Spirit, through Jesus Christ.— He heard our prayers and took away our old wicked hearts, and gave us new hearts.— He helped us to forsake our old crooked ways, & to overcome our great enemy the Fire-waters.—

When the Great Spirit found us, we had no fields, no houses, no cattle, and were altogether destitute of the comforts of this life, but since our eyes have been opened to see this good way, we have been very anxious to have lands to cultivate, to have houses to live in, and to enjoy all the blessings & comforts that our white Brothers enjoy, and to live like the good white farmers.—

We have appointed our beloved Brother and Chief Kahkewaquonaby otherwise called Peter Jones, who first explained to us the words of the Great Spirit, to take these our words across the great waters with authority to make known all our wants, and to ask our Fathers & Brothers to help us in our poverty.—

We also give power to our Brother and Chief Kahkewaquonaby to speak for us to our *Great Father over the great waters and to tell him what is in our hearts about our lands.—

Fathers & brothers we wish always to be good friends with you and your children and to walk together in one path.—

Fathers and Brothers, we shake hands with you in our hearts.— This is all we have to say.

Their marks

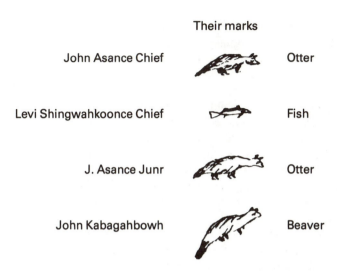

John Asance Chief		Otter
Levi Shingwahkoonce Chief		Fish
J. Asance Junr		Otter
John Kabagahbowh		Beaver

Lake Huron
Machedash Bay
Feby 17th 1831

1 True Copy   *The King [William IV][38]

Besides the acculturated preachers, nineteenth-century chiefs across Canada wrote letters, sent petitions, made speeches, and gave interviews to provincial and federal officials to make known the concerns and anxieties of their people. Surviving letters and minutes of general councils document the steady but subtle deterioration of their position from one of superiors and equals to that of 'brother' and lastly to 'child', forced upon them by government policies, as they made their slow but inextricable retreat before the advance of white settlement. In essence, Canadian Indian policy sought the elimination of the Indians through assimilation.

Whereas in the days of discovery, exploration, and early settlement Indians had figured prominently in the contexts of the fur-trade and colonial warfare, by the end of the nineteenth century they had become peripheral to Canadian development and history. Years of defeat, submission, and finally acceptance created a tragic picture of beleaguered men and women whose endless pleas and repeated requests went unheeded in the clash of two cultures where neither completely understood the other.

One important chief who protested eloquently for the redress of wrongs was Shinguaconse (c. 1773-1854), or 'Little Pine', of Garden River near Sault Ste Marie, who had fought with General Brock in the War of 1812. So concerned was he for the welfare of his people that he once walked all the way to York to ask the governor for teachers. In 1849, when Shinguaconse sent this letter to Lord Elgin, the Governor-General at Montreal, he expressed the dissatisfactions of the Indians:

When your white children first came into this country, they did not come shouting the war cry and seeking to wrest this land from us. They told us they came as friends to smoke the pipe of peace; they sought our friendship, we became brothers. Their enemies were ours, at the time we were strong and powerful, while they were few and weak. But did we oppress them or wrong them? No! And they did not attempt to do what is now done, nor did they tell us that at some future day you would.

Father

Time wore on and you have become a great people, whilst we have melted away like snow beneath an April sun; our strength is wasted, our countless warriors dead, our forests laid low, you have hounded us from every place as with a wand, you have swept away all our pleasant land, and like some giant foe you tell us 'willing or unwilling, you must now go from amid these rocks and wastes, I want them now! I want them to make rich my white children, whilst you may shrink away to holes and caves like starving dogs to die!' Yes, Father, your white children have opened our very graves to tell the dead even they shall have no resting place.

Father

Was it for this we first received you with the hand of friendship, and gave you the room whereon to spread your blanket? Was it for this that we voluntarily became the children of our Great Mother the Queen? Was it for this we served England's sovereign so well and truly, that the blood of the red skin has moistened the dust of his own hunting grounds, to serve those sovereigns in their quarrels, and not in quarrels of his own?

Father,

We begin to fear that those sweet words had not their birth in the heart, but that they lived only upon the tongue; they are like those beautiful trees under whose shadow it is pleasant for a time to repose and hope, but we cannot forever indulge in their graceful shade—they produce no fruit.

Father,

We are men like you, we have the limbs of men, we have the hearts of men, and we feel and know that all this country is ours; even the weakest and most cowardly animals of the forest when hunted to extremity, though they feel destruction sure, will turn upon the hunter.

Father,

Drive us not to the madness of despair. We are told that you have laws which guard and protect the property of your white children, but you have made none to protect the rights of your red children. Perhaps you expected that the red skin could protect himself from the rapacity of his pale faced bad brother.[39]

Shinguaconse blends much shrewdness and politeness with a consummate use of irony. As he fires one rhetorical question after another, he reminds the governor of Indian loyalty and kindness, skilfully contrasting these qualities with white deceit and hypocrisy. He pleads the cause of his people in the forcible and incisive traditions of protest literature and native rhetoric.

The Ojibway Catherine Soneegoh Sutton (Nah-nee-bah-wee-quay —'Upright Woman') was one of the few Indian women of her time to work for the rights of her people. Daughter of Chief Soneegoh of the Eagle Totem and Mary Crane of the Otter, Sutton (1823-65) was born near the Forks of the Credit River. Two years later her family moved to the Credit Indian village, where a Methodist settlement was started for Ojibway converts. Sutton attended the mission school there until 1837, when in the spring she accompanied her aunt, Elizabeth, the English-born wife of Peter Jones, to Britain. For a short time she attended school in England, where she developed a flair for poetry and penmanship and was present at Queen Victoria's coronation.

A year later she returned to Canada. In January 1839 she married an Englishman, William Sutton, who had immigrated to Canada in 1830, and for the next few years they served as Methodist missionaries. Around 1845 they moved to the Owen Sound area, where the Newash band gave them 600 acres of land. In 1852 they moved to the Garden River Reserve near Sault Ste Marie, where they superintended 'the working of a Model farm for the Benefit of the Indians', and two years later they went to Michigan, where William Sutton was engaged in making improvements on a mission.

In 1857 they returned to Owen Sound, where they found their property sold, surveyed, and laid out in townlots for sale. The Indian Department refused to recognize the validity of the Suttons' land title and also refused Mrs Sutton's request for her share of the Newash band's annuities 'on the ground of her having married a white man and having been absent from the country during the time for which she claimed payment.'

Mrs Sutton tried to buy back her land at the public sale, but she was told that Indians could not purchase the land. After three and a half years of petitioning the government, she decided to take her case to England.

To raise money for the trip and to enlist further support, Mrs Sutton began a series of lectures in both Canada and the United States. She captured the imagination of the press, and the *New York Tribune* reported on its front page her lecture about the poor and perishing Indian before the Society of Friends in Brooklyn.

Through the financial support of a group of New York Quakers, she was able to travel to England. On 19 June 1860 Sutton stood before the Queen, not as a subject appealing to her sovereign but as a chief's daughter—an Indian princess, as one royal person to another. The Queen noted in her private journal: 'She speaks English quite well and is come on behalf of her Tribe to petition against some grievance as regards land.' Mrs Sutton stayed in England for a year, and while there gave birth to a son, Albert.

In the end, as a result of the direct intervention of the British Government, the Suttons were allowed to buy back a portion of their land. Mrs Sutton continued to speak in letters, petitions, and lectures for native peoples' rights for only four more years: she died in 1865 at the age of 42. In the Grey County and Owen Sound Museum there is an excellent example of her mode of written protest. It is recorded in her journal, in response to an outrageous editorial she had read in a periodical called *The Leader*. Since it is signed, it is thought that it is a copy of a letter submitted to that paper for publication. Her effective command of English (it is not 'poor', as she says) and her protest, which is both intelligent and touching, are not at all weakened by her wayward spelling and punctuation. Its heading tells us that it was writtten on 8 September 1864 (to the date she adds the comment 'we had snow Storm') and it begins with a quotation from the hateful editorial:

> on the shores of Goulais Bay Lake Superior and the neighbouring one of Batchawana, one of these publick nusiances — an Indian reserve was laid of a few years ago under Lord Elgin's Government the reserve covered a portage of 30 miles on the Lake with a sufficient depth into the country to make up an area of 300 square miles of land — some of the best land in the country and so situated as to block up the means of access to the entire regions lying in the rear of it and all this for about a dozen of the most wretched, squalid, miserable specimens of human nature that I have ever seen: indeed a close inspection of, and a little acquaintance with, these creatures leads one to doubt whether they are human, but whether they are men or monkeys it matters not now, the present administration have found means to extinguish their title so far, that the country is now surveyed, and will soon be in market.

> I suppose the individual who published the above and Mr Charles Linsey, the great Hearo who tried last fall to frighten the Manitoulin Indians out of their sences and their Lands, are, one and the same—if they are not their certanly is a great family likeness between them I have lived for several years with in a few miles of Goulais bay and I have frequently seen

those Indians aluded to but I never took them for Monkyes neither did I ever hear such a thing hinted at by the white people I think they were allways, considered to be human beings, possessing living souls, I did not think monkeys lived so far north I allways understood that they were found in warm climates, when I was in England I went to the zoological garden were I saw a great maney monkeys and of various sises and kinds but I observed their was one trait coman to them all and a close inspection & a litle acquaintance with the Editor of the Leader has led me to the conclusion that the same trait stands out prominently in his natural disposition and character, and when I state what is the nature of that trait so comon to all the monkeys I ever saw I will leave you to guess who is by nature verey closly related to these four leged animals well I will tell you the trait wich I observed so comon to every variety of monkeys was an entire absence of humanity.

I have allso frequently seen the litle trained monkey exibeted in our canadian towns and vilages with pants red coat and cap, but every child could tell that it was a monkey because its tail would stick out and I noticed that after he had played of his money anticks he allways went round with his hat for a colection and as far as I can learn this is just what a certen creature does after he as performed something wich is pleasing to a certen party he expects them in return to throw something handsome into his cap.

The Editor of the Leader apears to think that every indian reservation is a publick nusiance so I conclude that if he could have his will, he would have every band of indians drove on to the baran waste of granite rocks north of Lakes huron and superior but why are indian reservations aney more a publick nusiance then large blocks of land bought and held by speculators I argue that Indians have a right to be paid a fair valuation for aney lands wich they may agree to surrender, I suppose the Leader would not have a word to say if a dozen or two poor hard working white men should get scatered through the Goulais bay teritory, while all the remainder was bought up and held by a few speculators untill those poor men by hard persevering industry had cleared up their lands and made roads and thus by the poor mans hard labour raised the value of the rich land speculators property—the Editor of the leader states that the present administration have found means to extinguish their title, my english his so poor that I frequently have to consult Webster and I find the word extinguish means to destroy to put an end to; to extinguish a claim or title, a wonderful feat surely for the present administration to perform and for the Editor of the leader to brag of; this shows another instance of the uter helplessness of the poor indian they apear to be at the mercy of such men as Mr Charles linsey our present administration can extinguish the red mans title at pleasure, what hope is their for the remnant that are yet left to whom can they go for redress who will help them or are they entirely without helper, I suppose Mr Linsey will answer these questions when the present administration give him a commission to go to manitolin with soldiers to subdue the Indians or monkeys as he calls them.

Catherine B. Sutton or *Nahnebahwequa*
Owen Sound[40]

Protest literature—the prose of letters, addresses, reports, and petitions—as well as autobiographies, histories, and travelogues dominated the period, but some poetry was also attempted.

An example is a poem entitled 'England and British America' by William Wilson, a talented youth who was sent to the Upper Canada Academy at Cobourg, where he excelled in Classics and wrote poetry with ease. But he died of smallpox in New York shortly after leaving the college. He recited his poem at a public examination on 19 April 1838, and it was published in the *Christian Guardian* on 23 May. It was also included in the chapter 'Capacity of the Indians for Receiving Instruction' in Peter Jones's *History*. Mainly a long patriotic tribute to Canada and the British connection, it is also a lament for the vanishing Indian written in heroic couplets, and is surprisingly adept for any young person; indeed, it is not all unlike the contemporary verse of Oliver Goldsmith. An extract illustrates:

> Here cataracts vast the echoing forests wake,
> And all the ground with quick vibrations shake;
> Where dread Niagara in thunder roars,
> As o'er the rocky steep his deluge pours,—
> Along whose banks the lonely Indian wound,
> And in the scene his kindred spirit found.
> Here boundless plains in fragrant verdure stretch,
> Bright landscapes there invite the artist's sketch;
> Here forests dark their stately branches wave,
> And rivers there in solemn silence lave.
> But though this land with ev'ry good is crown'd,
> And choicest gifts on ev'ry hand surround,—
> Though Nature here has wrought her grandest plan,
> Yet does the mind deplore the fate of man.
> Those lordly tribes that lin'd these mighty lakes
> Have fled, and disappear'd like wintry flakes.
> Lo! on the mountain-tops their fires are out,
> In blithesome vales all silent is their shout;
> A solemn voice is heard from ev'ry shore,
> That now the Indian nations are no more,—
> A remnant scarce remain to tell their wrongs,
> But soon will fade to live in poets' songs.[41]

The first literate Indians in southern Ontario were produced by the evangelical Christian movement. They had little formal education, but encouraged by their Church leaders and the relatively close-knit group to which they belonged, they wrote profusely and created the first body of Canadian Indian literature composed in English. Although few established literary reputations, their works are nevertheless valuable sources of historical and social information.

It should be remembered that their writing and speech-making were produced at a time when relatively few people in Upper Canada and the Hudson's Bay Territories—white or native—were literate, let alone literary. The accomplishment of Indians who became literate was all the more impressive because they had to bridge the gap between speaking and writing a language that for them had no spiritual or cultural roots. In many cases their favourite first form of literary expression was the letter. Silas Rand's comment about the Micmacs in 1850—'They are in the constant habit of corresponding among themselves by letter'—must have applied to other tribes as well.

When Indians began to write in such unfamiliar forms as the letter, autobiography, travelogue, diary, and journal, a break with the oral tradition was made. Christian converts began writing their tales of conversion and testimonials about the advantages of life as Christians, using Christian images and motifs and conventional Christian rhetoric. The Bible was their chief literary influence, and their writings reflect a derivative and imitative style.

The force and effectiveness of Indian speech—once heard around council fires and in orations among kinsmen and in negotiations with enemies—was now heard most often from the pulpit and in negotiations with white government officials. Although where the latter were concerned this eloquence fell on deaf ears, it was not totally lost. Nor could humiliation and subjugation erase the traditional respect for the word, even though it was written in an alien tongue and was used most often to protest the shocking way Indians were being dispossessed and disciplined.

Conversion meant absolute conformity to Western manners, morals, and religious dogma. Although on the one hand the new set of beliefs generated unbounded energy and invigorating thought that produced passionate sermons and lectures, as well as prose narratives that advocated assimilation into the blessings and benefits of Christianity and progress, on the other hand the new transformation caused considerable confusion and was not without its price in the form of emotional conflict. Very few were unaffected. Even Peter Jones, the moving spirit of the group of Methodist preachers, and probably one of its members who adapted best to the culture shock, went so far as to exclaim: 'Oh, what an awful account at the day of judgment must the unprincipled white man give, who has been an agent of Satan in the extermination of the original proprietors of the American soil!'[42]

The central theme of native literature at this time was 'the poor Indian'. However, cultural pride is also evident, with writers feeling called upon to explain and defend the native way of life in order to stir the hearts of Christian humanitarian reformers in the British Isles and the United States. Canadian native writers showed a passionate commitment to history, and not only recorded the historical tales and legends inherited from the past but also began setting down the history of their people to instruct and inform white readers.

Autobiography was also a popular literary form. Because of the great interest in Indians at the time, personal histories were in demand, and autobiography achieved great popularity. It was a new form, alien to an oral heritage where the communal and collective were celebrated.[43] As a result, autobiographical works retained many of the oral features of Indian pre-literate cultures. Personal experiences were juxtaposed with communal legend and myth, with the anecdote and little essay, creating a distinctive literary form that wove history, traditions, beliefs, and personal experience into unique works.

Letters, which often provided the only communication between scattered members of the group and isolated family members, were also written to government officials, white missionaries, and editors of Christian newspapers and the periodical press.

Above all, the literary accomplishment of this pioneering stage reveals the ability of native writers to master the English language. It also gives us a sense of their cultural identity, and contributes something of value not only to social historians but also to our early Canadian literature. For the first time in our literary history we hear the Indians express their views of the people and places of mainstream society in frank and cogent language. Despite their Christian and acculturated influence, their works are native accounts. Aboriginal in origin, form, and inspiration, their writings comprise the first body of Canadian native literature in English; and they offer the first written evidence of the ideas, responses, and feelings of individual Indians, as opposed to the collective responses contained in myths and legends. Moreover, in their efforts to share their experiences of two cultures they produced landmark works of their kind. Canada was not to witness another such florescence of native writing until modern times.

The Red Lake chief making a speech to the Governor of the Red River Settlement at Fort Douglas in 1825', a watercolour painting by Peter Rindisbacher (1806-34) (National Archives of Canada, C-1939)

Peter Jones in the 1850s (Courtesy Donald B. Smith)

John Sunday (Metropolitan Toronto Library, JRR 2450)

George Copway (Courtesy Donald B. Smith)

George Henry (National Archives of Canada, PA-125840)

Peter Jacobs

Catherine Sutton
(County of Grey/Owen Sound Museum)

THE ONLY ——►
CANADIAN MOHAWK INDIAN
NOW BEFORE THE ENGLISH PUBLIC IN A
CONCERT & LECTURE TOUR

J. OJIJATEKHA BRANT-SERO.
Ex-Vice-President Ontario Historical Society.

An advertisement for John Brant-Sero's lectures
(Ontario Archives, William Kirby Papers, MU 1638, A-19)

Pauline Johnson in evening dress (Brant County Museum, Brantford)
INSET: *Pauline Johnson in native dress (Brant County Museum, Brantford)*

III

1850-1914

Since Indians were an obstacle to settlement, Canada's Indian policy increasingly acquired an assimilationist and a coercive character. Indians were settled on reserves where they could be proselytized by missionaries and taught Euro-Canadian ways by government and church alike. To educate the young a system of residential schools, located off the reserves and operated by missionaries and Indian Affairs bureaucrats, was established. These schools prohibited Indian children from speaking their language or practising their customs and inevitably alienated them from the spiritual values of their communities.

Among the isolated educated natives in this period, a few—Peter Dooyentate Clarke, Francis Assikinack, Louis Jackson, and John Brant-Sero—managed to achieve publication. Peter Dooyentate Clarke (c. 1810-70), the son of a Wyandott woman and an officer of the British Indian Department, published a history of the Wyandott (Huron) Indians. In explaining the sources of his narrative, he wrote: 'The lapse of ages has rendered it difficult to trace the origin of the Wyandotts. Nothing new remains to tell whence they came, but a tradition that lives only in the memory of a few among the remnant of this tribe. Of this I will endeavour to give a sketch as I had it from the lips of such, and from some of the tribe who have since passed away.'[1] Clarke's *Origin and Traditional History of the Wyandotts, and Sketches of Other Indian Tribes of North America: True Traditional Stories of Tecumseh and his League in the Years 1811 and 12* (1870), published in Toronto, presents in a discursive and rambling style historical personages and events through a series of vividly dramatized tableaux. This extract illustrates:

One day, whilst Pontiac sat in his tent, near Fort Detroit, silently grieving over the overthrow of French supremacy in North America, and sullenly watching the English taking peaceable possession of the Fort, this Indian Chieftain, this stoic of the forest, conceived the plan of dislodging the English, not only at Detroit, but at all the other French military posts on the western frontier.

Forts Duquesne, Niagara, Detroit and Michilimackinac proved impregnable to his assaults. He succeeded, however, in capturing six other less strongly protected stations, viz:—Presque Isle, La Boeuf, Sandusky, Miami, Green Bay, and St. Joseph.

Pontiac at one time undertook to dislodge the English at Michilimackinac, in this wise: dividing his warriors into two equal parties; started them at ball playing near the fort, himself among them conducting the manoeuvering. At a given signal, when near enough, one party was to send the ball over into the fort, then both parties were to rush inside through the gates upon the unsuspecting soldiery, and take them by surprise, but the cunning Chieftain was baffled in this scheme. Strange to say, an Indian woman (of his own tribe), made a timely disclosure of the plot to the commandant, or in common phrase, this Indian women 'let the cat out of the bag.' Seeing the gates suddenly closed, and the officers and men who were on the ramparts looking at the ball play all disappear at once, and the 'big guns' *silently protruding their muzzles* through the port holes, Pontiac concluded that his plan must have been discovered, and that the sooner he and his *sporting party* made themselves scarce about the Fort the better.

Pontiac continued to annoy the English for some time after the latter had taken possession of Detroit. He at one time made a night attack on this fort and was repulsed.[2]

Another Indian who was a successful enough writer to get published was Louis Jackson, the foreman of a select group of Caughnawaga canoemen who led the British Boat Expedition for the relief of Khartoum in the Sudan, up the Cataracts of the Nile River, in 1885. His *Our Caughnawagas in Egypt: A Narrative of What Was Seen and Accomplished by the Contingent of North American Voyageurs Who Led the British Boat Expedition for the Relief of Khartoum up the Cataracts of the Nile* (1885) gives a short first-hand account of the expedition—the first time Canadians were sent overseas to assist in one of Britain's imperial wars. With an observant eye for detail, Jackson records 'novel' and 'unusual' sights and compares Egyptian social customs with Canadian. The British had expressly asked for the help of the Caughnawaga canoemen because they were experienced in shooting rapids:

Now came the tug of war, the shooting of all the cataracts. Coming up we used all eddies, now we had to avoid them, coming up also if unable to proceed we could draw back and try another channel, now, everything depended on quick judgment and prompt action, the more so as keel boats are not considered for rapid work. I ordered my captains to follow at such distances as to give them time to avoid following should the leading boat err in the choice of channel. After shooting the Dal cataract all safe I asked my captains how the boats behaved. All agreed that they were slow in answering their helm and required close watching. Travelling between the cataracts against a strong headwind was slow work and we longed for the next one to get along faster. Shooting the Dal, there had been much dodging of rocks and islands, which gave some excitement. In Akaska cataract we discovered a smooth, straight channel in the middle of the river and not very long.

This shooting of the rapids was a surprise to the Egyptian soldiers, a number of whom were stationed at every cataract. The natives came rushing out of their huts with their children, goats and dogs and stood on the beach to see the North American Indian boatmen. I had more leisure now to look round. I have not seen the place yet where I would care to settle down.[3]

Francis Assikinack (1824-63) was born on Manitoulin Island, Upper Canada, the son of Blackbird (Jean-Baptiste Assikinack), the celebrated orator-warrior of the Ottawas. Because he was bright, Francis was sent in 1840 to Upper Canada College in Toronto by Samuel P. Jarvis, then Superintendent of the Indian Department. The young man did not speak English, and became so discouraged after three months that he prevailed upon a fellow-student to seek permission for him to go home because he thought he could never master another language. The request was denied—fortunately, because in his eight years at the College he not only learned English, but some Latin and Greek as well. In June 1849 Assikinack was urged by the government to become an interpreter for the next Superintendent of the Indian Department, Thomas Gummersall Anderson, since it was felt that he should put his education to work. After one year as an interpreter he was sent to Manitoulin as a schoolmaster. He stayed until 1854, when he returned to Toronto to work as chief clerk in the Indian Department. In September 1863 he became seriously ill with tuberculosis and went back to Manitoulin to die.

While he was in Toronto, Assikinack wrote three essays for the *Canadian Journal* that demonstrate his style at its easiest when he is describing Indian customs (it becomes rather turgid when he writes about the language of the Odahwah and retells legends) and reveal his divided loyalties between his tribal background and his acculturated condition. The most interesting is entitled 'Social and Warlike Customs of the Odahwah Indians'. Besides discussing such matters as methods of war and the treatment of prisoners—no doubt learned from his father—he also describes the social customs of young people:

With regard to matrimonial affairs it may be remarked that the Indians do not seem to have much appreciated what is called 'keeping company' nowadays, as the choice of a wife was entirely left to the parents. The young bridegroom may never have seen, spoken to, or been acquainted with the girl until she was introduced to him as his bride. Generally speaking, when the eldest brother died, his younger brother was required to marry his widow; in all other cases it was not thought lucky for a young man to marry a widow; and in case the woman should die first her sister had to supply her place, provided the parties were not already married. The degrees of relationship extended a great way among the Indians; and it was prohibited by custom to contract marriage within the forbidden bounds . . .

Another discipline to which the young people were subjected, in addition to that of fasting, constituted a useful training for future life. They were required to bathe at daybreak every morning for about a month in the spring, whilst the water was cold. This was done with a view to render them hardy, robust, and capable of standing all sorts of weather. Unhappily the ancient discipline by which the Indian youths were thus trained to hardihood and self-denial, is no longer practised. It is a matter of regret that the young Indians of the present day have almost entirely lost the virtues of sobriety and self-respect practised by their predecessors. Self-indulgence of the grossest kind has taken the place of self-denial. Too often they frequent the low grog-shop, where they lose all sense of shame, and are rendered mean and beggarly, as well as useless members of society. It is scarcely necessary to remark that there were good speakers among the Indians formerly; but I have too much reason to believe, that there are no such speakers to be found among them at the present day. In my opinion it was chiefly owing to their deep contemplation in their silent retreats in the days of youth, that the old Indian orators acquired the habit of carefully arranging their thoughts; when, instead of the shoutings of drunken companions, they listened to the warbling of birds, whilst the grandeur and the beauties of the forest, the majestic clouds, which appear like mountains of granite floating in the air, the golden tints of a summer evening sky, and all the changes of nature, which then possessed a mysterious significance, combined to furnish ample matter for reflection to the contemplating youth.[4]

Dr Peter Martin (1841-1907), whose Mohawk name was Oronhyatekha ('Burning Cloud'), also had a book published. He was born on the Six Nations Reserve near Brantford, Ontario, and went to school there until he was ten years old. He was then sent to the Indian Industrial School near Brantford, where he learned English and the shoemaker's trade. An outstanding student, he went to the Wesleyan Academy in Massachusetts to continue his studies. On graduation he taught for two years at his reserve school and then furthered his education at Kenyon College in Ohio. On the Canadian visit of the Prince of Wales (later Edward VII) in 1860, Oronhyatekha was chosen by the Six Nations chiefs to present their address to the Prince. When the two conversed, and Oronhyatekha said that he wanted to become a doctor, the Prince was so impressed that he invited him to study medicine at Oxford University under the supervision of his physician, Dr Acland, Professor of Medicine. On his return to Canada, Oronhyatekha, now Dr Martin, first practised medicine at Frankfort in eastern Ontario and then in Stratford, London, and Toronto. He married Ellen Hill, great-granddaughter of Joseph Brant. Greatly interested in fraternal organizations—he was Supreme Chief Ranger of the Independent Order of Foresters from 1881 until his death in 1907—he published the *History of the Independent Order of Foresters* (1894). His portrait hangs in St Edmund's Hall at Oxford University, the only North American Indian to be so honoured by Oxford.

Another prominent native of his day was John Ojijatekha ('Burning Flower') Brant-Sero (1867-1914), whose mother was a descendant of Isaac Brant, Joseph Brant's first son, and whose father was a Bay of Quinte Mohawk. He was born on the Six Nations Reserve, attended the reserve school, and later went to the Mohawk Institute near Brantford, where he learned to be a carpenter. Realizing the value of an education, and wanting 'to learn the business ways of the whites', Brant-Sero took a business course and learned shorthand and typing.

He then went to Toronto, where he became well known as an actor and an assistant to David Boyle, curator of the Archaeological Museum. His knowledge of Mohawk and the various dialects of the Iroquois enabled Brant-Sero to furnish the museum with translations of the myths, songs, and traditions of his people. In 1891 he went to England, where he appeared as Bill Morley in *On the Frontier*. In 1900 he went to South Africa to enlist in the Boer War but was refused. He then returned to England and wrote the following letter to *The Times* of London (2 January 1901):

BRANT-SERO'S STORY

Sir, will you allow me space in your columns, as a humble Canadian Mohawk Indian, hailing from the Six Nations Reserve, Brant county,

Ontario? I have just returned from South Africa, disappointed in many respects, but I do not wish these lines to be understood as a grievance. I went to that country from Canada hoping that I might be allowed to enlist in one of the mounted rifles; however, not being a man of European descent, I was refused to do active service in Her Majesty's cause as did my forefathers in Canada.

Reaching South Africa about the middle of August, I attempted to join, as a Canadian, at East London, in Kitchener's Horse, Roberts' Horse, Driscol scouts, and at Queenstown the Cape mounted rifles, the Orange River Colony police and again Driscol scouts. Here one young Englishman resigned his position to make way for me, but it was hopeless, my credentials were never questioned, I easily satisfied the officer where I came from; that was the trouble. I was too genuine a Canadian. One medical officer who examined me pronounced me unfit; on my questioning him the nature of my unfitness he simply remarked, very good-naturedly, 'There is nothing serious; don't you worry.' After all my failures to handle the rifle, I managed to secure employment at the Queenstown remount depot No. 4. My duties consisted in taking animals up to the front and bossing the Kaffirs. I was on the civilian staff. I have had my share of tent life, army rations, and dodging sand storms during my stay at the seat of war. At various times I visited Springfontein, Bloemcontein, Aliwai North, Colesberg, Stormberg, De Aar and Bethulie. On one occasion the Boers were considerate enough to let me sneak past Bethulie bridge with 200 entrained mules before they blew up the rails. However, it was not their fault; the circumstance was purely accidental.

At Springfontein, just after the siege of Philippolis, a Boer, a sentry, captured me as I had to get my Kaffirs to identify me. Shortly after that, seeing it was useless remaining in the country, I resigned, and, armed with my honourable discharge, I proceeded to Cape Town, where, upon my arrival, I again made attempts to join a mounted corps, and met the same refusals. . . .

The history of the Mohawk and others of the Six Nations Confederacy residing in Canada is well known in Canada, in fact, a history of Canada cannot be written impartially without recounting the warlike deeds of the Six Nations. We believe we have an interest in the empire, bought by the blood of our ancestors. The name of Captain Joseph Brant (Thayandanegea) is imprinted upon the mind of every student and traveller. It was under his banner the Mohawks left their once beautiful homes in the Mohawk Valley, New York state, trekking northward to Grand River and the Bay of Juriste [Quinte], where they might enjoy a comfortable retreat safe to follow the customs of their forefathers. Here for over a century they have lived, cultivating their farms and their progress is the pride of all true Canadians. They are not degenerating, neither are they decreasing, but upon the other hand, in common with the Indian population of Canada they are rapidly increasing in numbers. There is scarcely a calling, trade or profession in which these Indians are not represented. In social life, politics and literature we occupy no small place.

J.O. Brant-Sero
8 Dartmouth Street, Westminster, S.W.
Dec. 30[5]

While in England, Brant-Sero lectured on the Six Nations and in 1901 read a paper, 'Dekanawidah, the Law-Giver of the Caniengaha-gas', before the Royal Anthropological Institute of Great Britain and Ireland, which was later published in *Man*.

Brant-Sero perceived himself as the Six Nations' historian, dedicated to making known their 'hitherto untold lore'. He went on tour in Canada, the United States, England, and the Continent, singing sacred and sentimental songs, reciting in Mohawk and English, and lecturing on Canada, its early history, settlement, development, immigration, industrial progress, social life, and Indian affairs. He lectured 'with great success' before the Royal Saxon Geographical Society in Dresden, Germany, on 'The History and Character of the Mohawk Tribe . . .' 'It is said to have been the first time a real Canadian Indian ever addressed a European scientific body.'[6] Wherever he lectured he received accolades. In Leeds, England, he gave 'A wonderful speech, full of intelligence, and rising to real eloquence as he described the habits, homes and traditions of the great Indian race.'[7]

There was a great deal of interest at the time in the Six Nations as descendants of the first Loyalists, and the Ontario Historical Society welcomed Mohawks as members. Indeed, the Society supported Brant-Sero's desire to have his people recognized as founders of the province along with the white United Empire Loyalists. Brant-Sero was second vice-president of the Society from 1898 to 1900. His publications include 'Some Descendants of Joseph Brant' in the *Ontario Historical Society Papers and Records* (1899); 'The Six Nations Indians in the Province of Ontario, Canada' in the *Wentworth Historical Society. Transactions* (1899); 'Indian Rights Association After Government Scalp', in *Wilshire's Magazine*; and 'Views of a Mohawk Indian' in the *Journal of American Folklore* (1905). Brant-Sero's prose combines a sense of the enduring past with the realities of the present in a straightforward, rather flat style. He wished to set the historical record straight in Canadian history books and was ambitious to write a history of the Six Nations, which he apparently never accomplished.

Brant-Sero must have known (though there is no evidence of this) a Mohawk contemporary, also from Brantford, who was the most popular native writer at the turn of the century and the first strong poetic voice in English: Pauline Johnson—the first Canadian woman, the first Canadian Indian, and the first Canadian writer to be honoured by a commemorative Canadian stamp in 1961 on the 100th anniversary of her birth. Emily Pauline Johnson (1861-1913), the daughter of a Mohawk Indian Chief, George Henry Martin Johnson, and his wife Emily Susanna Howells—an English relative of the American writer William Dean Howells—was born on the Six Nations Reserve near Brantford. Except for two years at the school on the reserve and another two years at Brantford Collegiate, Pauline was educated at home by a governess and by her mother, who introduced her to the literature of Byron, Scott, Longfellow, Tennyson, Browning, Keats, and Shakespeare. From her father and her grandfather, John Smoke Johnson, who for forty years was the speaker of the Great Council of the Six Nations Confederacy, she learned native legends and history. She must also have been influenced by the scholars, artists, and writers who frequently visited her parents' home, Chiefswood.

Although she had written poetry and stories since childhood, it was not until Johnson turned twenty that her first poem, 'To Jean', was published by the New York magazine *Genius of Poetry*. Her poetry began appearing in American, British, and Canadian magazines, including *The Week*, whose literary editor, Charles G.D. Roberts, was one of the first to appreciate her talent. He wrote: 'You are the original voice of Canada by blood as well as taste, and the special trend of your gifts.' In 1889 two of her short poems—'In the Shadows' (a canoe song) and 'At the Ferry ' (a musical lyric), both inspired by the Grand River—were accepted by William Douw Lighthall for his anthology *Songs of the Great Dominion* (1889). Her poems were admired by the well-respected English critic Theodore Watts-Dutton, who praised the originality and freshness of the new Canadian voice.

But it was not until 1892 when, under the name Tekahionwake ('Smoky Haze of an Indian Summer'), her grandfather's name, that Johnson leapt to fame when she thrilled a select literary group in Toronto with her recitation of 'Cry of an Indian Wife', a narrative poem of the Northwest Rebellion. Several prominent literary figures also read, but Johnson stole the show. The audience demanded an encore and Johnson recited her highly dramatic 'As Red Men Die'. Once again the audience broke into wild applause. This first triumph was to be the beginning of a successful sixteen-year road career. By the summer of 1894 Johnson was able to leave Canada for England to seek publication.

As a result of the praise the *Athenaeum* gave to her readings, Johnson's name became well known in London literary circles and she was able to get her first book of poetry *The White Wampum* (1895) published by The Bodley Head. It contained the poem by which she is best known, 'The Song My Paddle Sings', which generations of Canadian schoolchildren later memorized.

During the next fifteen years Johnson dazzled her audiences with dramatic recitations of such favourites as 'The Song My Paddle Sings', 'Ojistoh', 'A Cry from an Indian Wife', 'The Sea Queen', 'The Firs', and 'As Red Men Die' in order to support herself as a writer. It was the age of the platform entertainer and the custom was to have several artists provide the entertainment in order to give variety to the program. For her concerts from 1892 to 1897 Johnson's partner was Owen Alexander Smily, an accomplished English 'music-hall' entertainer. When this partnership ended, Johnson was joined by Jackson Walter McRaye, who recited the *habitant* poetry of William Henry Drummond. But wherever the partners went, whether from coast to coast in Canada, or in the United States (where she was billed as an American Indian for the Chautauqua circuit) or England, it was Johnson, 'The Mohawk Princess', who was acclaimed and celebrated by her Victorian fans. She attracted the wealthy minor aristocracy both in Canada and abroad—the Earl of Aberdeen, the Marquis of Lorne and Princess Louise, Lord Ripon, Britain's Colonial Secretary—and fascinated the London artistic and literary circles with her compelling personality and stage presence.

Johnson wrote some descriptive nature and landscape poems—such as 'In the Shadows', 'Shadow River', 'Marshlands', and 'Low Tide at St Andrews'—that celebrate the beauty of the Canadian scene and are admired for their singing rhythm and exquisite harmony. Although many of her lyrical poems were written in the Victorian romantic and sentimental manner, this lullaby, packed with images from nature, rises above the sterotype.

LULLABY OF THE IROQUOIS

Little brown baby-bird, lapped in your nest,
    Wrapped in your nest,
    Strapped in your nest,
Your straight little cradle-board rocks you to rest;
    Its hands are your nest,
    Its bands are your nest;
It swings from the down-bending branch of the oak;
You watch the camp flame, and the curling gray smoke;
But, oh, for your pretty black eyes sleep is best, —
Little brown baby of mine, go to rest.

Little brown baby-bird swinging to sleep,
    Winging to sleep,
    Singing to sleep,
Your wonder-black eyes that so wide open keep,
    Shielding their sleep,
    Unyielding to sleep,
The heron is homing, the plover is still,
The night-owl calls from his haunt on the hill,
Afar the fox barks, afar the stars peep, —
Little brown baby of mine, go to sleep.[8]

Johnson's Indian poems, in fact, are unique in subject matter, and are distinguished by dramatic energy and passionate intensity. They reveal her deep concern for the fate of the Indian people, especially her beloved Mohawks. 'Ojistoh', a narrative poem that takes place during the interal-tribal wars of the Hurons and the Mohawks, tells the gripping story of a faithful's wife's abduction, desperate ruse, and escape.

OJISTOH
I am Ojistoh, I am she, the wife
Of him whose name breathes bravery and life
And courage to the tribe that calls him chief.
I am Ojistoh, his white star, and he
Is land, and lake, and sky—and soul to me.

Ah! but they hated him, those Huron braves,
Him who had flung their warriors into graves,
Him who had crushed them underneath his heel,
Whose arm was iron, and whose heart was steel
To all—save me, Ojistoh, chosen wife
Of my great Mohawk, white star of his life.

Ah! but they hated him, and councilled long
With subtle witchcraft how to work him wrong;
How to avenge their dead, and strike him where
His pride was highest, and his fame most fair.
Their hearts grew weak as women at his name:
They dared no war-path since my Mohawk came
With ashen bow, and flinten arrow-head
To pierce their craven bodies; but their dead
Must be avenged. Avenged? They dared not walk
In day and meet his deadly tomahawk;
They dared not face his fearless scalping knife;

So—Niyoh! [God!]—then they thought of me, his wife.

O! evil, evil face of them they sent
With evil Huron speech: 'Would I consent
To take of wealth? be queen of all their tribe?
Have wampum ermine?' Back I flung the bribe
Into their teeth, and said, 'While I have life
Know this—Ojistoh is the Mohawk's wife.'

Wah! how we struggled! But their arms were strong.
They flung me on their pony's back, with thong
Round ankle, wrist, and shoulder. Then upleapt
The one I hated most: his eye he swept
Over my misery, and sneering said,
'Thus, fair Ojistoh, we avenge our dead.'

And we two rode, rode as a sea wind-chased,
I, bound with buckskin to his hated waist,
He, sneering, laughing, jeering, while he lashed
The horse to foam, as on and on we dashed.
Plunging through creek and river, bush and trail,
On, on we galloped like a northern gale.
At last, his distant Huron fires aflame
We saw, and nearer, nearer still we came.

I, bound behind him in the captive's place,
Scarcely could see the outline of his face.
I smiled, and laid my cheek against his back:
'Loose thou my hands,' I said. 'This pace let slack.
Forget we now that thou and I are foes.
I like thee well, and wish to clasp thee close;
I like the courage of thine eye and brow;
I like thee better than my Mohawk now.'

He cut the cords; we ceased our maddened haste
I wound my arms about his tawny waist;
My hand crept up the buckskin of his belt;
His knife hilt in my burning palm I felt;
One hand caressed his cheek, the other drew
The weapon softly—'I love you, love you,'
I whispered, 'love you as my life.'
And—buried in his back his scalping knife.

Ha! how I rode, rode as a sea wind-chased,
Mad with sudden freedom, mad with haste,
Back to my Mohawk and my home. I lashed
That horse to foam, as on and on I dashed.

Plunging thro' creek and river, bush and trail,
On, on I galloped like a northern gale.
And then my distant Mohawk's fires aflame
I saw, as nearer, nearer still I came,
My hands all wet, stained with a life's red dye,
But pure my soul, pure as those stars on high—
'My Mohawk's pure white star, Ojistoh, still am I.'[9]

Johnson wrote light verse for newspapers and magazines in order to earn a living—like Isabella Valancy Crawford, an earlier Canadian writer who also had to write for the popular market to support herself. Acutely aware of lowering her standards to appeal to popular taste, she wrote the following letter to Harry O'Brien, a young barrister and editor of the *Canadian Law Journal* who had criticized Johnson for catering to the applauding crowds:

My dear Mr. O'Brien: *Home, Feb. 4, '94*

Why do I write to you . . . to exonerate myself from a self-asserted failing, and yet I know you would partially understand me tho' not quite, not thoroughly.

I felt that you looked at me with unforgivable eyes when I tricked myself into the confession that I 'played to the public'. That I *must* make myself a favourite, whether it reflected credit upon my literary work or not.

More than all things I hate and despise brain debasement, literary 'potboiling' and yet I have done, will do these things, though I sneer at my own littleness in so doing. . . .

But where am I? Ah! I was writing of 'Literary pot boiling,' and dramatic padding, for which don't deny it, you feel a certain sense of disappointment in me. You thought me more of the true poet, more the child of inspirations than I have proved to be. The reason of my actions in this matter? Well the reason is that the public will not listen to lyrics, will not appreciate real poetry, will in fact not have me as an entertainer if I give them nothing but rhythm, cadence, beauty, thought. You will not like your friend (I am am I not?) to bend to public favour, when she has the power and ability to arise above it and yet you know that thank your guiding star and saint you have never *experienced* my reason for this vulgar 'catering' to an applauding crowd. Ye Gods, how I hate their laughter at times, when such laughter is called forth by some of my brainless lines and business. I could do so much better if they would only let me. I have had dreams of 'educating' the vulgar taste to Poetry, not action. *I will* do it some time, when this hard, cold soulless 'reason' for bending to their approval ceases to exist.

What am I writing? You see I am in a 'mood'. I often have them. I have no excuse for writing to you like this save perhaps the ever recurring haunting memory of your silent disapproval, when I confessed that I 'played to people.' Please do not think hardly of me. You do not know, your life has never been touched by certain grimnesses that people such as Owen and I have been surrounded with. Grimness, did I say? So grim that the hollow comedy of it has often struck us so strangely that we have laughed together until we were exhausted but that was a year ago. Now? Well, now we are trying to look an audience more honestly in the face, with the confidence that success, and demand, always assures. . . .[10]

Johnson's public appearances, and her talent as a performer, contributed in no small measure to the popularity her writing commanded during her lifetime. They also brought Canadian literature, and in particular Canadian Indian literature, to the people. In 1903 Johnson published *Canadian Born*, a second collection that included 'The Riders of the Plains', her tribute to the North-West Mounted Police. Although the book sold well, it received mixed reviews.

Johnson's reputation rests chiefly on her poetry. But she also wrote adventure stories for the juvenile market. Her tales of brave Mounties, trappers and cowboys battling blizzards, raging torrents, and ravenous animals, appeared in *The Boys' World*, an American magazine. She also wrote articles with such titles as 'Mothers of a Great Red Race', idealizing the lives of the women of the Six Nations, 'Winter Indoor Life of the Indian Mother and Children', 'Outdoor Occupations of the Indian Mother and her Children', and 'Heroic Indian Mothers' for *Mother's Magazine*. Two collections of her prose, *The Shagganappi* (1913) and *The Moccasin Maker* (1913), were published after she died. *The Shagganappi*, dedicated to the Boy Scouts, included the stories she wrote for *The Boys' World*, while *The Moccasin Maker*, dedicated to Sir Gilbert Parker, included those submitted to *Mother's Magazine* and included a biography of her mother, 'The Story of a Life of Unusual Experiences', as well as her popular 'The Legend of Lillooet Falls'. In his Appreciation of Johnson included in *The Moccasin Maker*, Charles Mair wrote:

> When her racial poetry first appeared, its effect upon the reader was as that of something abnormal, something new and strange, and certainly unexampled in Canadian verse. For here was a girl whose blood and sympathies were largely drawn from the greatest tribe of the most advanced nation of Indians on the continent, who spoke out, 'loud and bold' not for it alone, but for the whole red race, and sang of its glories and its wrongs in strains of poetic fire.[11]

Johnson wanted a good marriage above all else, but she was rejected because she was an Indian. However, she refused to hide her Indianness and preferred to be billed as Tekahionwake, the Mohawk

Princess. This cultivated Indian lady was as at home in the drawing-rooms of the rich and famous as she was in the Canadian wilderness. Her balancing of these two identities was even reflected in her platform costumes: a scalp-adorned buckskin dress was changed midway through her performance for an elegant dinner gown of satin and lace. Johnson made sacrifices to preserve her duality. Perhaps it was the consummate grace with which she responded to these antithetical pressures that was the main source of her fascination. She thought that nothing worthier could be said of a man than that he had been born in Canada, under the British flag, but she perceived herself as Indian 'by law, by temperament, by choice, and by upbringing'. She wrote: 'My aim, my joy, my pride is to sing the glories of my own people',[12] yet she did this in the Western cultural tradition, and her literary forms, her world view, and her attitudes to nature were European. It is difficult enough to be a woman of one world; it is more difficult to be a woman of two worlds.

The years of constant travelling from town to town, of gruelling one-night bookings, began to take their toll on Johnson's health. In 1909 she gave her farewell performance in Kamloops, B.C., and retired to Vancouver to become a freelance writer. In 1911 she published *Legends of Vancouver*, as told to her (for the first time, in Chinook) by Chief Capilano. The following year a number of her poems were published in *Flint and Feather*, which was revised and enlarged in 1914, a year after her death.

Johnson's writings peaked in popularity in the twenties. By the thirties they were mainly regarded as appropriate for school anthologies. Today they are considered dated and shallow—though 'Ojistoh' still has a compelling ring.

As more and more Indians learned to read and write, newspapers, newsletters, and periodicals of all sorts appeared to inform, instruct, and entertain their native and non-native readers. These were frequently initiated and sponsored by local missionaries and Indian-interest groups who recognized the power of the written word and the educational usefulness of print. Indian correspondents and subscribers were encouraged. Unfortunately these early papers had to struggle to survive, plagued as they were by infrequent publication, minimal staff and resources, poor distribution, and low circulation.

Petaubun (Peep of Day), an English and Ojibway publication, was started in 1861 at Sarnia, Ontario. It was published monthly in Ojibway and English by the Reverend Thomas Hurlburt, a Methodist missionary who was a fluent Ojibway scholar. Another Ojibway English paper was the *Pipe of Peace* published by the Shingwauk Home in Sault Ste Marie. It lasted from October 1878 to September 1879. Dr

Peter E. Jones, the son of Peter Jones, was editor of *The Indian*, published at Hagersville, Ontario, from 30 December 1885 to 29 December 1886. *Our Forest Children*, a monthly with the ironic sub-title 'And What We Want To Do With Them'—published by the Reverend E.F. Wilson, the energetic Anglican missionary at the Shingwauk Home—lasted from 1887 to 1890. It was followed by *The Canadian Indian* edited by E.F. Wilson and H.B. Small of Ottawa for the Canadian Indian Research and Aid Society. It too survived only a few years, from 1880 to 1892.

Writing, especially letter-writing, was emphasized at Shingwauk. *Our Forest Children* published regularly model letters by Indian students , who had been taught in the residential schools to be honest, polite, clean, and punctual—desirable traits for employment—and they wrote about these virtues. This indoctrination is revealed in Johnny Maggrah's typical composition in English on 'Honesty and Politeness', which takes the form of a miniature sermon.

Honesty is the truthfulness in a man. It is a thing we cannot see or feel. If honesty was in every person, the world would be in a different state than it is now. An honest man is loved by all who know him. Everybody speaks well of him. A good name is what a person needs. It is better to have a good name than being rich.

An honest person is he who is true to his neighbour and to his God. When he finds anything that does not belong to him, he does not put it in his pocket, but goes and tries to find out whose it is. Hundreds of men and boys have been sent to gaols for being dishonest; and hundreds of men and boys have got into high offices for their honesty. When a man looks out for a boy to work for him, he does not choose strong and active boys, but an honest boy.

Politeness is the man's character, for being polite often gives people a good situation. A polite person is kind and willing to assist others. He does not spend his time in pleasing himself, but rather in pleasing others. All Christians should learn to be polite, for Jesus was the politest man that ever lived; and if we want to be his followers, we must be polite too. Once a man wanted to choose out a boy among a crowd of boys to work for him. He got them to come into his office one by one. Some came in without shutting the door, and their feet dirty; others came in slamming the door, and did not seem to care how they spoke. The last boy came: before opening the door he cleaned his feet, knocked the door, shut it quietly, and took off his hat. The man at once noticed how the boy acted, and for this reason he choosed him. This boy was polite.[13]

Na-Na-Kwa; or Dawn on the West Coast was published in Kitamaat, British Columbia, between 1893 and 1895. *Kamloops Wawa*, a mimeographed Chinook magazine focusing on religious matters, was issued irregularly by the Reverend J.M.R. Le Jeunne between 1891 and 1904.

Despite the dearth of publications by Indians during this period, there was nevertheless a great deal of translating going on, particularly of historical documents into English. These were encouraged not only by learned societies such as The Royal Society of Canada and the Ontario Historical Society, but by two well-known Canadian authors, William Kirby and Gilbert Parker. The Kirby Collection in the Ontario Archives contains three letters, translated in the 1880s by the Mohawk clergyman the Reverend Isaac Bearfoot, from Joseph Brant to Daniel Claus (19 August 1779), John Deserontyan to Claus (3 December 1778), and Joseph Brant to Deserontyan (12 May 1779). At the same time Lydia Hill of Deseronto was also translating, as she makes clear in the following letter to William Kirby, written on 11 October 1888. It begins:

My dear Friend

I have at last finished translating this ancient manuscript for which I now return your book with the translation by today's post.

I hope you will get them safely and that you will find the work of some foundation.

The speech is so very peculiar that it was very difficult to form words into English yet by taking time we managed to get along.

Mother was a competent scholar in her time in Mohawk consequently she still understands the ancient way of speaking this language. Otherwise we could have hardly accomplished the task. I was confident of her knowledge therefore I urged with my assistance to master the subject and now we have it & is considered a first rate translation. I am not surprised that scholars of fame would give up the work for it is so tedious unless the mind is determined to do.

I have always believed in the motto, Where there is a will there is a way. . . .[14]

While the beginnings of a native journalism received its slow start in the late nineteenth century and produced letters and essays by young Indians, historical events also served to generate writing in English—and French. In the early days of British settlement in Canada there were several conflicts between Canada's native peoples and the newcomers. When the Earl of Selkirk established the Red River Settlement on lands granted to him by the Hudson's Bay Company, the Métis viewed this as a direct threat to their trade with the rival North West Company. In June 1816 some 70 Métis, under Cuthbert Grant, approached the Settlement, bringing pemmican to the men of the North West Company. When the governor, Robert Semple, went out to meet them at a place called Seven Oaks, with settlers and Hudson's Bay Company men, there was a skirmish, and Semple and about 20 of his men were killed. Fort Douglas, the headquarters of the Settlement, surrendered. Pierre Falcon (1793-1876), the 'Bard of the Prairie Métis', was there and composed his famous 'La chanson de la Grenouillère' ('Chant de vérité'), a rousing song describing the clash and the Métis 'victory'. This is one of six mocking songs by Falcon known to us, treating various local incidents, that have given this folk poet an important place in the literary history of the West as its first native-born writer.

The mapping by government surveyors of the Red River district, without regard for Métis land-holdings, led to Louis Riel's establishment of a provisional government at Fort Garry in 1869-70. Riel (1844-85) was a prolific writer in French, though he could read and write English. His letters, diaries, poetry, and political and religious writings could fill four or five volumes of up to 500 pages each. His poetry especially reveals his political and family concerns, his deep religious faith, and his pride in his mixed heritage.

The treaties to which the native leaders affixed their names and marks recorded the terms by which their ancestral lands were surrendered. Treaty-making sessions were spectacular pageants enacted with the drama, formality, and etiquette that characterized Indian ceremonial observances through the centuries. Set speeches, feasting, dancing, chanting, and the beating of drums to ancient rhythms, as well as the discharging of arms and magnificent exhibitions of horsemanship by mounted braves, combined to make these events—which often lasted for days—impressive and memorable to the white officers of the Crown and their ladies.

Apart from their historical significance, the addresses of the chiefs during these proceedings—which, of course, expressed the opinions of their tribes—are models of eloquence. These lengthy, polished, and dramatic discourses reveal the same high degree of statesmanship, courtesy, and respect that distinguished the utterances of chiefs of old. Speeches were delivered by master orators, and when the interpreter was a good translator the oratorical excellence was preserved.

Although speeches dealt with immediate concerns in a direct and concrete manner, the beautiful ancient metaphors of *road*, *chain*, *fire*, *hatchet*, and *pipe* were used again and again to express the ideas of peace and friendship as well as the traditional analogies to the natural world—*sun*, *forest trails*, *trees*, and *water*, all images drawn from the lives of the people whose ancestral lands were being lost.

One of the ablest chiefs to speak during treaty negotiations was

Crowfoot (1830-90), the most influential chief in the Blackfoot Confederacy during the difficult period of transition that saw the disappearance of the great buffalo herds from the Canadian plains, the coming of the North-West Mounted Police, the negotiation of Treaty No. 7, the laying of the railroads, and the North West Rebellion of 1885.

According to Indian legend, 'Bear Ghost'—as Crowfoot was called when a young brave—had a vision in which a 'buffalo-man' appeared to tell him he was to lead the warlike Blackfoot in the paths of peace. The young warrior—tall and straight, with the eye of an eagle and born to command—obeyed. He followed a policy of peace as he led his people without bloodshed from a nomadic free life on the plains to a life confined to reserves dominated by white Indian agents, because he realized that war with a powerful white enemy was futile. So successful was his diplomacy and statesmanship that he was considered by whites to be the greatest single influence in the preservation of peace between Indians and whites.

The Blackfoot were the last Indians on the open plains to sign a treaty with the government, Treaty No. 7, on 22 September 1877. But it was not until Crowfoot had signified willingness to sign that the other chiefs of the Blackfoot Confederacy would agree to the terms. Crowfoot's speech, addressed to Lieutenant-Governor Laird and the government commissioners, is a fine specimen of eloquence, expressing both strength and vision:

While I speak, be kind and patient. I have to speak for my people, who are numerous, and who rely upon me to follow that course which in the future will tend to their good. The plains are large and wide. We are the children of the plains, it is our home, and the buffalo has been our food always. I hope you look upon the Blackfeet, Bloods and Sarcees as your children now, and that you will be indulgent and charitable to them. They all expect me to speak now for them, and I trust the Great Spirit will put into their breasts to be a good people into the minds of men, women and children, and their future generations. The advice given me and my people has proved to be very good. If the Police had not come to the country, where would we be all now? The Police have protected us as the feathers of the bird protected it from the frosts of winter. I wish them all good, and trust that all our hearts will increase in goodness from this time forward. I am satisfied. I will sign the treaty.[15]

While the government was negotiating the major Indian treaties and pre-empting land for railways, it was ignoring the claims of the Indians and Métis who, historically, had established roles as buffalo hunters and provisioners to the Hudson's Bay Company. The land base promised by the government was not fulfilled, and thousands of Métis were forced to leave for land further west, in present-day Saskatchewan. The buffalo were disappearing. Alarmed at the advance of white settlement, the Métis were understandably concerned about title to their land and their very survival. But once again the government ignored Métis grievances. This failure led the Saskatchewan Métis to take up arms under Louis Riel and his military leader Gabriel Dumont in the North West Rebellion of 1885. It was doomed to failure. Riel was imprisoned and hanged—without reason, as many saw then, as we see clearly and shockingly now—on 16 November 1885.

Before his sentence was pronounced on 1 August, Riel was asked whether he had anything to say, and he replied, 'Yes, your honour.' He then embarked on a long, rambling speech in English that was nevertheless an eloquent and moving statement that recalls the finest Indian orations of the past. Here is an excerpt:

The day of my birth I was helpless and my mother took care of me although she was not able to do it alone, there was some one to help her to take care of me and I lived. To-day, although a man I am as helpless before this court, in the Dominion of Canada and in this world, as I was helpless on the knees of my mother the day of my birth.

The North-West is also my mother, it is my mother country and although my mother country is sick and confined in a certain way, there are some from Lower Canada who came to help her to take care of me during her sickness and I am sure that my mother country will not kill me more than my mother did forty years ago when I came into the world, because a mother is always a mother, and even if I have my faults if she can see I am true she will be full of love for me.

When I came into the North-West in July, the first of July 1884, I found the Indians suffering. I found the half-breeds eating the rotten pork of the Hudson Bay Company and getting sick and week every day. Although a half-breed, and having no pretension to help the whites, I also paid attention to them. I saw they were deprived of responsible government, I saw that they were deprived of their public liberties. I remembered that half-breed meant white and Indian, and while I paid attention to the suffering Indians and the half-breeds I remembered that the greatest part of my heart and blood was white and I have directed my attention to help the Indians, to help the half-breeds and to help the whites to the best of my ability. We have made petitions, I have made petitions with others to the Canadian Government asking to relieve the condition of this country. We have taken time; we have tried to unite all classes, even if I may speak, all parties. Those who have been in close communication with me know I have suffered, that I have waited for months to bring some of the people of the Saskatchewan to an understanding of certain important points in

our petition to the Canadian Government and I have done my duty. I believe I have done my duty. It has been said in this box that I have been
egotistic. Perhaps I am egotistic. A man cannot be individuality without
paying attention to himself. He cannot generalize himself, though he may
be general. I have done all I could to make good petitions with others, and
we have sent them to the Canadian Government, and when the Canadian
Government did answer, through the Under Secretary of State, to the secretary of the joint committee of the Saskatchewan, then I began to speak
of myself, not before; so my particular interests passed after the public interests. A good deal has been said about the settlement and division of
lands a good deal has been said about that. I do not think my dignity today here would allow me to mention the foreign policy, but if I was to explain to you or if I had been allowed to make the questions to witnesses,
those questions would have appeared in an altogether different light before the court and jury. I do not say that my lawyers did not put the right
questions. The observations I had the honor to make to the court the day
before yesterday were good, they were absent of the situation, they did
not know all the small circumstances as I did. I could mention a point, but
that point was leading to so many that I could not have been all the time
suggesting. By it I don't wish it understood that I do not appreciate the
good works of my lawyers, but if I were to go into all the details of what
has taken place, I think I could safely show you that what Captain Young
said that I am aiming all the time at practical results was true, and I could
have proved it. During my life I have aimed at practical results. I have writings, and after my death I hope that my spirit will bring practical
results. . . .[16]

Two Indian chiefs, Big Bear and Poundmaker, were also impli-
cated. Their eloquence in their defence is remarkable.

Poundmaker (c. 1842-86) of Stoney, Cree, and French blood,
adopted son of Crowfoot, was so named for his superior ability in
forming the pounds for trapping buffalo. Poundmaker was tall, dignified, and deliberate in speech and manner, with a striking face
framed by raven-black hair hanging in two large plaits to below his
waist. His native air of courtliness and distinction impressed all who
met him.

One of the ablest chiefs of the Cree Confederacy, Poundmaker
signed the treaty made in 1876 at Carlton by which the Indians along
the Cutknife, Battle, and Saskatchewan Rivers exchanged their old
freedoms for life on the reservations. Confined on the reservation,
Poundmaker, like Crowfoot, relied on diplomacy and statesmanship
to solve the many difficulties that arose. On many occasions it was
only his skilled leadership that prevented band members—hungry,

demoralized, and angry with existing conditions—from rising to open revolt.

Despite his efforts for peace. Poundmaker was arrested and convicted of treason for his alleged part in the Rebellion of 1885. He was sentenced to three years' imprisonment in Stony Mountain Penitentiary but was allowed, contrary to the rules, to keep his long locks. He was released in 1886, a dying man, and died four months after his release while on a visit to Crowfoot. At his trial, Poundmaker appealed to the jury with passionate eloquence:

I am not guilty. A lot has been said against me that is untrue. I am glad of what I have done in the Queen's country. What I did was for the Great Mother. When my people and the whites met in battle. I saved the Queen's men. I took the firearms from my following and gave them up at Battleford. Everything I could do was to prevent bloodshed. Had I wanted war, I would not be here but on the prairie. You did not catch me. I gave myself up. You have me because I wanted peace. I cannot help myself, but I am still a man. You may do as you like with me.[17]

Big Bear (1825-88) was a visionary leader of the Crees. Outspoken, fearless, and self-reliant, he repeatedly refused to sign away his people's liberty to settle on a reserve. The Reverend George McDougall was sent by Alexander Morris, Lieutenant-Governor of Manitoba and the North-West Territories, to see if the Crees along the North Saskatchewan River would accept a treaty. In his speech to him in 1875, Big Bear used a hunting metaphor to illustrate his refusal: 'We want none of the Queen's presents; when we set a fox-trap we scatter pieces of meat all around, but when the fox gets into the trap we knock him on the head; we want no bait, let your Chiefs come like men and talk to us.'[18]

Big Bear became the undisputed leader of all the free Indians left on the nothern plains. However, when his people were nearly starving to death, he capitulated and signed Treaty No. 6 in 1882, the last chief of the Northwest to do so. Signing the treaty did not bring the promised improvement. The discontent along the Saskatchewan erupted into rebellion in March 1885. Big Bear was accused of being responsible for the atrocities committed at Frog Lake and was charged with treason. In spite of evidence to the contrary, he was found guilty. Like Poundmaker, Big Bear received a three-year sentence to be served in Stony Mountain Penitentiary. Released in 1887, along with Poundmaker, he died that winter.

At his trial Big Bear pleaded not for himself but for his people:

I have ruled my country for long. Now I am in chains and will be sent to prison. . . . Now I am as dead to my people. Many of them are hiding in the woods, paralysed by fear. Can this court not send them a pardon? My own children may be starving and afraid to come out of hiding. I plead to you Chiefs of the White man's laws for pity and help for the people of my band.

I have only a little more to say. The country belonged to me. I may not live to see it again. . . . I am old and ugly but I have tried to do good. Have pity for the children of my tribe. Because Big Bear has always been a friend of the white man, you should now send a pardon to my people and give help.[19]

Indians across the country found their creative energies drawn into the political sphere in the spirit of protest and dissent. A few newspapers existed that would publish their letters. On the west coast the *Victoria Daily Colonist* (1858-) aired Indian grievances. In 1896 the Nootka Chief Maquinna (c. 1835-1901) dictated to a journalist a logical and well-reasoned argument for the preservation of the potlatch, which had been prohibited by an amendment to the Indian Act in 1884:

TO THE EDITOR:—My name is Maquinna! I am the chief of the Nootkas and other tribes. My great-grandfather was also called Maquinna. He was the first chief in the country who saw white men. That is more than one hundred years ago. He was kind to the white men and gave them land to build and live on. By and by more white men came and ill treated our people and kidnapped them and carried them away on their vessels, and then the Nootkas became bad and retaliated and killed some white people. But that is a long time ago. I have always been kind to the white men . . . And now I hear that the white chiefs want to persecute us and put us in jail and we do not know why.

They say it is because we give feasts which the Chinook people call 'Potlatch.' That is not bad! That which we give away is our own! Dr. Powell, the Indian agent, one day also made a potlatch to all the Indian chiefs, and gave them a coat, and tobacco, and other things, and thereby we all knew that he was a chief; and so when I give a potlatch, they all learn that I am chief. To put in prison people who steal and sell whiskey and cards to our young men; that is right. But do not put us in jail as long as we have not stolen the things which we give away to our Indian friends. Once I was in Victoria, and I saw a very large house; they told me it was a bank and that the white men place their money there to take care of, and that by-and-by they got it back, with interest. We are Indians, and we have no such bank; but when we have plenty of money or blankets, we give them away to other chiefs and people, and by-and-by they return them, with interest, and our heart feels good. Our potlatch is our bank.

I have given many times a potlatch, and I have more than two thousand dollars in the hands of Indian friends. They all will return it some time, and I will thus have the means to live when I cannot work any more. My uncle is blind and cannot work, and that is the way he now lives, and he buys food for his family when the Indians make a potlatch. I feel alarmed! I must give up the potlatch or else be put in jail. Is the Indian agent going to take care of me when I can no longer work? No, I know he will not. He does not support the old and poor now. He gets plenty of money to support his own family, but although it is all our money, he gives nothing to our old people, and so it will be with me when I get old and infirm. They say it is the will of the Queen. That is not true. The Queen knows nothing about our potlatch feasts. She must have been put up to make a law by people who know us. Why do they not kill me? I would rather be killed now than starve to death when I am an old man. Very well, Indian agents, collect the two thousand dollars I am out and I will save them till I am old and give no more potlatch!

They say that sometimes we cover our hair with feathers and wear masks when we dance. Yes, but a white man told me one day that the white people have also sometimes masquerade balls and white women have feathers on their bonnets and the white chiefs give prizes for those who imitate best, birds or animals. And this is all good when white men do it but very bad when Indians do the same thing. The white chiefs should leave us alone as long as we leave the white man alone, they have their games and we have ours.

I am sorry to hear the news about the potlatch, and that my friends of the North were put in jail. I sympathise with them; and I asked a white man to write this in order to ask all white men not to interfere with our customs as long as there is no sin or crime in them. The Potlatch is not a pagan rite; the first Christians used to have their goods in common and as a consequence must have given 'potlatches' and now I am astonished that Christians persecute us and put us in jail for doing just as the first Christians.

> Maquinna, X (his mark)
> Chief of Nootka[20]

But Victorian society in Canada was not ready to listen to its native peoples. It was too busy expanding from sea to sea, building railroads and factories and cities, surveying prairie lands and building a nation. It had no time to listen to the pleas of the Indians who had been shifted by the dominant white society from a position of allies and partners to conditions of dependence and, ultimately, subjection. By the late nineteenth century most of the natives of Canada had been forced by government policy onto isolated and remote reserves where, removed from undesirable influences and subjected to controlled culture change as Christians and farmers, they could better be 'civilized'.

A few isolated figures—such as Peter Dooyentate Clarke, Francis Assikinack, Louis Jackson, and John Brant-Sero—were able to get into print, and Pauline Johnson was able to achieve tremendous popularity as poet and platform artist. But the eloquent pleas of chiefs, trying to tell Canadians what was going on in the minds and hearts of a dispossessed people, went unheard.

IV

1914-1969

The decades between the First World War and the 1969 government White Paper on Indian policy was a barren period for native writing in Canada. The reasons for the scarcity of published works were many: the growing power of white control through the Department of Indian Affairs; government policies that were based on the assimilation and suppression of native cultures; a native population overwhelmed by the deluge of immigration that flooded the western Prairies and placed natives in ever more humiliating subjugation; the Depression and an increase in poverty; lack of unity among the scattered tribes across the country; and the commonly held belief that the natives were dying out. Finally, there was a notable lack of interest among publishers in anything pertaining to natives, although some of their narratives, as retold by non-natives, were published.

For example, two collections of Indian tales made a great impression early in this period. *Canadian Wonder Tales* (1918) and *Canadian Fairy Tales* (1922)—retellings by Cyrus Macmillan (1882-1953), who was born on Prince Edward Island—were published in England by The Bodley Head in two deluxe volumes with attractive illustrations, many in colour, by artists who had no knowledge of Indian life and simply remanticized it. Macmillan, a polished writer who later became Professor of English at McGill University, retold them as extensions of the European fairy-tale tradition, though he claimed to have received the stories from various authentic sources. The best are those about Glooscap. They were drawn from the Micmac tradition of his home territory, and no doubt from Silas Rand's *Legends of the Micmacs* (1894), and had a modern efflorescence in the collection *Glooskap's Country* (1955), which remained in print for two decades.

As recently as 1974 The Bodley Head reissued Macmillan's two books in one volume, with illustrations by the Canadian children's-book illustrator Elizabeth Cleaver.

Another interesting sidelight on the subject of publications about native life in this period lies in the very popular writings of two imposters: Grey Owl (Archibald Stansfeld Belaney, 1888-1938) and Chief Buffalo Child Long Lance (Sylvestre Clark Long, 1890-1932), one an Englishman adopted by the Ojibway, the other an American adopted by the Blood. After the second of Grey Owl's four books, *Pilgrims of the Wild*, was published in 1935, he made two highly successful lecture tours of the United States and Britain. Buffalo Child Long Lance's *Long Lance* (1928) purported to be an autobiography of a full-blooded Blackfoot chief on the Canadian prairie.

There were two reasons for the success of these books. Both authors personified the romantic Indian—they were handsome, and looked 'Indian'. But more significantly, Grey Owl's sketches of men and animals in a forest world, and Long Lance's account of a life of freedom on the plains satisfied complacent notions of the happy Indian, at one with nature, held by white readers who were far from ready to be confronted with the realities that at least a few native writers were willing and able to impart. It came as a great shock when, many years later, both men were revealed to be bogus Indians. (They were, however, sincere and authentic in their depictions of many aspects of native life and of nature.) A much more realistic glimpse of West Coast native life was given by the painter Emily Carr in *Klee Wyck*, published in 1941, but her endearing, slightly sentimental sketches of Indians she knew kept them at a distance, and of course she was white.

In his *Tales of an Empty Cabin* (1936) Grey Owl included a letter written in Canada by Ana-Quon-Ess, who had been in the Great War, to his former nurse in England. A remarkable outpouring of love for the native way of life that sometimes reaches lyrical heights, it illustrates not only his enjoyment of letterwriting (which was happily not affected by his shaky command of the language), but also the spirit of self-confidence his wartime experience had given him.

Dear Miss Nurse: *February 3rd, 1918.*

Nearly four months now the Canada geese flew south and the snow is very deep. It is long timesince I wrot to you, but I have gone a long ways and folled some hard trails since that time. The little wee sorryful animals I tol you about sit around me tonight, and so they dont get tired and go away I write to you now. I guess they like to see me workin. I seen my old old trees and the rocks that I know and the forest that is to me what your house is to you, I have been in it agen and am going back there in three days more, till Spring and the rivers run open agen and then I come out in canoe about last of April. I wisht youd ben here to see when I got back. The Injuns was camped and had their tents at the Head of the lake. I went up. They come out and looked at me and the chief took me by the hand and said How, and they all come one at a time and shake hans and say How. They ast me nothin about the War but said they would dance the Morning Wind dance, as I just came from East and that is the early morning wind on the lakes. Then they dance next night the Neebiche, meanin the leaves that are blown and drift before the wind in the empty forest. The white people, they got wise to it and come up, but a lot of them beat it away. The woman that teaches the white schol she fainted, which was comecal as we didnt mean nothin, ony they heard the yellin and drums and come up to see and they seen it in good shape. I kill 43 beaver now, 1 otter, 7 fisher, and a few wolves, and some moose and deer, have now meat for all winter, buckskin clothes and got my wound fixed so I can snowshoe as good as ever and wear moccassins. Comin out yestdy we made the last 18 miles in 5 hours in deep snow. Gee Im lucky to be able to travel the big woods agen. To us peple the woods and the big hills and the Northen lights and the sunsets are all alive and we live with these things and live in the spirit of the woods like no white person can do. The big lakes we travel on the little lonely lakes we set our beaver traps on with a ring of big black pines standin in rows lookin always north, like they was watchin for somethin that never comes, same as an Injun, they are real to us and when we are alone we speak to them and are not lonesome. only thinkin always of the long ago days and the old men. So we live in the past and the rest of the world keeps goin by. For all their moden inventons they cant live the way we do and they die if they try becase they cant read the sunset and hear the old men talk in the wind. A wolf is fierce, but he is our brother he lives the old way, but the Saganash is sometime a pup and he dies when the wind blows on him, becase he sees only trees and rocks and water only the out side of the book and cant read. We are two hundred years behind the times and dont change very much. . . . I have took a lot of pictures and will send you some. One is my friend (he is an Injun though, you mind the time you seen his letter). I am hunting at a place called Place-where-the-water-runs-in-the-middle becase the water runs in at the centre of the lake. I will send picture of it. I will show you the Talking Hill in a picture as so long as the old timers dont see me takin it. I wonder if all this means anything to you I hope you wont laugh at it anyway. It is now Seegwun when the snow is all melt of the ice and it thaw in the daytime and freeze at night, making a crust so the moose breaks through and cant run. This is the days when we have hardship and our snowshoes break through the crust and get wet an heavy an our feet is wet everyday all the time wet. The crows have come back. Between now and the break up is pleasant weather in the settlements but it is hell in the woods. White men dont travel not at all now and I dont blame him. March 20th/18 Well I lay up today all day in my camp and it is a soft moon, which is bad beleive me, so I write some more to your letter. I travel all day yestdy on the lakes in water and slush half way to my knees on top the ice. It will be an early spring. My wound is kinda gone on the blink, to hard goin. . . . Well the spring birds waken me up in the morning, but they eat my meat hanging outside too, but they are welcom to it, a long time I didnt see them and I am too glad too be back wher I can get meat and be wher they is birds to eat it I can get some more when thats done. They have sent a runner in twice for me to go onto that Govt. job fire ranger, but I am happy here and I want to be free. Thats a way better than money an I guess I go ranging this summer. I caught a squirrell in a trap by accident I had set for a fisher [ojig]. He was dead and I felt sorry. I made my dinner in the snow right there an sat an think an smoke an think about it and everything until the wind changed an blow the smoke in my face an I went away then. An I wondered if the tall black trees standing all aroun an the Gweegweechee [whiskyjacks] in the trees and the old men that still travel the woods thats dead long long ago I wondered if they knowed what I was thinking about, Me, I kinda forgotten anyhow. Theys a bunch of red birds outside feeding. I guess youd find them pretty, red with stripes on their wings. Well Miss Nurse this is somewheres around the last of March. Half of the snow is went now and the lakes are solid ice about 4 or 3 ft thick. That all has to go in about one month. The sun is getting warm. . . . Did I ever tell you about my throwin knife I had, well I got it back it lays along side of me as I write, the edge all gapped from choppin moose bones with. I would sure like to show you this country with its big waters and black forests an little lonely lakes with a wall of trees all around them, quiet, never move but just look on an on an you know as you go by them trees was there ahead of you an will be there after you are dead. It makes a person feel small, ony with us, that is our life to be among them things. I kill that lynx today and somehow I wisht I hadnt. His skin is only worth $10 and he didnt act cross an the way he looked at me I cant get that out of my mind. I dont think I will sell that skin no. . . . I was on a side hill facing south and in spots it was bare of snow and the leaves were dry under my feet an I thought of what I tol you onct, about bein sick. Once I walked amongst flowers in the spring sun and now I stand on dry leaves an the wind blows cold through the bare tree tops. I think it tells me that wind that pretty soon no one cannot ever hear me. That must be so becase I cannot see my own trail ahead of me. a cloud hangs over it. Away ahead not so awful far the trail goes into the cloud, the sun dies behind the hills, there are no more trees ony the cloud. I had a friend he is dead now. I wonder if he is lonesome. I am now. They wanted to send me to a Sanatoriom before I was discharged, but I said No sir, nothin doin. I would be dead in about a week. A man has a good chance here. I knowd a guy with punk lungs come up here expectin to celebrate his funeral an he didnt die for seven years. Say, you poor people over there gettin no meat. Dont think me mean to tell you, but we have 300lb of meat on hand now. Injuns can kill all they want for their own use. I wisht I could send you some. Hows the wee garden and the nieces coming along. Write and tellme all about them. My ears are open. . . . I will lisen to the song of a bird for a little while. Now the curtain is pulled down across the sun and my heart is black. A singing bird comes and sings an says I do this an I do that an things are so with me an I will lisen an forget there is no sun, until the bird goes, then I will sit and think an smoke for hours an say to myself, thats good, I am only an Injun and that bird sang for me. When the morning wind rises and the morning star hangs of the edge of the black swamp to the east, tomorrow, I will be on my snowshoe trail. Goodbye.

Ana-Quon-Ess.[1]

The early years of this century were the bleakest days in the history of Canada's native peoples, a time when their fortunes were at their lowest ebb.

In *John Tootoosis: Biography of a Cree Leader* (1982) Norma Sluman and Jean Goodwill tell how the Indians of the Plains were in 'massive shock' after they were forcibly removed to reserves. They tell how government agents and missionaries, backed up by the police, dominated every aspect of the lives of the people under treaty. 'At the turn of the century the prairie Indian reserves were just about the most isolated and silent places in Canada.'[2] After the First World War, when Indian soldiers who had fought beside other Canadians returned to the reserves, they did not find it easy to resume the segregated and disadvantaged life they had known before the war. They were no longer so mute and passive.

Frederick Ogilvie Loft (1861-1935) was born on the Tuscarora Reserve near Brantford, Ontario. Following three years in Caledonia High School, he spent two years in the vast lumbering regions of northern Michigan as a lumberjack and later as lumber inspector. Illness forced him to return home for a rest in 1884. Upon his recovery he took a course at the Ontario Business College in Belleville, Ontario, and graduated as a bookkeeper. In 1885 he joined the staff of the *Brantford Expositor* where, with his ready pen, good command of English, and keen interest in the affairs of his people, he became an authority on the history and traditions of the Six Nations.

In the general elections of 1886—the first Dominion election in which the Indians of the Six Nations were able to exercise their newly won franchise—Loft conducted a successful campaign in the interests of the Liberal candidate.

In 1887 he received an appointment in the bursar's office of the

Ontario Hospital in Toronto, a position he held for almost forty years. In June 1898 he married Affa Northcote Geare of Chicago, a cousin of Sir Stafford Northcote, later Lord Iddesleigh. At the outbreak of the Great War, Loft advocated, through the press, the raising of an Indian battalion to go overseas as a unit. In 1917 he was transferred from his own battalion to the Canadian Forestry Corps to recruit a company of Indians for the Corps, which he took overseas. While in England he received a private audience with George V. When he returned home he began the work of organizing the disparate tribes across Canada, founding a new national Indian organization that was known as the League of Indians. The following circular, dated 26 November 1919, was addressed to chiefs across Canada urging them to join:

Dear Sirs and Brethren:

For and in behalf of the League of Indians of Canada and its Executive, I have the honour to address you and the members of your band, to seriously urge upon the important necessity of all Indians becoming united into one great association; in this way to stablize our interests, protect and advance them in ways that will be of national benefit.

Union is the outstanding impulse of men today, because it is the only way by which the individual and collective elements of society can wield a force and power to be heard and their demands recognized by governments. Look at the force and power of all kinds of labour organizations, because of their unions. Now we see the great development and strength of the farmers, who are uniting to uphold and advance their interests. In a recent election in Ontario, they have been able to control the Government and Legislature of Ontario. How is this? Because each and all have combined to work together for an end, to elevate their position and noble calling as producers.

In politics, in the past, they have been in the background, scarcely heard or noticed in parliaments or in nature of laws passed, but now they are getting right into the front because they have wakened up to the great duty of uniting.

We as Indians, from one end of the Dominion to the other, are sadly strangers to each other; we have not learned what it is to co-operate and work for each other as we should; the pity of it is greater because our needs, drawbacks, handicaps and troubls are all similar. It is for us to do something to get out of these sad conditions. The day is past when one band or a few bands can successfully—if at all—free themselves from the domination of officialdom and from being ever the prey and victims of unfair means of depriving us of our lands, and even deny us of the rights we are entitled to as free men under the British Flag.

As peaceable and law-abiding citizens in the past, and even in the late war, we have performed dutiful service to our King, Country and Empire, and we have the right to claim and demand more justice and fair play as a recompense, for we, too, have fought for the sacred rights of justice, freedom and liberty so dear to mankind, no matter what their colour or creed.

The first aim of the League then is to claim and protect the rights of all Indians in Canada by legitimate and just means; second, absolute control in remaining possession or disposition of our lands; that all questions and matters relative to individual and national wellbeing of Indians shall rest with the people and their dealing with the Government shall be by and through their respective band Councils at all times to be consulted, and their wishes respected in like manner as other constituted bodies conducting public affairs.

All these matters are formulated in the constitution of the League, which was passed and adopted at the first congress of the League held at the 'Soo' Ontario, September 2-4th, 1919, which was attended by a large delegation from Ontario, and Manitoba was also represented.

Union then has started; it is for all who are not yet members to join with the forces to create a permanent national brotherhood with a great national policy of progess and advancement to lift ourselves up by our own effort to better conditions, morally, socially, politically and industrially. The aim also is to demand better educational advantages for our children, also to encourage our people to be farmers, stay on the land and work it, for it is the most independent way of living. We will co-operate with the Government, but we must have its sympathy, encouragement and assistance so as to make good. To force or coerce us will do no good; justice and fair dealing is what we ask for. We are men, not imbeciles; from our view and standpoint we must be heard as a nation when we have to speak for ourselves.

I urge your band and Council's early decision to join the League, if you are really concerned in the peace and welfare of your brother Indians in Canada.

Let me hear from you as soon as possible, or when you decide to join the League, send me $5.00 registration fees. This is only a first payment. For payment of yearly dues as a member, a band pays on the basis of 5 cents per head of the population.

Money is always required to pay for paper, stamps and other expenses. A fund to be created by us will be used to pay our children's fees in high schools. By doing this you are helping your race to get better schooling. Our success is in our own hands, so let us strive to be true to ourselves, our families, our brethren and our country. This is good citizenship.

When you write let me know how many are in your band and name and post office address of person I am to write to. Tendering my kind regards to all,

I remain in truth and regard your brother,

Chief F.L. Loft[3]

Loft's first circular was a powerful call to action and is typical of the reasoned appeals of his ancestors. It is also significant because it advocates self-help and voices the demands of modern-day native peoples: aboriginal rights, self-determination, and protection of the land base.

But the Department of Indian Affairs constantly challenged and undermined Loft's activities and the whole concept of Indian organization. 'Instead of recognizing such movements as positive evidence that Indian people were regaining strength and pride and the desire to help themselves . . ., the Department saw the organizers as disloyal, . . . even "bolshevicks", as one Indian agent put it.'[4] Loft's League failed during the Depression, partly because of the result of this bureaucratic opposition; but the seeds of his ideas had germinated, and other Indian organizations, and other lobbyists and activists, would carry on his work.

Another early native activist who devoted his talents to the service of Canada's Indians, particularly the Six Nations, was Levi General (1873-1925), lumberjack and farmer, whose other name was Deskaheh, Chief of the Bear Clan of the Cayuga Nation. General was from the Grand River territory of the Six Nations and was appointed to speak for them, to defend their rights in Ottawa, London, and Geneva. As an adherent of the Longhouse religion, Deskaheh insisted that the Six Nations retain their language and distinctive culture, and resisted the Canadian government's attempts in 1923 to unseat the Six Nations Hereditary Council and to institute an elected one. On a passport issued by the Council he travelled to the League of Nations in Geneva to obtain international recognition of the Six Nations as a sovereign Indian nation ruled by a hereditary council of Chiefs. But the League's Secretariat refused to allow him to address the Assembly, arguing that Canada had jurisdiction over the Six Nations. Knowing that if he returned to Canada he would be risking his freedom, Deskaheh spent the last two years of his life on the Tuscarora Reservation near Lewiston, N.Y. Disheartened, and suffering from a serious attack of pleuresy and pneumonia, he made his last speech before a radio microphone in Rochester on 10 March 1925:

Nearly everyone who is listening to me is a pale face, I suppose. I am not. My skin is not red but that is what my people are called by others. My skin is brown, light brown, but our cheeks have a little flush and that is why we are called red skins. We don't mind that. There is no difference between us, under the skins, that any expert with a carving knife has ever discovered.

My home is on the Grand River. Until we sold off a large part, our country extended down to Lake Erie, where, 140 winters ago, we had a little sea-shore of our own and a birch-bark navy.

You would call it Canada. We do not. We call the little ten-miles square we have left the 'Grand River Country.' We have the right to do that. It is ours. We have the written pledge of George III that we should have it forever as against him or his successors and he promised to protect us in it.

We didn't think we would ever live long enough to find that a British promise was not good. An enemy's foot is on our country, and George V knows it for I told him so, but he will not lift his finger to protect us nor will any of his ministers. . . .

We want none of your laws and customs that we have not willingly adopted for ourselves. We have adopted many. You have adopted some of ours—votes for women, for instance. We are as well behaved as you and you would think so if you knew us better. . . .

Your governments have lately resorted to new practices in their Indian policies . In the old days, they often bribed our chiefs to sign treaties to get our lands. Now they know that our remaining territory can easily be gotten from us by first taking our political rights away in forcing us into your citizenship, so they give jobs in their Indian offices to the bright young people among us who will take them and who, to earn their pay, say that our people wish to become citizens with you and that we are ready to have our tribal life destroyed and want your governments to do it. But that is not true. . . .

To punish us for trying to preserve our rights, the Canadian Government has now pretended to abolish our government by Royal Proclamation, and has pretended to set up a Canadian-made government over us, composed of the few traitors among us who are willing to accept pay from Ottawa and do its bidding. Finally, Ottawa officials , under pretence of a friendly visit, asked to inspect our precious wampum belts, made by our Fathers centuries ago as records of our history, and when shown to them, these false-faced officials seized and carried away those belts as bandits take away your precious belongings. The only difference was that our aged wampum-keeper did not put up his hands—our hands go up only when we address the Great Spirit. Yours go up, I hear, only when some one of you is going through the pockets of his own white brother. According to your newspapers, they are up now a good deal of the time.

The Ottawa government thought that with no wampum belts to read in the opening of our Six Nations Councils, we would give up our home rule and self-government, the victims of superstition. Any superstition of which the Grand River People have been victims are not in reverence for wampum belts, but in their trust in the honour of governments who boast of a higher civilization. . . .

We are not as dependent in some ways as we were in the early days. We do not need interpreters now. We know your language and can understand your words for ourselves and we have learned to decide for ourselves what is good for us. It is bad for any people to take the advice of an alien people as to that.

You Mothers, I hear, have a good deal to say about your government. Our Mothers have always had a hand in ours. Maybe you can do something to help us now. If you white mothers are hard-hearted and will not, perhaps you boys and girls who are listening and who have loved to read stories about our people—the true ones, I mean—will help us when you grow up if there are any of us left to be helped. . . .

This is the story of the Mohawks, the story of the Oneidas, of the Cayugas—I am Cayuga—of the Onondagas, the Senecas, and the Tuscaroras. They are the Iroquois. Tell it to those who have not been listening. Maybe I will be stopped from telling it. But if I am prevented from telling it over, as I hope to do, the story will not be lost. I have already told it to thousands of listeners in Europe—it has gone into the records where your children can find it when I may be dead or be in jail for daring to tell the truth. I have told this story in Switzerland—they have free speech in little Switzerland. One can tell the truth over there in public, even if it is uncomfortable for some great people.

This story comes straight from Deskaheh, one of the chiefs of the Cayugas. I am the speaker of the Council of the Six Nations, the oldest League of Nations now existing. It was founded by Hiawatha. It is a League which is still alive and intends, as best it can, to defend the rights of the Iroquois to live under their own laws in their own little countries now left to them, to worship their Great Spirit in their own way, and to enjoy the rights which are as surely theirs as the white man's rights are his own.

If you think the Iroquois are being wronged, write letters from Canada to your ministers of Parliament, and from the United States to your Congressman and tell them so. They will listen to you for you elect them. If they are against us, ask them to tell you when and how they got the right to govern people who have no part in your government and do not live in your country but live in their own. They can't tell you that. . . .

I could tell you much more about our people, and I may some other time, if you would like to have me.[5]

Deskaheh died shortly after he gave this address. Although his dissident voice employed an informal conversational style, it was still motivated by the same fervour of indignation that characterized earlier voices of protest. By this time, as Deskaheh observed, the issues had become a matter of life and death to the native peoples and the maintenance of their traditions. Indeed, the spirit of Deskaheh was present in the spring of 1990 at Askwesasne, a 9,500-member Mohawk community straddling the Canada-U.S. Border, where underlying the tensions that erupted into violence was the historic issue of their sovereignty.

Just as Loft had returned home after the Great War with a desire to organize the Indian people, so too were a number of Second World War veterans anxious to lobby for reform. When veterans such as Walter Dieter, Omer Peters, Malcolm Norris, and James Brady returned to Canada they dared to make their voices heard as they struggled against an intolerant and often racist society. They followed the traditional pattern of Indian protest, speaking in public and writing letters, reports, and petitions to various levels of government. As a consequence, polemics—whether in speech, essay, or letter—dominated the imagination and absorbed the intellectual energies of many talented natives as they responded angrily and bitterly, in direct and forceful language, to their problems.

An influential and educated Indian who was to play an important role in the increasingly complex world of Indian politics was the Squamish leader Andrew Paull (1892-1959), the founder of the North American Indian Brotherhood, who was born on Mission Reserve No. 1, Burrard Inlet, British Columbia. He received his formal education at a Roman Catholic mission school and worked as a longshoreman, sports writer, and radio announcer. He also managed sports teams, played several musical instruments, and organized an orchestra. He worked for a time in the office of a local attorney, where he developed an interest in law as it concerned Indians and memorized long passages of laws, legal rulings, and documents related to Indian affairs. Whether at the local, provincial, or national-policy level, Paull was a major spokesman for Indian rights in Canada. An indefatigable worker and prolific writer, he wrote letters on behalf of individuals and groups to various levels of government and to the newspapers. He even edited and published his own newspapers, *The Thunderbird* (1949-55) and *The Totem Speaks* (1953). His appearance before the Special Joint Committee of the Senate and House of Commons on 27 June 1946 notably revealed his dramatic style of oratory and the new aggressive, confrontational stance of the most vocal natives:

The Witness: And I might as well warn you that I am going to say a few disagreeable things, so you might as well be prepared.

The Chairman: I am sure that you want to be quite polite in your presentation.

The Witness: I will do it in as systematic way as possible. As I was saying, we asked for a Royal Commission to investigate 'you' and to investigate 'me'. And now, I wish this to be on the record; that this Royal Commission was asked for and recommended by the churches, by the attorneys general, men of learning, and was asked for by members of this committee also; to investigate you and to investigate *me*. And now, the parliament of Canada in its wisdom and in its judgment, and usurping the authority which it has, decided not to have a Royal Commission but to appoint a committee to investigate itself. Now, put that on the record will you, please?

Now, you are sitting here as a committee investigating yourselves. We have another complaint against you which is that you have appointed a committee, an august committee, a committee which we respect, but you have no Indians on your committee. We asked for a Royal Commission and that Indians be appointed to that Royal Commission. All right, if that is on the record we will pass that up. I just want you to know that you are a committee here to investigate yourselves. . . .

From that we will go on to another subject: is the Indian a British subject, or is he a ward of the government? That is a subject I should like you to determine in your mind now; is the Indian a British subject or is he a ward of the government? We have had court decisions to this effect, that the Indian is a British subject. And we have had court decisions that the Indian is a ward. And now, through legislative determination—whatever you wish to call it, can you split the personality of a human being in this country, whether he is an Indian, a white man, or whatever he is? Now, who is able to do that? You have done it. The minister just says that the Indian is a British subject, and the courts say that the Indian is a ward of the government. Is the Indian a super human being that he can be two kinds of people? That is something this committee will have to determine and settle before they make a decision. Now, I did not come here prepared with a lot of decisions or anything like that. I haven't got anything of that kind with me, but if you want us to support it we will be glad to supply you with that at some other time. An invitation has been extended to me to speak on generalities. Now, by the decision of the Deputy Minister of Justice, the Indian was asked to pay income tax because, in the opinion of the Deputy Minister of Justice, the Indian is a British subject. And now, I would like to put into the mind of every member of this committee, this question: how would you like to be taxed just on the opinion of a civil servant? We say that an Indian can only be taxed by an act of Parliament, because under Section 91 of the British America Act the Parliament of Canada has the charge and the management of lands reserved for Indians; and until you have sufficient intestinal fortitude to pass an Act in the House of Commons to tax Indians then it is ultra vires of the British North America Act to impose income tax on Indians. I do not think it is necessary for me to repeat that. The Parliament of Canada was entrusted with the charge and management of Indians. Now, a delegate cannot entrust his duty to another delegate, as those of you on this committee who are members of the bar know. That is a truism; a delegate cannot transfer his responsibilities to another delegate. And now, I will leave this matter of taxation for further discussion at a later time; but, as I say, it all turns on the point of whether the Indian is a British subject or a ward of the government. I have the greatest respect for the intelligence of the members of this committee, and I am confident that they know all the details of the Indian Act and everything connected with it. I presume you know what the Indian Act is. The Indian Act is an imposition, the carrying out of the most bureaucratic and autocratic system that was ever imposed upon any people in this world of ours. That is what the Indian Act is. And now, perhaps some of you have heard about William of Orange. The system that is in vogue as administered by some of our Indian agents is something worse than the system that was instituted by William of Orange in Ireland. Now, William of Orange ground the Irish people beneath his heel to such an extent that the Irish people could not express themselves; and yet when they left Ireland and came to Canada or the United States they became judges, jurists, members of parliament, senators, members of congress, and even policemen. Yet in their own country they could not even be policemen. Now, that is the system that is now carried on under the administration as it is carried out under the Indian Act. May I say that since Mr Hoey took over the administration of Indian Affairs there has been a remarkable change. I would like to say at this time that I wish to compliment him on the manner in which he has conducted Indian Affairs. I should like to extend some measures of congratulation to Major MacKay [Commissioner for Indian Affairs in British Columbia]; and I would like to take off my hat, my feathered hat if I had one, to the Hon. J. Allison Glen [Minister of Mines and Resources] for bringing this committee into being. He has had the courage to struggle with this situation and to bring this investigation into being, and all Indians in Canada take their hats off, or their feathered bonnets, to Mr Glen.

Now this committee will have to decide whether the Indian is a British subject or a ward of the government before it can successfuly deal with its duties. The next point I would like to deal with is the matter of treaties. . . .[6]

The protests of such early activists demonstrate a continuity of theme and style, grievances masked in humour, the same vein of dry sarcasm, the same irony, understatement, and teasing mockery that distinguished native literature of protest.

In 1958, for the first time in Canadian history, an Indian, James Gladstone (Blood), was appointed to the Senate. This was followed in the 1960s—a decade of protest and radical change in North America—by more reforms for the natives of Canada. Friendship Centres opened up in Toronto and Winnipeg to facilitate the shift of natives into these cities. And governments began to fund native associations and newspapers. Among the periodicals and newspapers were: *Native Voice* (1946-), published by the Native Brotherhood of British Columbia; *Indian Time* (1950-9), published by the Pan-American Indian League, Vancouver; *Indian News/Nouvelles Indiennes* (1954-82) published by the Indian and Inuit Affairs Program, Ottawa; *Indian Outlook* (1960-3), published by the Federation of Saskatchewan Indians; *Native People* (1968-), published by the Alberta Native Communication Society for Edmonton; *Kainai News* (1968-), published in Hobbema, Alberta; *Toronto Native Times* (1968-81), published by the Canadian Indian Centre of Toronto; *Akwesasne Notes* (1969-), published by the Mohawk nation in Roosevelt Town, N.Y.; *The Indian Voice* (1969-), published by the British Columbia Indian Homemakers' Association, Vancouver; and *The First Citizen* (1969-72), a community newsletter published in Vancouver. They provided a forum for the new politically conscious Indian organizations that were being founded. Native speakers emerged, and the oration once again became a vigorous literary form. Idiomatic and rhetorical speeches were recorded in native and non-native newspapers and journals alike. Journalistic prose, in the form of reports and essays, also became popular as native activists began to utilize such forms as their vehicles of attack on, and criticism of, the dominant society.

During the sixties singers too played an important role in the Indian protest movement across Canada. Willie Dunn (Ojibway), Buffy St Marie (Cree), Winston Wuttunnee (Cree), Shingoose (Micmac), and Alanis Obamsawin (Abenaki) all sang their own protest songs at folk festivals and wherever they had an audience.

The few books by natives in the first six decades of this century were mostly life histories or collections of legends written in the as-told-to-tradition, with the aid of a collaborator or editor. *From Potlatch to Pulpit* (1933) was an autobiography of the Reverend William Henry Pierce, a missionary to the natives on the northern coast of British Columbia, who ended his memoirs in 1910 when he was fifty-four. The book was edited by the Reverend P.J. Hicks.

Smoke from Their Fires: The Life of a Kwakiutl Chief (1941; reprinted 1968) by Charles James Nowell, edited by the anthropologist Clellan Stearns Ford, appeared as a result of a scientific field study on Vancouver Island during the summer of 1940. Nowell, who was born in 1870, tells the story of his life against the background of a disappearing culture. Despite his education and extensive contact with white culture, Nowell continued to hold his Kwakiutl beliefs and values.

Settlement of Indian tribes on reserves and the coercive education of Indian children in residential schools meant that many more Indians read and wrote English. Despite the harshness and cruelty that often existed in residential schools, they did produce a number of highly literate graduates in the twenties and thirties. And, with the encouragement of a single teacher who emphasized writing skills, Dan Kennedy, Mike Mountain Horse, Joe Dion, Victoria Calihoo, and Edward Ahenakew became interested in creative writing. They wrote their reminiscenses, life histories, and narratives in scribblers and workbooks and on foolscap. Sometimes they were fortunate enough to have a story or two published in farm papers or local newspapers, commercial magazines, trade journals, or in magazines sponsored by the growing political organizations that were springing up across the country. But on the whole, their manuscripts had to wait for publication until the 1950s and later, when white supporters like Hugh Dempsey of the Glenbow Museum deliberately sought them out. But by the time they were published, many of their authors had died. For example, Edward Ahenakew began a book in 1923 that was not published until 1973—as *Voices of the Plains Cree*. Mike Mountain Horse's book-length manuscript entitled 'Indians of the Western Plains' was completed in 1936 but wasn't published until 1979 as *My People the Bloods*. Victoria Callihoo, of Gunn, Alberta, wrote her articles on the Iroquois of Alberta and the Buffalo Hunt in the 1940s but could find no publisher until 1959, when they were published in *The Alberta Historical Review*. Walter Wright of the Kitselas band in British Columbia narrated the history of the legendary city of Tum-L-Hanna, and the migration westward to the Kitselas Canyon, to Will Robinson in 1935-6, but it was not published until 1962, as *Men of Medeek*.

It was not until 1967 and after that a few natives were fortunate enough to get into print immediately. The Saskatchewan History and Folklore Society published *Payepot and His People* (1959), a biography of the last great Cree war chief and medicine man, Payepot, as told by Abel Watetch to Blodwen Davies. In 1960 Ethel Brant Monture, a great-great-granddaughter of Joseph Brant, published the biographies of three celebrated Canadian Indians under the title *Canadian Portraits: Brant, Crowfoot, Oronhyatikha, Famous Indians*. Monture fused their biographies into their historical and cultural contexts.

Legends of My People, the Great Ojibway by the well-known native artist Norval Morriseau (and edited by Selwyn Dewdney) appeared in 1965. Morriseau's text, which was converted 'into academically acceptable English', offered the myths and legends of the Ojibway of Lake Nipigon and the Thunder Bay district. The Indian who was changed into a thunderbird, the sacred bear beliefs of the Midewewin Society, the shaking-tent rites, the Windigo, bad-luck stories, love charms, sexual lore, and healing practices all appear in his book.

The next year saw the publication of *Here Are the News* by Edith Josie, a Loucheux correspondent for the *Whitehorse Star* from Old Crow, Northwest Territories. Josie's book is a collection of some of her columns dealing with the day-to-day activities of her isolated Indian community, written the way she spoke.

Canada's centennial year, 1967, witnessed the publication of *Son of Raven, Son of Deer* by George Clutesi, the well-known British Columbia artist, author, and actor. It is a collection of traditional stories of the Tse-Shaht tribe (which Sheila Egoff described as 'often closer to Aesop' than to the condensed, elliptical tonalities of recorded West Coast oral literature). Clutesi was a member of the West Coast Tse-Shaht tribe and a resident of Port Alberni, British Columbia. He was born in 1905, raised on the reserve near Port Alberni, and received his elementary education at the Indian residential school. He left school at Grade 7 and then educated himself by reading extensively and by carrying on his traditional family role as tribal orator. In the role of author he addressed scores of youth groups, students, and adults, and appeared on radio and television. He received an ACTRA award as best actor for his role in the 1966 television drama *Dreamspeaker*. In 1973 he was made a member of the Order of Canada. He died on 5 March 1988 at the age of 83.

The first anthology of Canadian native literature was *I Am an Indian* (1969), edited by the non-native Kent Gooderham. It offered a wide assortment of literary forms: legends, essays, stories, and poems by such native writers as Duke Redbird, Chief Dan George, Howard Adams, Alma Greene, Ethel Brant Monture, George Clutesi, Red Peter Kelly, Edith Josie, and the Reverend Edward Ahenakew.

Two Articles (1969) by Wilfred Pelletier—an important native activist in the sixties—consists of two essays: 'Childhood in an Indian Village' and 'Some Thoughts About Organization and Leadership'. In the first, Pelletier uses his own experiences in Wikwemikong, Manitoulin Island, where he was born, to illustrate the ways Indian children are taught by their parents and to show the differences between white and native methods. In the second he contrasts white and native ways of organization. Both provide useful insights for the understanding and appreciation of native culture.

Guests Never Leave Hungry: The Autobiography of James Sewid, a Kwakiutl Indian (1969) was tape-recorded in unstructured interviews by the anthropologist Dr James Philip Spradley; the transcript was then edited, rearranged, cut, and 'the syntax altered a little'. Sewid, whose command of English was sufficient for the purposes of Spradley's research (according to Spradley), was a successful entrepreneur who owned his own fishing boat and hired his own crew to work it, yet kept his tribal identity as well. Spradley's research project was intended 'to provide an autobiography of a non-Western individual who had successfully adapted to culture conflict.'

With these few publications, and more and more articles on native issues appearing in newspapers across the country, the 1960s can now be seen as the threshold of a new wave of assertive action and creative energy.

V

1970-1979

The 1970s heralded a phenomenal explosion of creative writing by Indians. Its enormous range—poetry, song, autobiography, short fiction, novels, drama, storytelling, retold traditional narratives, history, essays, and children's literature—makes this period a turning-point in the development of literature in English by Canada's first peoples. The support that was now being shown them made Canadian publishers eager to publish, and even to seek out, native authors.

During the late sixties and early seventies the influence of American civil-rights activists, and the spectacular activities of the American Indian Movement at Wounded Knee, South Dakota, in 1973, drew the attention of the mass media to the plight of native peoples. The *Statement of the Government of Canada on Indian Policy* (1969), the controversial 'White Paper' that recommended the abolition of special rights for native peoples, mobilized for the first time native leaders all across the country in a bitter confrontation with the federal government.

An immediate and angry reaction to the government proposals came from the Alberta Cree, Harold Cardinal (b. 1945), in *The Unjust Society: The Tragedy of Canada's Indians* (1971). He argued stridently for the retention of special rights within the strengthened contexts of treaties and the Indian Act. His book, which gained national prominence, has become a classic on the Indian situation in Canada. Arguing a minority point of view, William Wuttunnee—a Cree lawyer from Calgary, originally from Saskatchewan—opposed special status as a barrier to progress, and in his controversial *Ruffled Feathers: Indians in Canadian Society* (1971) advocated instead integration into the mainstream of Canadian society, individual development, and a radical change in the psyche itself. Another reaction to the 1969 White Paper was *Bulletin 201* (1970), edited and published by the Anglican Church of Canada, which included responses by such native writers as Dave Courchene, the Reverend Ernest Willie, Walter Currie, Harold Sappier, and the Reverend Adam Cuthand, who wrote the Preface. In *Prison of Grass: Canada from the Native Point of View* (1975), by the militant Métis patriot Howard Adams—who dedicated his book to the memory of his great-grandfather, Maxime Lepine, 'a guerrila warrior who sacrificed his life in the struggle against imperialism'—examined Canada's Métis policy from earliest contact to modern times. In prose that is passionate though clichéd, Adams, who grew up in a Métis community in Saskatchewan, goes so far as to advocate 'the sophisticated level of guerilla warfare' as a partial solution to Métis liberation. Adams' book has also become a classic in Canadian native history.

In Harold Cardinal's second book, *The Rebirth of Canada's Indians* (1977), his anger had subsided considerably. His style was still hard-hitting, but he made it abundantly clear that the solution was not in Adams' gun barrel but in the creation of 'a bridge of understanding' between natives and non-natives. He suggested a number of important changes both must make before aboriginal independence and self-determination could be achieved. These included changes in the structure, role, and goals of Indian organizations beset by internal conflicts and factionalism; a return to traditional religious values and philosophy based on the wisdom of the elders; and the need for a revised Indian Act and freedom from the bureaucracy of Indian Affairs officialdom. He also made concrete suggestions concerning three vital aspects of native life in Canada: culture, education, and economic development.

Although the decade began with books of protest and defence written from partisan motives, works of history with varying degrees of popular appeal also began to be appear. In *The Feathered U.E.L.'s* (1973) Enos T. Montour (Delaware), a retired United Church minister who was once a saddle-back preacher on a circuit in Saskatchewan, preserves tribal memory and recreates some memorable occasions in the lives of the first Indian Loyalists and their descendants. His book traces the life of Hiram and Lottie Logan, a pioneer couple on the Six Nations Indian Reserve, and covers the time of the Seven Years' War, the Fenian raids of 1866, and the two world wars. Montour combines fully dramatized scenes with dialogue and folksy, entertaining anecdotes to record his lively history.

In his slim volume *A Social History of the Manitoba Métis* (1974), Émile Pelletier records the social history of the descendants of white and

Indian intermarriage, the Métis of the Red River Valley. With primary materials, maps, and statistical tables Pelletier sets out to prove, in an affirmative and optimistic text, that the demand for aboriginal rights of the Métis has a strong legal and moral basis. In *The Métis, Canada's Forgotten People* (1975) D. Bruce Sealey (Métis) and Antoine S. Lussier (Métis) trace the history of the Métis from their beginnings to the present. They describe how this once-proud and free people with a unique identity gradually became disinherited and disillusioned, rejected by whites and Indians alike, living in material poverty and without hope. The authors tell the sad story in a temperate and controlled tone.

Two histories with the voices of prophecy and vision were published in 1974 and 1977 respectively. In *The Fourth World: An Indian Reality* (1974) by George Manuel (1921-89) and Michael Posluns, Manuel traces the Canadian Indians' struggle for recognition, drawing upon his own background as a Shuswap from British Columbia, and offers his vision of a fourth world where the values of special-status people are integrated with those of all peoples. Self-educated, Manuel was an influential political leader who helped unite Indian people across Canada into a strong political force. He helped found the Native Brotherhood of British Columbia and the Union of B.C. Indian Chiefs. In 1976 he became the founding president of the World Council of Indigenous Peoples. *These Mountains Are Our Sacred Places: The Story of the Stoney Indians* (1977) by Chief John Snow (b. 1933) records the past and present history of his people, as well as his own work in tribal government and in the pan-Indian movement. It is the familiar story of a group of Indians trying to survive with freedom and dignity after the arrival of the Europeans, an unhappy story of enduring administrative abuse and neglect, misunderstandings, and broken treaties. Chief Snow, however, is optimistic about a future based upon a renewed philosophy of self-determination and spiritual revival. His quiet and moving prose often achieves a lyrical beauty and a biblical resonance.

The seventies witnessed a burst of autobiographical works. As more often than not they were written in the as-told-to-tradition, with the help of a collaborator or editor, it is difficult to know for certain just how much manipulation of style and content occurred, unless the degree of help is specifically stated. With or without collaboration, however, the narrators invariably conform to the native autobiographical tradition that blends personal, tribal, and mythological history, and moves back and forth among them. The life stories of natives are never told sequentially but in a loose style incorporating history, oral tale, myth, and practical advice. The episodic life is their reality because their lives are governed by special events. Hence an autobiographical narrative tends to be a long story composed of a number of events told in a discursive oral-storytelling style.

Buffalo Days and Nights (1976) by Peter Erasmus (1833-1931), as told to Henry Thompson in 1920, is strong as both history and autobiography. Erasmus was born in the Red River Settlement, the fifth child of a mixed-blood mother and a Dane who fought in the Battle of Waterloo and came to Rupert's Land in the service of the Hudson's Bay Company, which he left to become a river-lot farmer. During a long life as translator, guide and interpreter, mission worker and teacher, explorer and mapper's assistant (he was the last surviving member of the Palliser Expedition), miner, trader, government employee, and celebrated buffalo hunter, Erasmus became a legend in his own time. His life spanned the period when Rupert's Land became provinces of Western Canada and the open buffalo plains were transformed into townsites and farmsteads. In 1920, when he was 87, Erasmus related the first half of his eventful life to Henry Thompson, who carefully recorded it in shorthand. The book that resulted, *Buffalo Days and Nights*, is a remarkable first-person account of a critical period in Canadian history when the free roving life of the western plains disappeared forever.

The posthumous memoir *Trapping Is My Life* (1970) by John Tetso (1927-64), a Slavey Indian who lived near Fort Simpson, where the Laird River meets the Mackenzie, first appeared as monthly articles in the early 1960s in the *Catholic Voice*, the publication of the Oblate Missionaries. Written in an unpretentious style, it is packed with woodland lore and evokes Tetso's passion for the outdoors and the hunt.

An Indian Remembers: My Life as a Trapper in Northern Manitoba (1971) by Tom Boulanger (Cree), who was born at Oxford House, Manitoba in 1901, tells of almost seventy years spent in the North—trapping, fishing, trading, and freighting. His stories—such as the Christmas dinner with moose steaks and moose nose, considered a delicacy, and his wife's delivery of their son in a lonely tent in the middle of winter—are fascinating. His idiosyncratic English, as if he were telling the story orally, appears intact and does not detract from the pleasure of reading his text.

Forbidden Voice: Reflections of a Mohawk Indian (1971) is by Alma Greene, whose Mohawk name is 'Forbidden Voice'. A clan mother of the Turtle clan of the Mohawks, she recalls some of the tales that are told on the Six Nations Reserve on the Grand River, combining personal, family, and tribal history with Mohawk myths in an attempt to define both herself and her people.

In *Chiefly Indian* (1972) Henry Pennier, who was born in 1904 near the Chehalis Reserve on the Harrison River in British Columbia and worked as a logger for forty years, divides his autobiography into sections entitled 'I remember my kid days', 'I remember my 1920s days', 'I remember my 1930s days', and 'I remember the now days'. The editor, Hubert L. McDonald, says that he retained as much as possible the unique flavour and idiom found in the original manuscript. *Recollections of an Assiniboine Chief* (1972) by Dan Kennedy, edited by James R. Stevens, is a collection of Kennedy's writings during the twenties, thirties, and forties, some of which were published as magazine and newspaper stories. Kennedy (1874-1973) was an Assiniboine from Carry-the-Kettle Reserve in Alberta. The name Ochankugahe ('Path Maker') was bestowed on him by his grandfather to commemorate and perpetuate his own exploits. (As leader in his youth of a war party across the blizzard-swept plains in the dead of winter, the grandfather had made a path, thus earning his name.) In a style that is both engaging and insightful, Kennedy writes unprententiously—with wisdom, subtle humour, warmth—as he tells of the Cypress Hills Massacre of 1872-3, of Sitting Bull and the Messianic Religion, Almighty Voice, Chief Piapot, why Indians camp in a circle, the arrival of the railroads and the French and German immigrants, and the Sun Dance, a ritual that was eventually forbidden by the Canadian government; he also includes important autobiographical material dealing with his childhood and his schooling. His book is a rich resource.

Devil in Deerskins: My Life with Grey Owl by Anahereo (Mohawk) was also published in 1972. Anahereo was born at Mattawa, Ontario, in 1906. In 1926 she married Grey Owl—the Englishman Archie Belaney, who had been adopted by the Ojibway and given the name Grey Owl—before he wrote the first of his many popular books, Anahereo lived with him in the wilderness, trapping and hunting. But she disliked the brutality of trapping and influenced Belaney to abandon it: they established a beaver sanctuary in northern Quebec and then in Prince Albert National Park, Saskatchewan. Her adventures, combined with her revealing portrait of Grey Owl, make for a highly readable book.

Geniesh: An Indian Girlhood (1973) by Jane Willis, who was born in 1940 on an island where the Fort George River meets the eastern shore of James Bay, recalls her life as a child growing up in the care of her loving Cree grandparents. Then, with increasing bitterness and anger, she tells of her ten-and-a-half years in Anglican boarding schools for Indians, when she spent less than a year and a half with her family and was forbidden to speak her language. Disillusioned with life and people and ashamed of her heritage, she finally determines to take pride in her Indian heritage.

For twelve years I was brainwashed into believing that 'Indian' was syn-
onymous with 'sub-human', 'savage', 'idiot', and 'worthless'. It took almost that long for me to regain my self-respect, to feel whole once again.
Now I can, once again, say with pride, 'I am an Indian'.

Willis's account of her early life and education does not rise above autobiographical protest because she has not moved beyond bitterness
and the desire to condemn. Nevertheless her gift for remembering
and recording and her sharp eye for detail are noteworthy.

The Days of Augusta (1973) by Augusta Evans (Shuswap) was edited
by Jean Speare. Evans, who was born at Soda Creek in the Cariboo
region of British Columbia in 1888, tells her life story of hardships
and pleasure in poetry and short fiction. Her sensitive responses to
the experiences of a long life include poems about a hold-up, a
Christmas at the mission, her premature babies, her grandparents,
tobacco costing 35 cents a plug, and the death of a son, as well as stories about the smallpox epidemic of 1860, catching a sturgeon, and a
girl who was taken prisoner. The aged narrator's colloquial English,
which the editor has wisely not altered, merely adds to the intimacy
of a life history that is told bravely and touchingly.

First Among the Hurons (1973) by Max Gros-Louis (b. 1931) is an autobiography of a Quebec chief who played a vital role in the James
Bay project. It was written in collaboration with Marcel Bellier and
translated from the French by Sheila Fischman. The nature of the collaboration is not specified, but the book blends Gros-Louis's personal
and tribal histories with his Indian-rights activities in a cohesive and
forceful style.

For *No Foreign Land: The Biography of a North American Indian* (1974)
by Wilfred Pelletier (Ottawa), a white friend, Ted Poole, tape-recorded Pelletier's story during a fishing trip as he talked informally
about his life and his feelings. With the colloquial idiom of Pelletier's
language retained (the narrative is in the first person), Pelletier's personality and opinions emerge clearly as he tells of his youth, his experiences with racial prejudice, his assimilation as a businessman, his
work as a hunter's guide, and of his ultimate decision to reject, in
large measure, the 'Western European's way of life' and to return to
the ways of his childhood.

In 1975 the (American) Liberation Support Movement Center be-
gan its Life Histories from the Revolution Series with *Bobbi Lee: Indian
Rebel—Struggles of a Native Canadian Woman*, recorded and edited by
Don Barnett and Rick Sterling. It is a first-person account of the first
twenty terrible years in the life of Lee Maracle, a British Columbia
Métis. Such chapter titles as 'Turbulent Childhood', 'Early Rebellion',
'With California Farmworkers', 'Problems at Home', 'Hippie Lifestyle

1967', 'Toronto: Anti-War Demonstrations and Racism', 'Red Power', 'Street Patrol', 'Harassed', and 'Confronting White Chauvinism' indicate the book's ugly and uncomfortable subject matter and the narrator's intense feelings of outrage and hostility. This protest autobiography bristles with shrill revolutionary rhetoric and the diction of industrial warfare that spare neither reader nor author embarrassment.

Forty Years a Chief (1977) by George Barker was translated from the Saulteaux by Boniface Guimond into spare, standard English. Barker, who was born in 1896 on the Bloodvein Reserve, on the east shore of Lake Winnipeg, was raised by his grandmother and received little formal education. The panoramic treatment of his life—as hunter, trapper, and fire-ranger, as chief of the Hollow Water Indian Reserve, and as President of the Manitoba Indian Brotherhood—includes explanations of the medicine dance and advice on trapping fur-bearing animals and about the wild-rice business.

My Tribe the Crees (1979) by Joseph F. Dion (1880-1960), edited by Hugh A. Dempsey, is partly a history of the Crees and the Métis. Dion, a nephew of Big Bear, was born on the Keehewin Reserve. Farmer, writer, and prominent political leader among the Crees and the Métis, he taught school on the reserve for a number of years. He provides much detail about his childhood, his Roman Catholic education at Onion Lake and young manhood, small-pox epidemics, starvation after the buffalo disappeared, forest fires, problems with the Department of Indian Affairs, and the formation of Indian and Métis organizations. Interestingly, Dion saw the early reserve days around the turn of the century much more favourably than in the 1920s and 1930s. He also includes his mother's account of the Northwest Rebellion of 1885, which provides some new insights.

My People the Bloods (1979) by Mike Mountain Horse, also edited by Hugh A. Dempsey, is drawn from a book-length manuscript that Mountain Horse completed about 1936. Mountain Horse (1888-1964) was born and raised in his Blackfoot tribe and attended an Anglican boarding school. He joined the Canadian Army during the First World War and served overseas in France. On his return to Canada he worked at various Royal Canadian Mounted Police detachments in the Lethbridge area. He began his writing career in the 1920s and wrote for local newspapers. Dempsey says that changes in the text were minimal, though he did omit negative descriptions of such traditions as the Sun Dance ('this barbarous ritual', 'this revolting custom')[1] reflecting the racist attitudes of mainstream Canadian society in the 1930s, which Mountain Horse had felt he needed to use in order to get his manuscript published.

The decade's most acclaimed native autobiography was *Halfbreed*

(1973) by Maria Campbell. Campbell (b. 1940) recalls her childhood spent in a strong, vibrant, and close-knit Métis community that was forced to live a marginal existence in shanties on Crown land along the roads north of Prince Albert, Saskatchewan. Despite her extreme poverty and the terrible racism of white people in the area, Campbell recalls some happy times in family and community events. At the spiritual centre of her life was her wise Cree great-grandmother, her beloved Cheechum. Even though 'dad was always drunk, mom always pregnant', after visiting her Indian relatives she was 'always glad to get back to the noise and disorder of [her] own people.' Circumstances changed when her mother died, Cheechum had to leave the family, and Maria was left to take care of six younger children. At the age of fifteen she married a white man to keep the welfare people from taking the children, but her husband soon reported them to the welfare agencies and they were placed in foster homes. Her marriage eventually failed and Campbell, cut off from the support of Métis community life, tried to survive in an urban world of alcohol, drugs, and prostitution. Overcoming extraordinary odds, and with the help of a few good friends and the hovering spirit of her Cheechum as well as her own remarkable strength of will, Campbell was eventually able to find spiritual and economic freedom and her true identity as a Métis woman. At the age of thirty-three she was resilient enough to rise from her stereotypical self-destructive behaviour towards healing and taking responsibility for her own life. From saying: 'My parents and I never shared any aspirations for the future', she became able to say: 'If I was to know peace I would have to search within myself.' Campbell offers no definitive solution to the plight of her people, but she manages to be optimistic. She knows that tomorrow will come and it will be better. Cheechum's prophetic words, 'You'll find yourself, and you'll find brothers and sisters' were understood and fulfilled. Interestingly, in her struggle for rehabilitation her assertiveness was attacked by the Métis male community. (As a result of the American Indian movement of the 1960s, many young Indian and Métis men had acquired a sense of pride that was as much macho as native and subsequently became oppressive to native women.)

Campbell weaves into her personal history descriptions of Métis social customs, the traditional role assignments of men and women, and the differences between the Indians and the Métis:

They were completely different from us—quiet when we were noisy, dignified even at dances and get-togethers. Indians were very passive— they would get angry at things done to them but would never fight back, whereas Halfbreeds were quick-tempered—quick to fight, but quick to forgive and forget. . . .

We were always the poor relatives . . . They laughed and scorned us. They had land and security, we had nothing.

Campbell also discusses the linguistic characteristics of Mischif, the patois spoken by the Métis. She celebrates community life, capturing the fun-loving spirit of the Métis at weddings, week-end dances with fiddler music, and sports competitions. Her account rises above the level of mere autobiographical protest because she sees her life in the larger context of distinctive Métis culture.

Written during the height of native activism, *Halfbreed* reflects the political climate of the early 1970s. Campbell views her own life and struggles as a continuation of Métis resistance. It is ironic that she chose as her title the word that has been used by both whites and Indians in Canadian society as a label of scorn. Instead of rejecting the term of abuse, she wears it as a badge of merit and pride. In her introduction she states that her purpose was to explain 'what it is like to be a halfbreed woman in our country. I want to tell you about the joys and sorrows, the oppressing poverty, the frustrations and the dreams.' She does just that and more. Her searingly honest account of human misery, courage, and hope is told in a stark, unsparing prose, unfiltered and undiluted. Though the chronological flow of her memoir, broken by Cheechum's appearances in and out of narrative sequence, is difficult to follow, and the second half about her struggle for survival after her marriage failed lacks the rich detail and the strong narrative line of her childhood years, the strengths of *Halfbreed* outweigh the weaknesses. Rich with a sense of place and time, it is a disturbing testimony to the ugliness of racism that is part of Canada's social history.

In order to make Indian oral narratives acceptable and easy to read for non-natives, white compilers and editors have made considerable alterations: plots were fashioned from variations of a tale: tales were pruned, polished, and rearranged; native oral storytelling techniques such as repetition, the pauses and stops of the narrator's voice, and the vocables of a participating audience were often disregarded; syntax and grammar were also changed. Many white children who are now adults became familiar with such altered narratives, during the many years when the native voice was silent, through books like *Sketco the Raven* (1961) by Robert Ayre, *Once Upon a Totem* (1963) by Christie Harris, *Tales of Nanabozho* (1963) by Dorothy Reid, and *Glooscap and His Magic* (1963) by Kay Hill. Not only were such adaptations distortions, but readers were unaware of their cultural significance. Natives considered it unfortunate that such an intrinsic element of native culture as their oral literature was lifted and made use of in ways they never intended. Lenore Keeshig-Tobias explains:

Stories, you see, are not just entertainment. Stories are power. They reflect the deepest, the most intimate perceptions, relationships, and attitudes of a people. Stories show how a people, a culture, thinks.[2]

Fortunately in the 1970s a few books were published in which natives themselves recorded their oral traditions. Basil H. Johnston's first book, *Ojibway Heritage: The Ceremonies, Songs, Dances, Prayers and Legends of the Ojibway* (1979), records a number of ancient ceremonies and myths that have given the Ojibway their cosmology—the meaning and purpose of their being and directions for living—as well as their perception of the world. They are presented in an expository manner that is illuminating.

Medicine Boy and Other Cree Tales (1978) by Eleanor Brass, illustrated by Henry Nanooch, is a collection of legends and stories told to Mrs Brass as a child. Included are the Wesuketchuk (Whiskyjack) stories and tales about the coming of the first horses, and about the white buffalo. Eleanor May Brass, a descendant of two chiefs who signed the Qu'Appelle Treaty No. 4—Chief Gabriel Côté (Saulteaux) and Chief Okanese (Cree)—was born in 1905 on the Peepeekisis Indian Reserve near Balcarres, Saskatchewan, and grew up in the File Hills Colony of southern Saskatchewan. She attended an Indian boarding school for a time and then went to a public school at Abernethy. 'This was a terrible experience for me, as I encountered a lot of discrimination,' she writes in her autobiography (discussed on page 149). Later she went to a high school in Canora but did not graduate. She began working on her father's farm and later as a waitress at the Plaza Hotel in Balcarres. Her marriage in 1925 to Alex Brass took her to Regina, where she wrote articles for the *Regina Leader-Post* and did a series of school broadcasts over the CBC based on the legends she wrote. For a short period she worked for the Department of Agriculture as an information writer for television, radio, and the press. After she retired she moved to Peace River, where she was active in the local friendship centre. As a writer, puppeteer, and storyteller she ably communicated the Cree culture to her own people and, in this book, to all Canadians.

In 1971 some of the people of Ksan, Hazelton, British Columbia—a rugged and isolated territory that was probably among the last to be affected by Europeans—taped, transcribed, and translated the tribal stories. They wrote a single version from the variations, using details that were accepted by the majority of their elders, and published the collection as *We-gyet Wanders On: Legends of the Northwest* (1977), which was published by Hancock House in Saanichton, B.C.

Most other story collections in this period were also collaborative efforts, as told by tribal elders to white anthropologists or editors. The stories in *Sacred Legends of the Sandy Lake Cree* (1971) were related to James R. Stevens by the elders of the Sandy Lake Reserve, a remote community in northern Ontario. Most of these 68 tales are very short and tell of queen mosquitoes, giant seagulls, thunderbirds, the Windigo, and Wee-Sa-Kay-Jac (Whiskyjack), the Cree trickster/transformer/culture hero.

Wild Drums: Tales and Legends of the Plains Indians (1972), by Alex Grisdale as told to Nan Shipley, includes a short autobiography of Grisdale, who was born in 1895 on the Brokenhead Reserve in Manitoba. Most of the tales tell of life before the white man among the Assiniboine, Cree, Sioux, Saulteaux, and Blackfoot.

Voices of the Plains Cree (1973) by Edward Ahenakew (1885-1961), edited by Ruth Buck, is a collection of stories about the Plains Cree—some traditional, some relating to their history. In Part One we hear the voice of Chief Thunderchild (1849-1927), the last of the chiefs who signed Treaty No. 6 in 1869, who recalls battles with the Blackfoot, fights with the Sarcees, tales about horse stealing, buffalo chases, encounters with bears, and the great Sun Dance. These stories are very well told, combining adventure and excitement with a component of pride in ancient traditions and a moving, even lyrical response to natural beauty. In Part Two, Ahenakew uses his fictional character 'Old Keyam', a Cree word meaning 'What does it matter?' or 'Who cares?', as a mouthpiece for his own commentaries on white injustices and the Indians' own lethargy. The Reverend Edward Ahenakew was born on the Sandy Lake reserve near Prince Albert, Saskatchewan. Graduating in theology from Emmanuel College, Saskatoon, in 1910, he was ordained an Anglican priest in 1912 and sent to a mission station at Onion Lake. When the influenza epidemic swept his reserve in 1918-19, the suffering of his people induced him to study medicine. However, a serious illness curtailed that ambition and he was sent to Chief Thunderchild's reserve to recover his health in 1923.

Visitors Who Never Left: The Origins of the People of Damelahamid (1974), by Chief Kenneth B. Harris in collaboration with Francis M.P. Robinson, is a collection of eight traditional narratives dealing with the origin and history of the Gitskan Tsimshian Indians of northern British Columbia. Harris translated them into English from his mother's modern translation of the ancient Gitskan, in which they were recorded in 1948 by Harris's uncle. According to Robinson, 'they have not been tampered with in any way and are given exactly as translated by Harris.'

Over a quarter century ago the Chilliwack Indians of the Upper Fraser Valley in British Columbia told stories of their tribe to anthropologist Norman Lerman. For *Legends of the River People* (1976) Betty Keller set thirty of the stories in the context of a feast to celebrate the building of a great cedar-plank house in the traditional style.

Shuswap Stories (1979), from the Kamloops and Chase dialect areas of south-central British Columbia, is a collection of thirty-six stories originally taped in the Shuswap language during 1971-5 and then translated into English by Charley Draney and Aimee August. Edited by Randy Bouchard and Dorothy Kennedy, the book includes many stories about Coyote, the trickster/transformer culture-hero of the Shuswaps, and such other stories as 'How Fish Came Down from the Upper World', which explains why the rainbow trout has red on both sides of its body, and 'The Boy and the Frog' and 'The Boy and the Monsters', which belong to the post-contact period when there began to be a strong influence of European folktales on traditional Shuswap tales.

Basil H. Johnston is one of the leading native short-story writers. He was born in 1929 on the Parry Island Indian Reserve, Ontario, and is a member of the Ojibway tribe of the Cape Croker Indian Reserve in Ontario. He was educated in reserve schools, at Loyola College in Montreal, and trained as a teacher at the Ontario College of Education in Toronto. From 1962 to 1969 he taught history at Earl Haig Secondary School in North York and in 1969, encouraged by the late Dr E.S. Rogers, he joined the Royal Ontario Museum to initiate a program of Indian history studies. He currently works in the Department of Ethnology at the Museum and specializes in Ojibway language, history, and mythology. He lives in Toronto but maintains a house on the reserve.

Johnston is a prodigious writer and his numerous short stories, essays, articles, and poems have appeared in native newspapers and *The Educational Courier, Canadian Fiction Magazine,* and *Whetstone.* In 1978 he published *Moose Meat and Wild Rice,* a collection of twenty-two stories arranged in four thematic parts: 'The Resourcefulness of the Moose Meat Point Ojibway', 'Christianity, Religion, and Worship at the Moose Meat Point', 'Getting Along and Ahead Outside the Reserve', 'With Housing, Education, and Business . . . Poof!' The stories deal with life on and off the fictional Moose Meat Point Indian Reserve near 'Blunder Bay'. A recurring theme is the clash between white government bureaucrats, clergymen, and missionaries, all of whom are excessively overbearing, and the Moose Meaters, who are impulsive, imaginative, proud, and patient. Johnston punctures the pretensions of Indians and whites alike. The narrator of 'The Kiss and the Moonshine', who has studied the techniques of the screen's great lovers, has finally decided to apply 'West European kissing' methods upon his girlfriend. On the night she drives him to his uncle's house on the reserve, he is determined to make his move—'manly, direct, forceful and swift'—but he accidentally leans on the car horn. He tears himself loose from the girlfriend, 'knocking off her hat and getting a button from [his] coat sleeve entangled in her hair. She screamed. The car horn promptly stopped.' The narrator's uncle mistakes the horn for a police raid and runs out of his house in his underwear and rubber boots to get rid of two pails of moonshine. And so there was no kiss and no moonshine.

Many of the protagonists of these stories are stereotypes—the welfare bum, the comic drunk, the shiftless and irresponsible—but Johnston exposes the absurdities of his characters with such good-humoured teasing caricature that the reader forgets about their stereotypical behaviour and enjoys them as human beings. Johnston has a gift for comic outrageousness, focusing on ridiculous incidents that satirize the inconsistencies of acculturation:

When and where the white people could drink and be merry, the Moose Meaters could not; when and where the white people could play cards and gamble, the Moose Meaters could not without committing sin; when and where white people could dance, the Moose Meaters could not without pain of sin. How difficult it was to try to be white. How hard to become acculturated. . . .

But no matter the gravity of their offences in moral or legal terms, the Moose Meaters, having been induced to advantages and promises of acculturation, practised those delights that were considered illegal and venial; surreptitiously, circumspectly, and stealthily perhaps, but practise and enjoy them they did. Damn the consequences.[3]

Johnston also focuses on humorous confrontations between Moose Meaters and whites, and on the misunderstandings that arise, in scenes of raucous and rascally comedy. Like their archetypal trickster figure, the Moose Meaters may be tricked, beaten up, wounded, and ridiculed, but they are resourceful and tenacious enough to outwit and outmanoeuvre the other guy. They are truly 'westernized in outward appearance but in soul and spirit very much still Ojibway.'[4] Johnston has a sure sense of the way they think and talk. His ability to focus on the comic situation, and his unnerring ear for the quirky syntax and pronunciation of natives on reserves speaking English, give the stories an authentic and distinctive Indian voice without betraying the essential dignity of his characters. In 'A Sign of the Times' the Moose Eaters outmanoeuvre one of the white bureaucrats who has come to their reserve:

After a few more guests described themselves, an elderly matron, hair streaked with blonde, got up at the official table. 'My name is Olga Shaposhnikoff employed by the Ontario Department of Health. The Department will assist in family planning and provide diet and nutrition courses.' She slithered back into her seat and smiled. Her message was translated into Cree and Ojibway. The linguists scribbled some more.

Big Flossie got up again. 'I wanna ast dat woman some questions,' she said tugging at her tam.

'By all means,' the chairman acknowledged, 'that's what she's here for.'

'Mrs, whatever you name is,' she did not quite finish . . .

'It's Miss Olga Shaponshnikoff,' the lady from the Health Department broke in somewhat coldly.

'How many kids you got?' Big Flossie demanded.

'Why? What has that got to do with the services our Department can offer and render?' Miss Shaposhnikoff stammered.

'Look Miss whatever you name is,' Big Flossie shot in, placing her hands on her hips and scowling at the same time. 'Don't git smard wid me; maybe old me, but I kin skin you anyday. Jis remember dat. Always de same. White peoples come 'ere tells us poor Indians what to do, ast us questions. An' when us Indians ast questions, youse neber answer. Dis time youse gonna answer. De chairman up dere said youse peoples gonna answer.

'Maybe Miss whatever you name is, you kin get away wid dat wid de mens aroun' here. Dey is scared; just sit dere an listen an' say nudding. Well, dey kin jis sits dere like sheeps. Not me. I'm not scaret of dem, me. I'm not scaret of you neider. So Miss whatever you name is jis' remember dat dis is my reserve an' if you don' answer my questions, I fin' you outside apter, and I'll shake some answers from you. Now. How many kids you got?'

'None,' Miss Shaposhnikoff spluttered.

'Dats bedder! You married, you?' Big Flossie examined.

'No,' Miss Shaposhnikoff answered in a quivering voice.

'You take dem pills, you?' Flossie interrogated.

'No,' Miss Shaposhnikoff replied, quaking.

'Den, how come youse gonna teach us dis family planning. Youse aint married; youse ain't got kids, youse don' take pills; youse don' hab a house. How you gonna teach us dem tings? Eh? Eh? Eh?'

'I read and do research,' Miss Shaposhnikoff returned.

'Well, me, I don' hab no education. I raisit ten kids. I keep house, I keep clean. I feed my husband. I happy me. You happier, you, wid no kids? Is womens who hab no kids happier? Only time us take pills and medicine is w'en wese sick. Is dat de bes' your Department can do? If dat's de bes', den we don' need you dammed help.' Big Flossie sat down. The interpreters went to work. Miss Shaposhnikoff blanched and paled.[5]

Johnston's characters enjoy outwitting each other as well as the whites with whom they come in contact. Their lively affirmation of life attests to an indestructibility born from a strong sense of identity that grows out of a particular place and culture. Johnston's stories—which are told as fiction but are based in fact and give life to a world of comedy most of his readers would never have seen or heard—are dedicated 'especially to the white man, without whose customs and evangelistic spirit the events recounted would not have occurred.'[6] Whether in short stories or in poems, retold myths and legends, historical and critical essays, or works on the Ojibway language, Johnston articulates the feelings of a Canadian native author, motivated by a sense of mission, who wishes to share his Ojibway heritage with those whose culture and heritage may be very different, but who wish to enlarge their understanding.

More and more native writers are producing literature designed specially for children. Children's stories *per se* did not exist in traditional times, but they have become a favourite medium of expression for contemporary native writers. This popularity is probably due to requests of publishers who have long been issuing collections of Indian stories, or single stories in picture-storybook format, by whites.

In 1970 Patronella Johnson published *Tales of Nokomis*, illustrated by Francis Kagige, a collection of fifteen Ojibway tales told in the context of native children visiting Nokomis, their grandmother. Mrs Johnson, who was born on the Cape Croker Reserve in Ontario, recalls several ancient legends associated with the Ojibway culture hero, here called Nanabush, whose grandmother was Nokomis.

Maria Campbell has written three books for children: *People of the Buffalo* (1976), *Little Badger and the Fire Spirit* (1977), and *Riel's People* (1978). *People of the Buffalo* and *Riel's People* are in a series about the lifestyles of North America's native peoples, published by Douglas and McIntyre in Vancouver.

In *People of the Buffalo* Campbell tells how the Plains Indians lived. She describes their food, storage, utensils, clothing, transportation, warfare, beliefs, and ceremonies. She also explains that they were 'deeply spiritual' and teaches that in order to know who you are and where you came from, you must return to a spiritual way of life. The book is illustrated by Douglas Tait and Shannon Twofeathers. In *Riel's People*, illustrated by David Maclagan, Campbell drew on her own background to tell how the Métis lived. She includes accounts of the rebellions of the late nineteenth century and the life stories of Louis Riel and Gabriel Dumont. The book is suffused with a pride that comes from belonging to Ka-tip-aim-soot-chic, 'the people who own themselves'. *Little Badger and the Fire Spirit*, also illustrated by David Maclagan, recreates for children the traditional Indian myth of how humans were given fire. The story, which is symbolic on several levels, is put in the context of eight-year-old Ahsinee's leaving the town of Lac La Biche to visit with her grandparents, who still live very much in the traditional way, and hearing the story from them. This structure enables Campbell to make the past a living oral tradition. Little Badger is a blind Indian boy who brings fire to his people. For his quest he seeks the aid of Grey Coyote to guide him on his dangerous journey. He is befriended by Mountain Goat, Mountain Lion, Grizzly Bear, and the Rattlesnake, the four strange creatures who stand guard over the fire spirit that dwells inside the mountain cave. By using animals who befriend Little Badger, Campbell stresses the idea of the harmonious affinity between nature and man. Little Badger's blindness is also symbolic. According to Campbell, 'He is like I was for so many years; I didn't see when it was so obvious. I had all kinds of helpers . . . but I couldn't see. And then one day I woke up; I could see.'[7] And by including Cree words in the myth, Campbell hopes to arouse the curiosity and excitement of young native readers in their native language.

A number of biographies were also published in the 1970s. *Red on White: The Biography of Duke Redbird* (1971) by Marty Dunn is about Gary James Richardson (Duke Redbird)—painter, poet, actor, political activist, and filmmaker—who was born in 1939 in Southampton, Ontario, the sixth and last child of Jack and Kathleen Richardson. When he was nine months old, his mother died while saving her children from a fire that destroyed their home. Duke was then put in a white middle-class foster-home in St Catharines, where he remained until he was eleven with the Jukes family. (His nickname at school, Duke, developed from that name; later he legally took the name Duke Redbird, the surname combining the native symbol for 'messenger' (bird) with his pride in being a 'Redman'.) When his foster-father died he moved from foster-home to foster-home, often running away, always trying to find his birth-father and family. He spent a difficult youth on the move in Ontario and the United States, chasing jobs. For several years he was in the forefront of Indian political organizations and was sought-after as a speaker on radio and television. But he soon lost faith in political organizations and turned to his old love, the mass media, as actor, script-writer, and film producer. (As a freelance filmmaker Redbird directed a number of documentaries on native issues, including *I Am the Redman* and *The Ballad of Norval Morriseau*.) He also gave poetry readings and lectures on drama at Glendon College, York University, Toronto. In *Red on White* Marty Dunn describes Redbird's early life of foster-homes, street gangs, and odd jobs, and follows his later chequered career in various types of work, from operating a discothèque in Toronto to writing the theme poem for the Indian pavilion at Expo, to taking the Thunderbird Dancers to the Mexican Olympics and writing and acting in various radio, television, and film productions. We hear Redbird's prophetic voice insisting that the Indian must teach the white man new ways. 'To be Indian is to be unique, is to be a person who is related to the world and to himself in a special way, a unique way that is indigenous to this continent and is quite different from what the western European feels his relationship to the world to be . . . Indians are motivated at a creative, passive, spiritual level—as opposed to the academic intellectual approach of most Western Europeans.'[8] Redbird is now retired as a political activitist and operates a wilderness retreat in Ontario, where he paints 'spirit loon' decoys in the style of Norval Morrisseau and sells them in his antique shop.

Great Leader of the Ojibway: Mis-quona-queb (1972), edited by James R. Stevens, is by James Redsky (b. 1899), the last of the Midewewin holy men on the Shoal Lake Reserve, who traces the history of the last great war leader of the Ojibway in the eighteenth century. More documentary than literary, the book includes a section devoted to the Midewewin society and another containing explanations of Ojibway customs, such as the Shaking Tent. In the introduction Redsky tells about his childhood, schooling, employment, and experiences in the First World War.

Chief Peguis and His Descendants (1973) is by Chief Albert Edward Thompson, a direct descendant of the celebrated Chief Peguis of Red River who led a band of two hundred Ojibway from their homelands around Sault Ste Marie to Red River in the late 1790s and were known thereafter as the Saulteaux. Pioneer families at Red River called Chief Peguis 'The Friend of the Colonists', and his story was given to the author by his grandfather, the Reverend Chief W.H. Prince, but the original was lost while Chief Thompson was overseas during the First World War. As a result, Thompson spent more than five years recreating the chief's story.

Fifty Dollar Bride: Marie Rose Smith—A Chronicle of Métis Life in the 19th Century (1977) is by Jock Carpenter, granddaughter of the prairie pioneer Marie Rose Smith (1861-1960), whose reminiscences in numerous diaries and writings form the backbone of the book. Smith was born at Fort Garry into a family who lived the traditional Métis life—following the buffalo, hunting, trading, and making pemmican. At the age of sixteen she married a much older man against her wishes. She bore him seventeen children during a marriage that entailed prairie wanderings between the Red River Settlement and Pincher Creek, Alberta, where the family finally settled. Carpenter's narrative provides fascinating and authentic insights into pioneer prairie life. Unfortunately it stops in late 1917 and Marie Rose lived another forty-three years.

A few publications on a miscellany of subjects and in various literary forms also appeared in the 1970s. *Defeathering the Indian* (1975) by Emma La Roque, a Cree-Métis from Alberta, is an indictment of Indian education in Canada. Two collections of essays were published by the Neewin Publishing Company Ltd of the Nishnawbe Institute in Toronto, an Indian educational, cultural, and research centre: *For Every North American Indian Who Begins to Disappear, I Also Begin to Disappear* (1971) and *Who Is Chairman of This Meeting?* (1972). Both contain essays by Wilfred Pelletier, an Odawa born in 1927 on Manitoulin Island. In the former, Pelletier discusses the methods Indians must use to survive in an 'alien' society. He also gives an Indian viewpoint on the white educational system and its drastic impact on the Indian children who attend it. His two essays in *Who Is the Chairman of This Meeting?*, 'Dumb Indian' and 'Time', both stress important differences between white and Indian attitudes. Pelletier has done much to try to show the causes underlying the conflict between two cultures.

The Only Good Indian: Essays by Canadian Indians (1970), edited by Waubageshig (Harvey McCue), is an anthology containing essays dealing with aboriginal rights, 'red power', Indian education and identity, a few protest poems by Duke Redbird, a short play by Nona Benedict, as well as the well-known essay by Chief Dan George, 'My Very Good Dear Friends . . .', and an extract taken from *Citizens Plus*, often called 'The Red Paper', prepared in 1970 by the Indian chiefs of Alberta in response to the federal government's White Paper.

Indians Without Tipis: A Resource Book by Indians and Métis (1973), edited by Bruce D. Sealey (Métis) and Verna Kirkness (Cree), was funded by Project Canada West, a western consortium for curriculum development in the area of Canadian studies, and was designed to provide information and curricula materials to assist teachers and pupils in developing a knowledge and appreciation of people of native ancestry. It contains a number of articles by native writers and leaders such as Bruce Sealey, Verna J. Kirkness, Dave Courchene, Ahab Spence, Joe Keeper, Antoine Lussier, George Munroe, and Jim Wemigwams on 'Indian Culture', 'Education of Indian and Métis',

'The Dilemma of Language', 'The Settlement of the Americas', and 'Indian Contributions to the World', as well as a narrative poem by Elizabeth Cuthand entitled 'Billie', the sad story of a young native woman who left the reserve for the city 'to make dreams realities'. The editors admit in the Foreword that, '. . . intermingled with straightforward descriptive passages, there are others that reflect in strong, emotional words the frustrations of "a conquered and oppressed race".'[9]

In 1978 Duke Redbird completed his masters degree at York University on the history of the Métis in Canada, and his thesis was published as a small book entitled *We Are Métis: A Métis View of the Development of a Native Canadian People* (1980). It was his first book, although he had written many poems that appeared in anthologies, and articles for the new magazines that were being founded.

The following periodicals provided outlets for the growing number of native writers across Canada who were submitting their poems, short stories, letters to the editor, and articles to them: *Saskatchewan Indian* (1970-) published by the Federation of Saskatchewan Indians; *Tawow* (1970-80) published by the Department of Indian Affairs, Ottawa; *Micmac News* (1971-) published in Sydney, Nova Scotia; *Yukon Indian News* (1974-) published by the YE SA TO Communications Society, Whitehorse, Yukon; *Wawatay News* (1974-) published in Sioux Lookout, Ontario; *The Native Perspective* (1975-8) published by the National Association of Friendship Centres, Ottawa; and *Ontario Indian* (1978-) published by the Union of Ontario Indians.

Native poetry lagged behind prose in the 1970s. However, among the poets who managed to get published were Sarain Stump, Duke Redbird, George Kenny, Rita Joe, Ben Abel, Chief Dan George, and Daniel David Moses.

Sarain Stump (1945-74, Shoshone-Cree-Salish) combined poetry and drawings to convey his feelings and experiences in *There Is My People Sleeping* (1970). He laments the loss of the traditional way of life.

Duke Redbird's early poetry, drawing upon his mixed Ojibway and Irish heritage and his troubled adolescence and youth, is protest verse of strong rhetoric in which he reacts passionately against the misery and oppression of Canada's native people. In poems such as 'The Beaver', 'A Red Nation', and 'I Am the Redman' Redbird lashes out against an insensitive white society; they reflect the political turmoil of the period when he was a militant social activist. In 'I Am the Redman' Redbird's ironic tone and symbolism, derived from an urban and industrialized society, bristle with contempt and pride:

I AM THE REDMAN
I am the Redman
>Son of the forest, mountain and lake.
>What use have I of asphalt?
>What use have I of brick and concrete?
>What use have I of the automobile?
>Think you these gifts are devine
>That I should be humbly grateful?

I am the Redman,
>Son of the tree, hill and stream,
>What use have I of china and crystal?
>What use have I of diamonds and gold?
>What use have I of money?
>Think you these from heaven sent,
>That I should be eager to accept?

I am the Redman,
>Son of the earth and water and sky.
>What use have I of silk and velvet?
>What use have I of nylon and plastic?
>What use have I of your religion?
>Think you these holy and sacred
>That I should kneel in awe?

I am the Redman
>I look at you White Brother
>And I ask you:
>Save not me from sin and evil,
>Save yourself.[10]

In contrast to his angry protest poetry, Redbird's *I Am a Caanadian*—printed in a limited edition of 2,000 copies and presented in Ottawa to Queen Elizabeth on the occasion of her Silver Jubilee on 17 October 1977—is an exuberant sixty-line prose-poem celebrating the provinces and the people of Canada.

A younger Ojibway poet, George Kenny, was born in 1951 on the Lac Seul Indian Reserve near Sioux Lookout, Ontario, where he received his elementary- and secondary-school education. He graduated from Grade XIII at the Great Lakes Christian College, Beamsville, in 1971, received his Teacher's Certificate from Hamilton Teacher's College in 1974, and in 1984 received his B.A. from the University of Waterloo. He was Information Officer for the Ontario Federation of Indian Friendship Centres in Toronto (1976-9) and is currently Co-ordinator of the Skills Development Program in the

Indian Friendship Centre of Thunder Bay. His *Indians Don't Cry*
(1977) is a collection of eighteen short poems and eight short stories
about contemporary life on the Lac Seul Reserve and in the towns of
northern Ontario and Manitoba where natives go to live. Kenny
writes about what he knows: family, humiliation, loneliness, death,
confusion, disappointment, departed love, frustration, rejection, and
thwarted hopes. The harsh realities of life for Indian people are fil-
tered through the prism of an acutely sensitive social consciousness.
But rather than a cloying sentimentality, there is a stoic acceptance of
suffering; the poems are gentle, restrained, and the dominant mood
is one of heroic endurance and calm. Here is a loving tribute to his father:

LEGACY
John, an Indian who never went
to jail
was the memory left for us,
my sisters and I.
not a car for our use
not a house worth thousands
not bonds in our names
not a nickel did come our way
on a death-winning day.

John, an Indian who never took
welfare
was the legacy left for us,
my sisters and I.
not a boat for our pleasure
not lands worth tens of thousands
not trust funds in our accounts
not a dime did come that day
when death passed our way.

John, father, human being who
loved us
is the faith we cling to,
my sisters and I.

Love that died, having tried
its best to give us
shelter, food, clothing
so we could survive to know
the misery,
the misery and the ecstacy,

the ecstacy
of living, life.[11]

Rita Joe (Micmac) was born in Whycocomagh, Nova Scotia, in 1932. As a foster-child she moved from home to home and from one reserve to another. She is now a grandmother who loves to look after her grandchildren. She says that she writes always with children in mind, and for others to understand the rights of her people to education and dignity. *Poems of Rita Joe* (1978) contains 26 untitled poems, a few with Micmac translations. Rita Joe's reflections on her life and the changes experienced by a once-proud and self-sufficient people reveal thoughtful sensitivity. Although her poems convey a strong sense of self, Rita Joe also articulates the hapless plight of the Indians as she pleads for understanding:

> I am not
> what they portray me.
> I am civilized.
> I am trying
> To fit in this century.
>
> Pray
> meet me halfway—
> I am today's Indian.[12]

Chief Dan George (1899-1981), or 'Teswahno', was a Coast Salish descendant of six generations of Tse-Lall-watt chiefs, one of twelve children on the Burrard Indian Reserve. At the age of five he was sent to a Roman Catholic boarding school. At sixteen he left the school to work as a logger, and then later worked as a longshoreman until 1946, when he was injured in an accident. From 1951 to 1963 he served as chief of the Squamish Band of Burrard Inlet. From 1959 to his death Dan George distinguished himself as an actor, on radio and television, and in some eight Hollywood films, always portraying with great effectiveness wise and dignified natives. Soft-spoken, gentle, and philosophical in addressing audiences, he often spoke on behalf of native rights and environmental groups. 'A Lament for Confederation', which he delivered at Empire Stadium in Vancouver on Canada's centennial birthday, is of almost biblical nobility and beauty. In *My Heart Soars* (1974), a collection of prose-poems, Dan George pleads the cause of his people with warmth and nobility, trusting in the common humanity of natives and whites:

> Already signs of new life are arising
> among my people after our sad winter
> has passed. We have discarded our broken
> arrows and our empty quivers, for we know
> what served us in the past can never serve
> us again![13]

Another collection, *My Spirit Soars* (1982), was published posthumously.

The Highway Book Shop in Cobalt, Ontario, published several works written by Indians in the 1970s. In 1972 it published *Wisdom of Indian Poetry* and *Okanagan Indian*, poems and short stories by Ben Abel, who was born in Westbank, British Columbia, in 1938. He attended Kamloops Indian boarding school for five years and then entered the work force. His poetry, which has appeared in *The Malahat Review*, deals with animals and the beauty of nature, love, and politics, as well as with contemporary society. Abel tends to be didactic, but his messages are more often than not oblique, couched in gentle and lyrical language.

> INDIAN
> I am only a Shadow
> You cannot see me.
> You can only hear me.
> You hand me
> a bottle of wind,
> and
> I will disappear,
> I am not known . . .
> only in shadows.[14]

Highway Book Shop also published *Sweetgrass: A Modern Anthology of Indian Poetry* by three brothers of the Keon family—Orville, Wayne, and Ronald—as well as *Thunderbirds of the Ottawa* by Orville and Wayne. In 1977 the Book Shop was brave enough to publish *Native Sons*, a collection of poetry and one legend by eight inmates of the Guelph Correctional Centre. Subjects focus mainly on lost love, rejection, and environmental concerns. The voices of this prison literature are sad, but there is no anger, no bitterness. Many are elegiac in mood and inclined to be didactic.

Many Voices: An Anthology of Contemporary Canadian Poetry (1977)— edited by two non-Indians, David Day and Marilyn Bowering—

includes poets of native ancestry from across Canada: familiar names such as George Clutesi, Duke Redbird, Jeannette Armstrong (Bouveau), and Sarain Stamp, and less-familiar ones, such as Fred Favel, Leo Yerxa, the Keon brothers, Skyros Bruce, Edward John, Gordon Williams, and Susan Landell. The anthology offers poems about nature and animals, about contemporary Canadian society and traditional customs and ceremonies. There is free and conventional verse, concrete poetry, and spoken poems revealing an Indian world characterized by pride, rejection, loneliness, and the voice of prophecy and vision. There is anger but little bitterness. In the variety of tone, mood, attitude, and technique there is a certain unity of impression derived from the way Indians have been treated by white society in Canada.

Daniel David Moses is a singular new voice in poetry. His first collection, *Delicate Bodies* (1978), did not receive the critical attention it deserved, and yet Moses—poet, playwright, critic, and short-story writer—is one of the best of Canada's young native writers. He was born in 1952 on the Six Nation lands of the Grand River in southern Ontario. He attended elementary school on the reserve, graduated from Caledonia High School, received his Honours B.A. in Fine Arts from York University, and his Master's degree in Fine Arts from the University of British Columbia, where in 1977 he won the Creative Writing Department's prize for playwrighting. He returned to Toronto in 1979 and worked at a number of jobs, including security guard at the Art Gallery of Ontario and assistant immigration officer at Pearson Airport. He works with organizations that help to promote the literary and artistic efforts of native writers and to gain recognition for their works. He is also founding member of the Committee to Re-establish the Trickster. His poetry, short fiction, and plays have been published in a number of literary magazines: *The Antigonish Review, The Malahat Review, The Canadian Forum, Fiddlehead, Waves, Impulse.* He was anthologized in *The Last Blewointment Anthology, Volume II* (1986) edited by Bill Bissett, and in *Harper's Anthology of Twentieth-Century Native American Poetry* (1988).

Delicate Bodies is arranged in two sections: 'Songs and Conversations' and 'A Calendar'. In the first, joyful presentations of nature and rural life—a river on the reserve, chores in winter, frost, rain, geese migrating south—are rich in images, with visual and emotional impressions juxtaposed. Moses effectively fuses nature to human relationships, as in 'Digging among these trees with their sun / dry, mosses, it is the cured wood of old / love, my love for you I've uncovered' ('Late Song'). One of Moses' favourite subjects is his grandparents:

A VISIT IN MIDSUMMER
You now are little
more, Grand
father, than the blue wool
rumples of your blanket and the berry
blue veins threading
through the skin of your untanned
feet. You are not

fat enough. Your body's
receding, though your hands are still
the same size, and in your pillow
the same hollow is full
of your head with its dried
apple face and insistent
breath. In the dull after

noon of this upper
bedroom your glasses are clean
ponds your eyes rise
though, black as the eyes of
the God of All Frogs, so wise
they can take the whole
ceiling in. Your voice, an old

leaf, scratches the air. You can't live
for ever, it says. I pour you more
tea and through the window we
hear the maples and spruces are
sifting the gusts from the August
thick atmosphere. The sky is so much
rushing, and soon it will rain here.[15]

Moses writes about the places and people he knows, on and around the farm where he grew up and in the city where he works. He sees colour, texture, and movement with the eyes of a painter. His mood is romantic and nostalgic; his quiet, casual tone is made fresh by his spontaneous joy in ordinary things and in the processes of rural life and nature.

The seventies saw the birth of native drama—an art form at once ancient and modern because traditional Indian practices were basically dramatic, a fusion of music, dance, and ceremony. Three writers—Duke Redbird, Nona Benedict, and George Kenny—attempted this literary form.

Edward Ahenakew, 1956 (Saskatchewan Archives Board, R-B 7063)

Maria Campbell, c. 1973

Duke Redbird

Basil H. Johnston

Rita Joe
(Raytel Photography, Sydney, N.S.)

Jeannette C. Armstrong
(Redivo Photography Ltd, Penticton

Beatrice Culleton

Marie Annharte Baker

Ruby Slipperjack
(Bill Davis Photography, Thunder Bay)

Thomas King
(Francisco Photography)

Drew Taylor

Jordan Wheeler

Daniel David Moses (© 1989 Chris Buck, Toronto)

Tomson Highway

Wasawkachak, a play by Duke Redbird with music and lyrics by Shingoose, was produced in Montreal by the Pendulum Theatre Company in 1974. It illustrates the power of love. A demi-god chooses to sacrifice immortality to become mortal in order to marry the blind girl he loves. The Great Spirit is so moved by his sacrifice that he restores the girl's sight.

The Dress by Nona Benedict—a Mohawk who was born on the St Regis Reserve and graduated from General Vanier High School in Cornwall—was included in Waubageshig's anthology *The Only Good Indian*. It is a one-act play that explores the conflicts of native young people caught between tradition and mainstream culture. The characters include the Native, who has successfully assimilated into the white world of big business, the young worker and secretary who are trying to assimilate, and a young girl whose concern for native beliefs and values is symbolized by her creation of a traditional dress.

The theme explored in *The Dress* is also dramatized in George Kenny's play *October Stranger*, much of which is based on Kenny's poem 'I don't know this October stranger' and on the characters and situations that are found in Kenny's *Indians Don't Cry*. His characters are also caught between two cultures. The tension from this dilemma is dramatized when several young people must decide whether to leave or stay on the reserve. *October Stranger* was written in collaboration with the director Dennis Lacroix and was expressly created for performance at the Sixth International Amateur Theatre Association Festival in Monaco in September 1977 by members of Kematewan, an all-native theatre company from Toronto mobilized for the purpose.

Drama was in its infancy in the 1970s, but would make a great impact in the next decade.

VI

1980-1989

The 1980s were a decade of productive and impressive creative output that even surpassed the great upsurge of literary activity in the 1970s. A younger generation of university-trained writers with a singular sense of purpose and commitment began producing exciting and original works. An amazing vitality emerged as all across the country writers came to the fore and often gathered together: Tomson Highway, Lenore Keeshig-Tobias, Daniel David Moses, and Drew Taylor in Toronto; Lee Maracle, Vera Manuel, Margo Kane, and Verna Kirkness in Vancouver; Jeannette Armstrong in Vernon; Marie Annharte Baker and Sue Deranger in Regina; Maria Campbell and Beth Cuthand in Saskatoon; and Thomas King in Lethbridge—all of them generating enthusiasm and encouraging native writers, staging festivals to introduce new native plays and playwrights, forming aboriginal writing groups and conducting workshops to hone writing skills. The result is that native writers all across the country have been imbued with a feeling of optimism and dedication. Contributing greatly to this feeling are a number of small—some relatively new, some left-wing, some obscure—publishers that have made a strong commitment to publishing the work of native writers. These include Fifth House Publishers in Saskatoon; Pemmican Publications in Winnipeg; Talon Books and Press Gang Publishers in Vancouver; Theytus Publications in Penticton; Canadian Dimension, Briar Patch, and NeWest Press in Edmonton; and The Women's Press in Toronto. Books are also published by native groups such as the Saskatchewan Indian Cultural College and the Gabriel Dumont Institute of Native Studies and Applied Research.

Indian life in Canada is changing rapidly. More and more Indians are moving from the reserves to the cities and this change is reflected in the literature. Native writers continue to be concerned with their social, political, and economic history, attempting to distinguish once and for all right from wrong, truth from fiction—to set the record straight. But now the problems that cities engender, because of skin colour and self-fulfilling stereotypes, have become the new subject of their literature. Understanding themselves in this challenging social context is their task.

One of the younger generation of novelists is Beatrice Culleton (Métis), who was born in St Boniface in 1949, the youngest of four children of Louis and Mary Clara Mosonier. At the age of three she became a ward of the Children's Aid Society in Winnipeg and grew up in foster homes there. She spent several years in high schools and then studied clerical accounting at George Brown College, Toronto, where she is currently residing. In 1983 she published her first novel, *In Search of April Raintree*. (It was reissued in 1984 as *April Raintree*, with the graphic rape scene cut for high-school use.)

Set in Winnipeg, it is the story of two Métis sisters, April and Cheryl Raintree, whose parents are alcoholic: 'It seemed to me that after the welfare cheque days, came the medicine days. That was when my parents would take a lot of medicine and it always changed them.' The death of a baby sister prompts the Children's Aid Society to intervene and the two girls are placed in foster homes. They become separated from their parents and each other and are raised by different foster parents to develop in totally opposite directions. Cheryl is encouraged to study the history of her people, while April grows up to be ashamed of her Métis heritage. In a meeting with Cheryl, who looks Indian, April, who looks white (she resembles her half-Irish mother), explains to her younger sister:

I am ashamed. I can't accept . . . I can't accept being a Métis. That's the hardest thing I've ever said to you, Cheryl. And I'm glad you don't feel the same way I do. I'm so proud of what you're trying to do. But to me, being Métis means I'm one of the have-nots. And I want so much. I'm selfish. I know it, but that's the way I am. I want what white society can give me.

April finishes school with a degree that qualifies her for a decent job and soon marries a successful businessman from one of Toronto's wealthy old families. Cheryl, on the other hand, is unable to function in mainstream society. She is rebellious and even militant. She wants to be a social worker to help her people. But she becomes disillusioned and descends into a life of alcoholism, violence, and prostitution on a wilful path of self-destruction, the stereotyped native-girl syndrome.

April returns to Winnipeg when her marriage fails, and is assaulted and raped after being mistaken for Cheryl. This brutal experience haunts her and forces her to confront her true self and her Métis heritage. In the meantime Cheryl's nightmare life is so hopeless that she commits suicide by jumping off the same bridge her mother did, thus ironically fulfilling the predetermined stereotype. Cheryl's suicide forces April to come to terms with her identity. Wiser and stronger, she takes responsibility for Cheryl's young son and resolves to make a better life for themselves and her people.

In Search of April Raintree is composed of a series of vignettes in an episodic structure. Drawing on her own childhood and youth, Culleton portrays two life stories in a graphically and mercilessly vivid manner that is shocking in its details of abuse and its anger and at the same time moving. Culleton allows her protagonists none of the spiritual support that Cheechum provides for Maria Campbell in *Halfbreed*, nor do they have any contact with traditional Métis life. But while *April Raintree* is depressing, it is elevated from melodramatic cliché by its daring honesty and its energy. It does justice to its dispossessed second-class citizens and we are grateful for that.

Culleton followed this with *Spirit of the White Bison* (1985), a novel for children (see page 179).

Jeannette C. Armstrong's novel *Slash* (1985) was written to give the native perspective on the North American Indian protest movement of the sixties to the eighties for a contemporary Social Studies unit for grades eight to eleven. Armstrong was born on the Penticton Indian Reserve in 1948 and was educated first in the traditional ways by Okanagan elders. Her formal education includes a Diploma of Fine Arts from Okanagan College and a Bachelor of Fine Arts Degree from the University of Victoria. After graduation in 1978 she returned to Penticton and began working for the En'owkin Centre—a native cultural and education association run by the six bands of the Okanagan Nation, in conjunction with Okanagan College and the University of Victoria—as a consultant, researcher, and writer. In 1989 she became the director and prime mover in the establishment of Penticton's En'owkin International School of Writing, the first credit-giving creative-writing school in Canada to be operated for and by native people. She was actively involved in the Indian movement of the sixties and seventies and in *Slash* tried to eradicate misconceptions, and to recount the historical details accurately and clearly.

When the story opens Thomas Kelasket, also known as Slash, is an acutely sensitive boy in Grade VI from a happy stable family living a traditional life on a good reserve. His troubles begin when he is forced to attend a town school off the reserve. He studies hard and makes good marks, but he is confronted with culture shock. Trying to come to grips with racial prejudice, he begins to question and think. 'I don't know who is right anymore,' he confesses to a friend. Slash has become a troubled teenager. He is caught up in the political ideological world of the militant period of the American Indian movement in the 1960s and following, when 'a strong feeling of unity persisted among the people. Nobody questioned which Band or which Tribe a person belonged to; everybody was Indian.' It was an exciting time 'when people brought out the drums and sang the protest songs and the friendship songs'; when 'people grew their hair, and wore chokers and beads and blue jeans.' It was a time when the RCMP issued a report 'which said that Indian people were the biggest threat to national security since the F.L.Q. thing in Quebec.'

Slash indulges in all the passionate and tense restlessness of a period when oppressed and powerless people, moving together, changed themselves and their country profoundly and permanently. He travels back and forth between the United States and Canada, joining sit-ins, blockades, protest rallies, occupations, caravans, and demonstrations, participating in discussion after discussion, and always listening to a variety of points of view from the most assimilationist to the most radical. And always there was never any agreement, no tidy solution.

For Slash the two decades were an educational experience characterized by frustration, confusion, and pain. Like the archetypal hero in search of truth, Slash the political activist emerges from his experience stronger and wiser, choosing to return home to the community of his reserve, where he realizes that his old Chief had said the same things he had heard from the Elders and medicine people of the different tribes he visited across North America. 'I thought about how much farther ahead I would have been if I had listened to my own parents teach me those things while I was growing up. Instead it hadn't been good enough. I had to look for other solutions. I realized that there were people like me who had all that teaching right at home and had completely missed the point.' Like the archetypal hero, Slash had to suffer before he reached wisdom. With a better understanding of the whole Indian-rights movement, he is content to settle down in the hope that the next generation, as symbolized in his young son, would gain some advantages: 'You are an Indian of a special generation. Your world will be hard but you will grow up proud to be an Indian,' he tells his son.

Slash brings together details of the scattered events of an extraordinary period—which probably would have been lost unless documented in its own time. Armstrong tries to make sense of what happened and illuminates the protest movement's structures and dynamics. Even though she goes off in too many directions and gets mired in factual data, lengthy explanations, and bewildering digressions (her book is not an easy read), she has honoured the past and has given us a hero who makes choices and suffers the consequences in his own pilgrimage from innocence to experience.

Another first novel of this period is *Honour the Sun* (1987) by Ruby Slipperjack, who was born in 1952 on a trapline near White Water Lake north of Armstrong, Ontario. She received her elementary education in Collins, Ontario, and in Sault Ste Marie, where she attended Shingwauk, a residential school. She went to high school in Thunder Bay and graduated in 1989 from Lakehead University with her B.A. and B.Ed. degrees. She lives in Thunder Bay with her husband and three children.

Honour the Sun is set in an imaginary small isolated community along the CNR line in northern Ontario. The narrator and observer is a ten-year-old Ojibway girl called 'the Owl', who writes of the warm, carefree, often humorous episodes of her childhood. As she turns thirteen, however, her happiness ends when her mother, once her source of love and strength, succumbs to alcoholism. And for the next three years the young narrator records her confusion and loneliness as she watches her mother and her community disintegrate—as 'The whole community drank and the kids just stayed out of the way.' Despite the horrible change, the Owl—who is now sixteen and going to boarding school away from the community—is reassured of the promise of a better world by the words her mother taught her: 'Honour the Sun, child, just as it comes over the horizon, Honour the Sun, that it may bless you, come another day . . .'

The Owl is perceptive, sensitive, and articulate. Her first-person narrative captures gently and simply both the joys of her childhood and her struggles with her community's alcoholism and violence, which help to transform her from an innocent little girl to an anxious and determined teenager. 'The railway line and alcohol-related accidents take so many lives,' she reflects at the age of sixteen. Although she can assess the cause of the accidents, she cannot analyse the reasons for the excessive drinking that plagues her once-idyllic community.

The story rambles episodically, in the present tense, through a repeating seasonal cycle from the summer of 1962, when the Owl is ten, to the summer of 1968 when she returns to the community from an urban school. The narrative voice of the child does not preach or make any sociological comment; there is no self-pity—just the straightforward telling of the story. *Honour the Sun* is suffused with the way members of an isolated native community in the northern-Ontario wilderness think, talk, and act. It is rich with a sense of place. One suspects that only an autobiographical source could have given such life to the narrative.

In *Breathing Water* (1990) by Joan Crate the Métis narrator, a sexy cocktail waitress newly married to her former boss, a Greek hotel owner with 'lots of money', has just given birth to a son whom she has named Elijah after her father. With a mother-in-law who refused to accept her and a husband whom she suspects is cheating on her, Dione finds marriage boring and difficult:

> The house makes me nervous. . . . I don't know what to do here so I turn on the dishwasher, the washer and dryer, the Vacuflo, the garburator, stereo, radio, and t.v. I want noise, I want voices.
>
> The Baby Blues, Mother calls it. Postnatal Depression the doctor said . . . I don't feel depressed, only watered down and foggy. Everything is undefined, and I need clarity, meaning. I need a voice to tell me.

The first-person novel is about Dione's quest for that voice. With her infant nearly always in tow, she lives dangerously, frequenting bars, drinking too much, having sensual pleasures with virtual strangers, and shop-lifting regardless of the consequences. Dione finally hears the voice in a sudden epiphany and is now able to disentangle reality from fantasy and sort herself out.

Dione's rite of passage to healing involves both physical and psychological escape. She meditates most of the time, letting her mind flow, musing about her past, retelling the Indian tales her negligent father told her as a child. By thus re-experiencing rather than denying childhood memories of her father, she frees herself from her obsessive shackles to him.

Breathing Water illustrates the profound significance of memory and the pull of blood and tribe. The novel has several flaws: the tales that zig-zag between past and present in the post-modernist style often slow down the narrative pace; the loose plot has the effect of a sprawling succession of episodes—many of which, however, are memorable. Crate's first novel displays an astonishing mastery of technique and of supple and evocative prose.

Thomas King's *Medicine River* (1990) is narrated by Will, a colourless, good-natured forty-year-old Métis photographer who has moved from Toronto to Medicine River, a small prairie town where he had lived as a boy. He soon gets involved with the native world of the community—the Friendship Centre, the basketball team, and the bar of the American Hotel—which King portrays in a lighthearted manner. Various local native characters make brief cameo appearances in accounts of births, weddings, funerals, as well as wife abuse, an RCMP arrest and a jail sentence, drinking, and suicide.

Will is more closely associated with the meddlesome, clownish Harlen Bigbear, who becomes his best friend, and Louise Heavyman, a liberated and successful accountant who gives birth to another man's child. (Will stands by her at the hospital—the authorities think he is the father.) But at novel's end Will is alone, while Louise is spending Christmas in Edmonton with her baby's father and Harlen is visiting his sister on the reserve.

In fragmentary recollections that intersect the present, Will re-experiences painful childhood memories of family life without a father, as well as memories of a later on-again-off-again relationship with a white woman. The ending is inconclusive. The reader is not sure whether Will's psychological journey has enabled him in the end to make peace with his unhappy early years or to bury the past—the memories are unexamined, neither probed for significance nor related to the present. Though the episodic presentation makes the plot seem an accretion of incidents,[1] King demonstrates his skill as a writer in individual scenes that are effective and often humorous.

Thomas King (b. 1943), of Cherokee, Greek, and German descent, has a Ph.D. in English/American Studies from the University of Utah. For nine years he taught in the Native Studies Department of the University of Lethbridge and is now teaching American Studies/Native Studies at the University of Minnesota.

More and more writers throughout the decade turned to the short-story form. Thomas King's short fiction has been published in a number of literary journals, including *Whetstone*, *The Malahat Review*, and *Canadian Fiction Magazine*. 'One Good Story, That One' is about a ruse played on an anthropologist who hears an Adam and Eve story and believes it to be an authentic Indian tale. The first-person narrative is in the style of telegraphic discourse that is characteristic of the oral storytelling tradition and reads best aloud. First published in *The Malahat Review* (Spring 1988), it was selected for *A Journey Prize Anthology* (1989). Another story, 'The Dog I Wish I Had, I Would Call it Helen', also first appeared in *The Malahat Review* (Winter 1989) and has also been chosen for *A Journey Prize Anthology* (1990). It focuses on the interaction between Jonathan, a precocious four-year-old who wants a dog, and Helen, his mother. The dialogue between mother and child, and the realistic domestic scenes, are so convincing that only the first-hand experience of raising an imaginative four-year old could have produced this delightful piece.

Achimoona (1985), published by Fifth House, is the first anthology of short fiction by native Canadians. It was the result of a series of writing workshops sponsored by Saskatchewan Education and conducted by Maria Campbell, who wrote the Introduction. *Achimoona*, a

Cree word for 'stories', includes a variety of short tales, ranging from realism to allegory and science fiction, by eight writers of diverse ages and backgrounds. All are set in the present, but they carry with them strong echoes of legends and times past. Many tend to be didactic in their social statements, and the quality is uneven, but stereotypes are happily missing.

Recurring themes are the interrelationship of men and nature, the reverence for all life, and the loneliness and rejection of the native child. In 'The Boy and the Eagle' by Peter Deranger, an oral storyteller and journalist, a young boy frees an eagle that is caught in a trap and the eagle later saves the boy, his sleigh, and dog from falling through the ice in the middle of a lake. 'The Hockey Game' by Wes Fineday, who 'comes from a family of oral storytellers and hereditary chiefs' from the Sweetgrass Reserve in Saskatchewan, focuses on a young Indian boy, living in a 'good Christian boarding home' while attending Grade 9 in Moose Jaw, who is maltreated by his landlady.

Three stories are by Jordan Wheeler (b. 1964), a singular new voice in short fiction. In 'The Pillars of Paclian' an angry young boy, who had just stepped on a worm, is led by another worm through his own backyard, where he experiences a series of transformations, becoming in turn a decaying tooth, the hydrogen atom in a water molecule, and the sun. The story is didactic in the sense that it teaches respect for all living things, but Wheeler's handling of the age-old transformation conceit of Indian storytelling is interesting. 'A Mountain Legend' is a suspenseful adventure story in which Jason, a city-born Indian boy, taunted by his two white friends, decides to climb a mountain. He gets into trouble and is rescued by the power of a myth. Wheeler cleverly weaves a traditional tale into a contemporary setting. 'Play With Me' is a children's story about a six-year-old Indian boy who calls a fireman to rescue a kitten from a tree. The fireman, who is also Indian, makes him proud to be an Indian, and their alliance earns the boy his schoolmates' acceptance.

John Cuthand (b. 1953) in 'Naska' shows his command of lyrical prose as he recounts the wonderful story of a powerful northern pike that ruled her domain in the South Saskatchewan River with pride of strength and courage—until the time came for her to die, and mighty Naska's body was reduced to bones and 'a toothy grinning skull'.

Darlene R. Frenette (b. 1949) created marvellous science fiction in 'A Feather Story: The Legend of the Laser Queen'. The fearless queen, who has conquered the terrible fog that arose when the earthquake tore a giant crack in the earth's surface, searches for other warriors who would learn how to dispel the fog and cross the great chasm in the world.

In Issue 16 of *Canadian Fiction Magazine* (1987) Thomas King brought together eighteen stories by fourteen writers, including Basil H. Johnston, Jeannette Armstrong, Daniel David Moses, and Gilbert Oskaboose. Their stories range from narratives set in contemporary urban centres and on the reserve to a legend about how the racoon got its markings and a modern-day parable, employing aesthetic structures from both the oral and Western traditions.

The theme of estrangement is at the heart of many of the stories. 'Run' by Barry Milliken—a Chippewa from Dutton, Ontario—is narrated by a fifteen-year-old boy who decides to run away from a home on the reserve that has become unbearable. Milliken depicts the stereotyped Indian family, but the story rises above stereotype in his lyrical account of the boy's reflections on running.

'In the Looney Bin' and 'Window' by J. B. Joe (Nootka) and 'Turtle Girl' by Beth Brant (Mohawk) lay bare the battered lives of Indian women worn out by alcoholism, poverty, and the abuse of men. The stories are depressing in their frank portrayal of human misfortune, but they are elevated by their authors' ironic wit.

'The Serpent's Eggs' by Gilbert Oskaboose (Ojibway) is a splendid story that articulates the chronological history—beginning with trapping and lumbering and ending with contemporary uranium mining—of industrialization in the lands between Elliott and Quirke Lakes in northern Ontario. Oskaboose's sensibilities have undoubtedly been coloured by living fifty kilometres downriver from the toxic dumps and radioactive wastes of the uranium mines of Elliott Lake, on the Serpent River Indian Reserve. The universality of his story—which has a moral in the manner of parables—haunts the memory. It possesses the clarity and simplicity of the myth-making imagination, and dry humour. The prose is lyrical, and resonant with biblical cadences:

And in a galaxy far far away, a tiny green planet hung in deep space, a single dewdrop that sparkled and shone in the gossamer web of another solar system, waiting for the white light from an incinerated planet as it sped across the dark chasm of a billion light years.

It was in the dead of winter when the light arrived, and, on the southern hemisphere of that tiny green planet, peaceful men tending their flocks on rocky hillsides looked up, and, Lo, a great shining light appeared in the eastern sky, and they were afraid, and stood in fear and awe, and wondered what this great sign could mean.

Thomas King's understanding of the Indian mind is wonderfully evident in his 'Bingo Bigbear and the Tie-and-Choker Bone Game'. A dispute between Big John and Eddie, the focus of the story, is finally settled in the Indian manner because 'being related was more important than some small difference of opinion or a little name calling.' King's second story in the collection, 'Joe the Painter and the Deer Island Massacre', suffers from artifice and overwriting. Narrated by Joe's Indian friend, it focuses on a pageant of the Deer Island Massacre when on 31 March 1863 a number of Indians were killed by whites. Staged by Joe with the help of his Indian friends, it was intended to celebrate the founding of San Francisco, but the pageant does not amuse the city fathers; it does not win the coveted prize. As Joe said, 'Most people can't manage honesty.'

'Gramma's Doing' by Daniel David Moses takes place in a funeral chapel where the narrator sits gazing at his grandmother in a casket, recalling past events and reliving childhood experiences through his fond memories of the old lady, who 'used to always be doing something, Gramma did. Now she's not.' In a moment of insight the mystery of death and life are revealed to the narrator: activity is being, and the creative person moves from one creative expression to another. The grandmother is now laughing at those who mourn her discarded physical form, for she has moved on to other activities. Moses' other story in the collection, 'King of the Raft', centres on a motherless boy who has been given too much freedom by a father who is mostly absent. The boy becomes a bully and 'king of the raft', but later dies in a traffic accident. The story is written as if the narrator is making it up as he goes along; one statement is followed by another that clarifies and modifies what went on before. This oral storytelling technique doesn't quite work—the story is confusing and the symbolism obscure—but the loose structure appropriately suggests the meandering flow of a raft downriver.

Women and Words: The Anthology/Les Femmes et Les Mots: Une Anthologie (1984) was a project of the West Coast Women and Words Society. It contains a story, 'Grandmothers Laugh Too', by Beth Cuthand (Cree) who was born in 1949 at La Ronge, Saskatchewan. (She attended the University of Regina and the University of Saskatchewan, where she graduated with a B.A. in sociology in 1986.) Her story portrays the familiar situation of a housewife stifled by domestic routine. Linda finally decides to see a girlfriend who helps her to make up her mind to confront her husband with the announcement that she needs to leave him for her own self-fulfilment. The story, told in a routine prose style, has a commonplace theme, except that the characters are now urban Indians.

Jordan Wheeler's three novellas in *Brothers in Arms* (1988) all deal with the relationship between pairs of native brothers and their efforts to re-establish contact after years of separation. 'Hearse in Snow' is about two brothers who are escorting the body of their father to a funeral on the reserve. Caught in a blizzard, they spend the night huddled with the casket in the back of the hearse. In the futuristic 'Red Wave', native networks of anarchist cells spring up across North America. Two brothers, one a journalist and the other a vengeful terrorist, accidentally meet after years of estrangement. 'Exposure' tells of two brothers, one dying from AIDS and the other a successful businessman who returns to the reserve to help his brother. In each story one brother has been able to succeed in the white man's culture; the other has been unwilling or unable to try. Their reunions, each under different circumstances, create the dramatic and emotional tension in the stories. Despite distance and maturity, they recall with both nostalgia and bitterness their traumatic childhood relationships in a series of alcoholic homes and Indian residential schools, and confess their innermost feelings to each other in 'soul searching' interaction. The reserve seems to be a spiritual retreat, a place to be returned to for healing. Wheeler explores the reserve-city syndrome with insight and imagination, contrasting each pair of brothers with knowing and convincing detail and a good ear for their speech. His stories are often awkward and disjointed, but Wheeler is an original talent who will surely only advance and grow as a writer. He was born in Victoria of Cree, Ojibway, Irish, English, Scottish, and French descent. Educated at St John's Ravenscourt School, Winnipeg, he lives there and works in video, film, and popular theatre.

Autobiography was a popular form in the 1980s. Beth Brant (Degonwadanti) is a Bay of Quinte Mohawk from the Theyindenaga Reserve in Deseronto, Ontario. Her *Mohawk Trail* (1985) is a miscellany containing autobiography, short stories, poems, and a reconstructed American Indian myth. Brant reminisces lovingly about her grandparents, while her portraits of her working-class parents and friends express passionate social concern through small details and penetrating compassion. Several stories enter the private world of physical love between girls and women. Brant's lesbian sensibility deals with the erotic exploration of female sexuality and, without a trace of self-consciousness, with the pleasures of lovemaking. Her prose ranges confidently in tone from the humorous to the poignant. Hers is a refreshingly down-to-earth literary voice. Born in 1941 and a high school drop-out, Brant married at seventeen and had three daughters. She has been writing since the age of forty when, after a trip through the Mohawk Valley, a bald eagle flew in front of her car, sat in a tree, and instructed her to write. She is co-founder of Turtle Grandmothers, an archive and library of information about North American Indian women and a clearing-house for manuscripts, published and unpublished, by Indian women. She lives in Detroit with her companion of eight years, Denise, and two of her children.

Florence Davidson (b. 1896), daughter of the noted Haida carver and chief Charles Edenshaw, told her life story when she was 81 years of age to the anthropologist Margaret E. Blackman, who spent more than fifty hours recording her on tape. The resulting life history—the first by a Northwest Coast Indian woman—was published in *During My Time* (1982). It is particularly interesting because Davidson lived through a significant period of Haida cultural history when traditional customs such as the puberty ceremony, arranged marriages, secret societies, and most forms of potlatching went from being practised to being gradually discarded.

Chief Charles Jones, in collaboration with Stephen Bosustow, tells the story of his long life in *Queesto, Pacheenaht Chief by Birthright* (1981). Born in 1876, he is thought to be the last of the pelagic seal hunters, having accompanied his father on a sealing expedition to the Bering Sea at the turn of the century. Hereditary Chief of the Pacheenaht people of Vancouver Island's west coast, Jones was one of the few remaining Indians of British Columbia who have lived through the transition from the traditional Indian to the modern Canadian way of life. His recollections include hunting seals, the arrival of the first white man and the first missionaries, the potlatch, his early schooling at missionary schools, the food they ate, and the clothes they wore. Jones also gives us insights into the beliefs, customs, and manners of his people before the arrival of the white man and after, when they were forced to adapt to the white man's laws, religion, and monetary system.

Eleanor Brass (b. 1905) is the author of *I Walk in Two Worlds* (1987), an account of her long life in Saskatchewan and Alberta. Her father, Fred Dieter, was a successful farmer and she learned little about her native Cree culture at home. She attended an Indian residential school, and later graduated from high school in Canora, Saskatchewan. She then spent several years in the File Hills Colony of southern Saskatchewan, where graduates of Indian schools were brought together in one place rather than returning to the reserves where English was spoken at home. At nineteen she married Harry Alexander Brass from the Colony. Unsuccessful as farmers, they moved to Regina. Mrs Brass then devoted her life to improving relations between Indians and whites, working chiefly in Indian Friendship Centres. She has included a few articles and stories she wrote for the *Regina Leader Post* and other newspapers and magazines in the fifties and sixties. 'They show that many things have changed since then, but many other problems facing the Indians are still with us.'

In *Indian School Days* (1988) Basil H. Johnston recalls his early years when, at the age of ten in 1939, he was taken from his family and placed in a residential school operated by Jesuit priests in the north-ern-Ontario town of Spanish. The school was run with exacting mili-tary discipline, and Johnston highlights a number of dramatic encounters between students and teachers as the boys try to cope with, or outwit, the stern white authorities. In a blend of sharp detail and comic force, Johnston manages to evoke a wonderful *joie-de-vivre* at the school, despite a system that imposed unpleasantness and even cruelty. Indeed, the autobiography reveals the external circum-stances of a community of students sharing similar backgrounds and bonded by friendship, rather than the inner personal development of any of the students or even the author, who may have deliberately chosen self-effacement in the manner of his ancestors. *Indian School Days*, however, is lively and amusing. Johnston is, above all, a story-teller with a love of humour and drama (like his Ojibway ancestors). He also loves language, sometimes getting carried away into over-blown rhetoric, but always catching the flavour of the boys' dialogue, its idioms and style. This gives his stories a distinctive flavour, but the dialogue can become tedious and the banter among the boys ex-hausting. Although the book carries the now-familiar message of white mistreatment of natives, Johnston does not make the students objects of pity. The book is warm, but never sentimental—though there is a touch of nostalgia.

The harsh existence to which native Canadian women have been doomed by race, colour, and their sex drove Lee Maracle, a Métis, to write *I Am Woman* (1988), a collection of informal autobiographical es-says with titles such as 'I Want to Write', 'Law, Politics and Tradi-tion', 'Black Robes', 'Heartless Teachers', 'Education', 'The Rebel', and 'Women's Movement'. Lee Maracle (b. 1950) was raised in North Vancouver and has lived in Toronto and Southern California. She married one of the founders of the Red Power Movement in Vancou-ver in 1968, and read books by Third World revolutionary writers. She is an advocate for native women and native rights, stating that 'our whole philosophy is based on our personal sovereignty and our collective will.' Merciless in its thrust, her book seethes with a pas-sionate sense of grievance as Maracle lashes out at the implacable forces that have been bent on keeping Indian women down:

We are not a violent people. But neither are we fools. Those not befog-ged by the powerless and obscure phrase-mongering of the oppressor, are sharply aware of their condition. They know they must fight. If they sit in the bars in vain attempts to drown their fighting spirit, it is because they are not sure how they are to fight and win. It is our history of losing that keeps us locked to the bar stools, not our fear of fighting.

To most of the élite, the re-writing of our history is equal to dignified betrayal. To the rebel it is the altering of her condition that will re-write her life onto the pages of a new history. Only rebellion, the spiritual cleansing of the bad blood that separates her from her womanhood can appease the rebel. But we need to know that we can win.

- Out of the telling of *I Am Woman*—her torrent of words and heavy preaching exposing a shameful record—Maracle herself emerges free and triumphant, having retrieved a life beaten from the wreck of experience. In the last sentence of the last chapter entitled 'Flowers', she says: 'It is the process of . . . articulation that I love.'[2]

Montreal-born Jovette Marchessault (b. 1938), a playwright and novelist who is proud of her Amerindian ancestry, is a radical lesbian feminist. Her novel *Comme une Enfant de la terre*, the first in a proposed trilogy, won the Prix France-Québec. In a translation by Yvonne Klein it was published in English as *Like a Child of the Earth* (1989); its sequel (*La Mère des herbes*) was published as *Mother of the Grass* (1989), also translated by Klein. Free-wheeling and unconventional in form, they are strongly autobiographical and amount to ebullient memoirs. Marchessault's account, in *Like a Child of the Earth*, of a childhood paradise on the banks of the St Lawrence—of family warmth, closeness, and laughter—and in *Mother of the Grass* of her education and working career, and of surviving painful experiences, are compelling; but even more interesting are her detailed visionary experiences and her authorial commentaries on such topics as birth, religion, the practice of the Roman Catholic faith, nuns, family violence in working-class Montreal, lesbian feminism, and poverty. And *Like a Child of the Earth* contains lyrical passages of despair over the colonial oppression of natives by Church and state:

The wind and the arrow bear witness to motion—and we, we began to understand that to remain unmoving as we were in our silence would be to make a lie of the authentic, natural sense of the word Kebec, which, in the language of the Montagnais, means: *Come to us, come to earth, set down here.*

Grandmothers are important figures of fascination and support in native Canadian writing and Marchessault's grandmother, painter of chickens and pianist extraordinaire, is no exception. Like Campbell's Cheechum, Marchessault's grandmother is her beloved pillar of strength and emerges as a truly memorable and endearing character. Marchessault also reveals a great deal about her love of books and language and words, her thinking and imaginative processes. She tells how she would 'dive' into books and, like a 'pearl-diver', would stay at the bottom exploring them:

Free words and attached words, words apt to copulate without pausing once, moist, sexy, well-built words spilling from a horn of plenty. I started up dialogues, I inaugurated more than one metamorphosis, and I danced a creative dance with these words which had newly landed in America. I had a passionate relationship with books. For the members of the Catholic tribes, this relationship reeked of scandal. I had to hide to read . . . reading is a waste of time . . . dangerous . . . the critical point . . . you'll make your head burst. You'd do better picking something everyone can relate to, like sports, or housekeeping, or vegetable gardening. Grandmother seemed to understand and she often asked me questions. I kept her in touch with my latest discoveries. Since the devil fascinated her above everything else, if, in the course of my prospecting, I stumbled over some rare, hitherto unrevealed piece of information, I hastened to share it with her. Succubi, incubi, they made my grandmother's eyes open, they sent her over the Moon. She wanted details and further information.

Marchessault's love of words sometimes leads to lack of control. She is prone to heap words on top of words, pack metaphors together in lists that gleefully spill over the brim. In this passage she is describing their rat-infested home:

Fat rats, noisy rats, snickering rats, rats that pillaged, rats that hung out, rats that harassed us, rats that skinned us very gently and tasted us a bit at a time. They were as wary and careful as politicians, and shady and artful and full of suspicion right to their whiskers. By night they galloped in the walls, leaping over obstacles and vaulting rusty nails, and throwing balls and squealing. By day they dove into darkness and ate electrical wiring. The tribe did all it could to get rid of them—cats, poison, traps, chasing, swearing, cursing, novenas, and lighting candles in front of the statue of St Jude, patron of lost causes. These rats stood mid-way between the atom and the roof of the world and therefore were indestructible.

Marchessault's two volumes of family history are unusually complex. They do not follow a linear narrative pattern but are a myriad of vignettes in which the narrator goes in and out of reminiscence and editorial commentary and analysis. At times these intrusions lack transition and make the narrative line difficult to follow. Authorial energy and the profusion of detail tend to overwhelm the reader, but both books are informed by Marchessault's ironic wit, irreverent tone, and a mind and imagination rich with ideas.

If Marchessault's two books are novels that read like autobiographies, *Inside Out: An Autobiography by a Native Canadian* (1990) by James Tyman (b. 1964) reads like a novel. Tyman's Métis mother took him out of the unhealthy environment she lived in and put him up for adoption when he was four. His new parents, the Tymans, who were white, gave him a happy childhood and a comfortable home. Two things blighted his early years, however. He was teased at school as a 'breed', and 'I got everything I needed, except a sense of identity. . . . I just didn't know who I was, or where I came from.' He committed his first crime, breaking and entering, at fifteen:

> To my family I was a hard-working, clean-cut youth. Then on weekends I was pulling three or four break and enters a night, just so I could buy friends and influence people with beer, drugs, and romping good times. Inevitably, my two lives crashed together. When the dust had settled, my roller-coaster emotional life had derailed. I had crossed the line. There was no turning back.

After numerous probations Tyman was confined to the Regina Correctional Center for 4 months. When the book ends in 1987 he is in the Saskatoon Correctional Center. (We are told that he is now seriously involved in rebuilding his life.) In between, his life was a round of drinking ('partying'), drug-taking, fighting, crimes, arrests, and imprisonment, and consorting with a stream of sad, affectless men and women who, like him, found it just as easy to pull a knife on someone as to buy him or her a drink. The reader, however, can't help liking Tyman and hoping he will pull himself out of his neurosis, while remaining unsympathetic to his bouts of self-destructive or criminal behaviour—which officials, with all their faults, usually tried to deal with compassionately. The book has many horrifying scenes of degradation and violence, but they are not sensationalized or offensive because the author never gives undue prominence to any one event; the narrative is evenhanded and detached—even unfeeling. Tyman says at one point that he was filled with hate, but this emotion does not colour his memoir, in which a desire to give a fair and accurate accounting seems to be uppermost; it reveals an exemplary control that was sadly missing in his life. The lack of depth and the superficial insights do not take away from a book that is adept in its use of language and quite novelistic in its narrative flair and convincing dialogue. One is surprised to read, in the endnote of the publisher (Fifth House), that Tyman wrote the text over six weeks in prison. However much editorial revision and polishing it received, *Inside Out* is highly successful on its own terms—a grim but hopeful odyssey.

Enough is Enough: Aboriginal Women Speak Out (1987) is a remarkable collection of interviews Janet Silman had with women activists from the Tobique Reserve in New Brunswick. The women recall their personal experiences while growing up on the reserve and their struggles to regain their full Indian status, rights, and identity. Their capacity for defiance, and their strategies for resistance and survival, contributed to the passing of Bill C-31 by Parliament in June 1985 that ended over 100 years of legislated sexual discrimination against native women. *Enough is Enough* helps illuminate how the dynamics of racial injustice in Canada shaped the lives of these women—and how their lives are reshaping the country.[3]

Although fewer in number than in previous years, collections of traditional stories were still being published. In *Tales the Elders Told* (1981), illustrated by Shirley Cheechoo, Basil H. Johnston tells nine delightful Ojibway creation myths. There is the story of the Great Spirit, who, at Nanabush's request, transformed stones into butterflies so that a set of twins would learn to walk and run in their attempts to capture the illusive creatures. And the story of a loon who made a foolish bet with a hawk because he was certain he could win a lacrosse game; he lost, however, and the hawk, by causing winter to come, forced the loon and his friends to fly south in winter forever. In *Ojibway Ceremonies* (1983) Johnston uses the context of the birth of a son, Mishi-Waub-Kaikaik (Great White Falcon), to Waubizeequae (Swan Woman) and Ogauh (Pickerel), in order to describe how, from babyhood to old age, nearly every action is governed by Ojibway tradition. As the baby grows up to adulthood, he participates in the rituals and ceremonies that mark the most important stages and events of Ojibway life, such as the naming ceremony, the vision quest, the Midewewin, and the ritual of the dead. Mishi-Waub-Kaikaik's life story ends in old age when, during a treaty-signing session, he warns his people against the selling of their land. Included in the book are three appendices giving the Ojibway texts for the petitions of the Midewewin (the Society of Medicine), the petitions of the Waubunowin (the Society of the Dawn), and the invocation before Council (the treaty-signing session).

Kwakiutl Legends (1981) were told by James Wallas (b. 1907) to Pamela Whitaker, a freelance writer who spent three years recording and researching stories about the trickster Raven, the culture-hero Deer who brought fire to the people, the thunderbird, mink, whales, and salmon, as well as creation stories. Wallas heard them from his uncle and other elders of his tribe who lived on Quatsino Sound and Hope Island in British Columbia. *Kwulasulwut: Stories from the Coast Salish* (1981)—translated by Ellen White (b. 1922), whose Salish name is Kwulasulwut ('Many Stars')—contains five stories: 'The Stolen

Sun', 'Grandma Goes Fishing', 'Hulitun, the Magic Hunter', 'Father Barbeques', and 'The Raven and the Racoon'. In the longest story, 'The Stolen Sun', the sun descends every evening to visit his people, goes home to sleep until it is time to rise again, and then is captured by a sea-gull who wants to be 'the light of the world in his place'. In 'The Raven and the Racoon', Raven teaches a shy racoon how to climb and how to fly; in return Racoon shows Raven how to catch fish. All the characters, human and animal, wander through natural and supernatural adventures, and each story discloses a traditional lesson in life.

Where the Chill Came From (1982) is a collection of thirty-one narratives about Windigo, 'a complex, voracious spirit-being who, they say, has wandered the subarctic forests and icy swamplands west of Hudson Bay throughout time', translated from the Swampy Cree dialect by Howard Norman from 1969 to 1980. Norman explains that in most instances his tales were part of 'announced performances'. A few of them were audience-participation events when an ongoing dialogue between narrator and audience prevailed, making the performance a collaborative telling.

Tagish Tlaagu (*Tagish Stories*), published in 1982, were narrated by Mrs Angela Sidney (b. 1902) at Tagish in the southern Yukon during the winter of 1978-9. Julie Cruikshank recorded them as they were told, in idiomatic English, with some minor changes. Cruikshank also provides important information regarding the philosophical and social context of the stories, as well as some linguistic clarification regarding Athapascan languages and reasons for certain features of the characterization, plot development, and structure of the stories, which include 'Crow Stories', 'The Woman Stolen by Lynx', 'Killer Whale', 'Wolf Helper', and 'Skookum Jim's Frog Helper'.

Micmac Legends of Prince Edward Island (1988) by John Joe Stark, with illustrations by Michael Francis and George Paul, contains stories about Glooscap, the trickster / transformer / culture-hero of the Micmacs.

In *Earth Elder Stories: The Penayzitt Path* (1988), Alexander Wolfe tells the Saulteaux oral history of the Pinayzitt family as he heard it from his grandfather, Earth Elder, who survived the smallpox and flu epidemics. Wolfe has retold his family's stories well: how his family participated in the signing of the treaties, how his people obtained the grass dance and were forced to stop performing the rain dance, and the last horse-stealing raid.

Write It on Your Heart: The Epic World of an Okanagan Storyteller (1989) contains the stories of Harry Robinson (1900-90), a retired rancher and an elder of the Similkameen reserve near Penticton, B.C., transcribed by Wendy Wickwire. Robinson learned the stories, and the method of storytelling, from his grandparents when he was a child. With great sensitivity and understanding, Wickwire presents them in a manner that captures their authentic flavour and sound, setting them typographically in lines structured to evoke the speech rhythms, repetitions, and dramatic pauses, without attempting to polish the English. Reviewing the book favourably, Thomas King wrote: 'In reading Robinson, one is virtually forced to read the story out loud, thereby closing the circle, the oral becoming the written becoming the oral.'[4] When oral literature is recast as written literature, the storyteller's *voice* and the *performance* aspect of the event are invariably lost. *Write It on Your Heart* manages to retain both: it faithfully captures the native oral-storytelling mystique. 'Coyote Tricks Owl' begins in this way:

> *Owl is bad. He preys on people. So Coyote*
> *devises a crafty plan to end Owl's killings.*

> The Owl is bad.
> He kills people.
> Owl, he's supposed to be big man.
> Big tall man.
> And he kills people, that Owl.
> He's tall and he got the power,
>   that Owl, he got the power.
> Was a big man.
> Tall and long arms.
> Big arms.
> Big man.
> Big person, the Owl was.
> Big woman or big man.
> And he can kill people.
> Kill 'em and eat 'em.
> He bad.
> And he can turn himself into a bird.
> Into an Owl.
> But in another way, it's a person.
> Big man or big woman.
> But he can change himself into Owl.
> And that's a bird.
> Then sometimes he could change himself or herself
>   into a big person
>   so he can kill people.

> So Coyote find that out.

All right.
He look for Owl.
They call that *sa-NEE-na*.
That's an Indian word, *sa-NEE-na*.

And he look around.
And he going along,
    and he see some people.
And he ask and they tell them,
    'You go that way.
    He was over there.
    And you can find 'em if you go over that way.'

So he keep going and get closer.
Finally he find 'em.
And this time
    when he found 'em,
        and he change into Owl.
He was Owl.
He was Owl Woman when he found 'em. . . .

The desire to write history books slackened somewhat in the 1980s. *We Are Métis* (1980), Duke Redbird's first published book (originally his M.A. thesis)—described as the first complete published history of the Métis people written by a Métis—presents in intemperate language a jargonistic view of Métis history and cannot be considered objective. *The Ways of My Grandmothers* (1980) by Beverly Hungry Wolf records the ancient ways of the Blood women, as well as some personal and tribal history. *Kipawa: Portrait of a People* (1982) by Kermot A. Moore—a Métis of Anishnabi (Ojibway) descent who grew up in the area of Kipawa, a native community in northern Quebec—describes the changes brought on by the fur-trade, lumbering, and tourism, and shows how traplines and the new tourist zoning systems have displaced the natives, disrupting their traditional livelihood of trapping, and forcing them onto the farm or into the factory. Moore also describes native methods of game conservation, and the land issues that forced the community to stage a blockade on one of the main highways in 1979. He weaves details of his own personal experiences and those of other community members into the larger context. An administrator in the Royal Canadian Air Force for twenty years, Moore resigned to take an active role in native affairs and to write native history. His second book, *The Will to Survive: Native People and the Constitution* (1984), which appeared two years after his death, discusses the fundamental rights of the aboriginal people of

Canada, and of the relationship of these rights to the Universal Declaration of Human Rights.

In poetry during this decade Duke Redbird's *Loveshine and Red Wine* (1981) includes some of his old poems of protest and indignation, like 'Kaleidoscopically', 'Mackenzie Delta', and 'The Beavers'. But most of the poems reveal a mellowed Redbird who has moved from bitterness and defeat onto such subjects and themes as the beauty of the landscape; love of family, home, and friends; and romantic love. Redbird has learned to feel better about himself in these poems. 'Alive as the Land' celebrates his wonderful affirmation of life as he rejoices in his new-found identity.

ALIVE AS THE LAND
Oh give me the rain and the wind,
And the mist of a summer draped lake,
Give me the warm arms of a morning dawn
And the tender kiss of a summer breeze,
Shaking the sunlight from the poplar leaves.
And give me the caress of a woman's hand
Soft as a moment, alive as the land.

I've climbed the mountain,
        and feared the stony path
I've reached the precipice,
        And I've laughed
At the crevices of life.
I've shouted my triumph at the granite wall
And watched my failures fall.
Lord I've loved the morning
And slept with the night,
I've touched the goodness,
And fondled the sin,
I've wondered at creation
And cursed some paths I've been.

In an interview with the author in 1977, Duke Redbird explained: 'I'm more concerned now with making statements about personal human development . . . I'm into a time of introspection, a time when people are thinking more about what is happening to themselves, [a time when] they are more interested in regaining some sense of morality, and honesty and beauty and some sense of what the basics are to human development.'[5]

In *Horse Dance to Emerald Mountain* (1987) Beth Cuthand (b. 1949), a

Cree, makes her pilgrimage to Emerald Mountain. But her odyssey is more than a physical journey; it is a spiritual quest as well, an allegory for an individual journey to enlightenment. She not only reaches Emerald Mountain, she has become 'Emerald Mountain / selfless / unfettered / free'—she has found herself. Cuthand's grandfather was given the privilege of performing the beautiful horse-dance ceremony, and Cuthand weaves a traditional ritual into a modern setting. Her rhythms successfully evoke the free flight of her stallion and its galloping, prancing, cantering, resting paces:

> V
> The horse returns
> head tossing
> hooves prancing
> impatient for the dance.
>
> We face east
> caching the light of the sun
> glinting
> gleaming
> glowing
> on the face
> of the Emerald Mountain
> I shiver
> the horse rears
> leaping forward toward
> our fate.
>
> galloping galloping galloping
> the dark blue mountains
> rise before us now
> steep
> treacherous
> testing the dance. . . .

Rita Joe's second book of poetry, *Song of Eskasoni: More Poems by Rita Joe* (1988), is her response to a variety of subjects, ranging from the disappearance of her brother Roddy, to Christopher Columbus's error and the imprisonment of Donald Marshall Jr for a crime he did not commit. Rita Joe juxtaposes her reflections with those of Micmac everyday life to create a textual counterpoint that makes the ordinary extraordinary. Expressed, once again, in uncomplicated simple and direct lines, her solution to the contemporary problems of Indian-white relations is based on the power of love and understanding.

MY SHADOW CELEBRATES
Though it was natural for me to create my leather dress
the beads and quill my ornamentation
You call it art,
It makes me feel wise with a sense of identity.

Though it was necessity I used bone, stone, and wood to
        carve my images
You call it art.
It makes me feel wise and a seer of beauty.

Though I created the mask for mystical purposes
The amulets my ritual objects
You call it art.
It makes me feel wise as my spirit flows with love.

My sketches have revealed the loneliness of fading away
The message passing the wind into all eternity.
You call it art.
My spirit shadow celebrates, 'You have found me!'

Nineteen poems by Daniel David Moses were included in the anthology *First Person Plural* (1988) edited by Judith Fitzgerald. In these poems Moses' imagination tends to work on a more abstract and reflective level than in his earlier poems in *Delicate Bodies* (1978).

SNOW WHITE
Yes, a charming conversationalist
so handsome and tall, it was all I could
do to lay still—at least until that mist
your breath had laid overhead had silvered.

I watched you try to kiss me through the ice
and my own reflection. How my face shone!
—like one of your spoons—which is why I guess
you thought I could be got by lip action.

You got caught instead. I saw how your kiss
froze and bled—and thought of a rose that had
lasted until the first frost. How your face
iced over as the chill spread! I felt sad.

But my head of coal-black hair looked so rich
in winter's mirror, I soon felt much better.
And a happiness this bright won't tarnish
or crack—thanks to my very best lover!

> You gave me a clear sky showing through ice,
> a looking glass where my face is a full
> and rising moon forever. There's no price
> you can put on something this beautiful.

Moses tries many poetic forms, ranging from the sonnet to the looser forms. His poems are characterized by a subtle understatement that contributes to their controlled elegance. He is not particularly interested in castigating whites for past injustices. There is no outright confrontation in his poems; the message is submerged in his surreal images. Underneath the wry humour and ironies, the reader senses a struggle to attain self-knowledge, as if Moses is feeling his way through the contradictions and puzzles of life. Individual in both style and thought, possessing a strikingly original sensibility and a probing intelligence, Moses is an arresting poet.

Joan Crate's collection, *Pale as Real Ladies: Poems for Pauline Johnson* (1989) contains poems about Johnson's personal and family life as seen through the prism of modern sensibilities and an acute sensitivity.

> IN THE CLOSET UNDER THE STAIRWELL
> Eva and I play with porcelain dolls.
> Their hypnotized eyes demand
> doilies for their table,
> embroidered pillows. Over
> their flaxen heads dangle woolen haloes,
> musty with the memory of Mother's angel arms,
> and a sky of neon beads strung across
> Father's smoke-skin coat.
>
> We will not allow our brothers inside,
> sweaty from games and thumping dance.
> They lurk, too bright, on the other side
> of our curtain door.
>
> For ourselves we steal Mother's
> tatted collars to subdue the riotous
> dresses our grandmother stitched.
> We curl our hair and dust talcum powder
> over cheeks and eyelids,
> turn pale as real ladies.

Crate's sardonic wit and sharply pointed images wonderfully capture the tensions within a family troubled by divided loyalties and Victorian prudery.

Seventh Generation (1989) is an anthology of poems by native poets. The significance of the title is explained by Tomson Highway in another context: 'Legend has it that the shamans, who predicted the arrival of the white man, and the near-destruction of the Indian people, also foretold the resurgence of the native people seven lifetimes after Columbus. We are that seventh generation.'⁶ Some of the poets in the anthology are known—Jeannette C. Armstrong, Lenore Keeshig-Tobias, A. Garnet Ruffo—but many are still relatively unknown: Marie Annharte Baker, Mary Sky Blue Morin, Charles Minitsoos, Kateri Damn, Henry Michel, Tracey Bonneau, Garry Gottfriedson, and Greg Young-Ing. They write about many things: the West Edmonton Mall, Toronto Transit, Vancouver, the Sundance, Sweetgrass, a hospital visit, lost love, eagles, a clown at a fair, bears at a dump, a phone-call, and home. There is nostalgia for past traditions and customs as well as political and social concerns. But the voices in the collection are pre-eminently political, drawing inspiration from history and the present plight of Canada's native peoples, and share common dreams, anxieties, and sorrows. There is no rage and no anger. But there is commitment, because these writers have something important to say. And although there is pain, it is expressed with restraint, at times with elegance, and occasionally with sardonic wit.

For example, images of past injustices and a suggestive irony of diction characterize Jeannette C. Armstrong's 'History Lesson', in which she recalls the history of Canada's 'discovery' and settlement. Armstrong concentrates on the negative aspects, and her history lesson emerges as an indictment of European conquest and colonization. In another poem, 'Dark Forests', Armstrong laments the untimely death of a young political activist of the American Indian Movement in a warm and loving tribute.

DARK FORESTS
It was spring when we met in Seattle.
We danced the blanket dance.
After the drums went quiet,
there was
warm sea
and
warm bodies.
I was nineteen.
You said you were from the owl clan.

Once on Centre Island
we smoked a joint
laughed awhile

at birds coasting through clear summer.
Then you told me about your son

It hurts that he will never know
his grandfather was owl Chief.

In your eyes
a night bird trembled
in a dark forest.

Wild roses blossom everywhere in the foothills.
We walked to the buffalo paddocks.
talked about this fall gathering of elders.
Your red hairband showed allegiance
to spilled blood
to A.I.M.
to Wounded Knee
to all of your hurts.

That night we watched Hopi dancers
invoke the Kachinas.
Then you went to the peyote ceremony
to speak to the relentless masters
known only in shadows
who breathed your name, owl man.

I have walked uneasy
down a long road
since they found you
covered in the first soft crow flakes,
laid out in your best,
eyes wide,
mouth slack,
your last master gratified.

And I remember
always
in the night
owls call to each other.

Armstrong is a woman of strong sympathies and warm passions. Her poetry is direct, unequivocal, and assertive, even aggressive. One can always rely on her to grapple with the grim realities of the contemporary native Canadian experience and tell the uncomfortable truths. No one has portrayed the native dilemma more energetically or with more emotional intensity.

An unpretentious freshness and economy of form and style characterize Lenore Keeshig-Tobias's three poems in the collection. Tobias (Ojibway) was born in 1950 in Wiarton, Ontario. She is a member of the Chippewas of Nawash, Cape Croker Indian Reserve. The oldest of ten children, she received her elementary-school education on the reserve and later attended Loretto Academy in Niagara Falls and Wiarton District High School, where she completed Grade XI. In 1983 she graduated from the Creative Writing Program at York University. Now living in Toronto, she has been assistant editor of *Ontario Indian*, founding editor of the short-lived *Sweetgrass*, and is currently the editor of *The Magazine to Re-establish the Trickster: New Native Writing*. In her poems in *Seventh Generation* she draws on her life on the reserve in 'I Grew Up' with an engaging child-like simplicity. 'Indians' reveals her sense of humour:

INDIANS
When I was
a kid back home,
we kids used to
play Cowboys and Indians.
We never wanted
to be the Indians
'cause they were
always the bad guys
and lost,
so we were all cowboys
back home on the reservation.

'Come, Lay Your Wounds' can be read as the invitation of a protective earth mother to her children or as an address to whites. Although the diction is plain and direct, the effect is heart-warming.

COME, LAY YOUR WOUNDS
though my bones grow
old under centuries
of decay and my heart
forgotten over the years

remember that
someday your bones,
your ashes will
rest with mine

and if by chance you
should come upon

my fragments while
you furrow and build

remember i have hoped
it so, i have wished
to touch the future and
breathe again today

you are my
future my past
i—your past and
your future too

remember your spirit
claims more and more
this earth and you
shall never be alone

come, lay your
wounds to be healed
come, lay your
wounds to the earth

'Chant for Mother and Child' by A. Garnet Ruffo, whose work has been published in eastern Canada and the United States, is a lyrical treatment of an old subject. The extended metaphor, in gentle images from nature, of a mother lavishing her love on her baby is punctuated by a melodic refrain that evokes eternity.

CHANT FOR MOTHER AND CHILD
I will be a sparrow   prairie grass flows
perched on your body
softness slowly rustling

I will be a wind   prairie grass flows
washing past
cooling you gently

and in the morning   prairie grass flows
I will be a dew
cleansing and
a rainbow arc
revealing
the many colours of our day   prairie grass flows

Mary Sky Blue Morin makes her poetry chiefly out of the traditions and ceremonies of her people. Her titles include 'I Dream of Buffalo

Days', 'Sweetgrass', 'The Sundance', 'The Women's Sweatlodge', and 'A Healing Time'. Modest and slight, her poems convey a strong sense of cultural values from which she obtains strength, as in the following poem, which evokes her acculturated impatience to learn from the elders, who are attuned to ancient traditions and to a slower, gentler pace:

RUNNING . . . TO CATCH UP TO SOMEONE WALKING
Teaching me traditions
at a furious pace
of a few short months
I had envisioned years.

So ignorant a feeling
to be running
running to catch up
to someone walking.

To cry tears for fear
of being left behind.
To be at his side
knowledge waiting.

So painful a feeling
to be running,
running to catch up
to someone walking.

Marie Annharte Baker (b. 1942, Saulteaux) contributes the interesting poem 'Moonbear'. Not only is the moon an important symbol to Indians, but in Indian cultures menstrual time is known as 'moon time', and the bear is the archetypal mother figure. In 'Moonbear' Annharte merges both metaphors to express her power as a woman and as a source of life. The poem brings to mind the pictographic style or 'x-ray art' of Norval Morrisseau, where the action is depicted as taking place internally.

MOONBEAR
My moon is a deep lake in me
down there little fishes swim
Too scared to see the shaking
Sunlight spears above their stare
She-bears birthing in my winter womb
Sleeping till spring to growl again
Shadows dancing before the nights come

Tomorrow the wind out there will be just right
Maybe a quick look to find a tourist dump
What happened since her earth eyes shut
Muzzle up and around for scents secure
Her baby wants her back, it is still cold
The iceface feel of my moon lake
Slips away as soon as there is more sun
My moon will grow within me to greet
Rising bears bringing warm faces to my lips.

'Moonbear' is among the poems in Baker's collection *Being on the Moon* (1990), which includes a cycle of moon poems.

Seventh Generation is an uneven anthology, but it offers insight, originality, and considerable experimentation with verse forms, with a preference for the loose conversational line and typographical innovations.

During the eighties Canada's alien judicial system still filled jails with natives, in numbers far out of proportion to the native population. Bruce Chester (b. 1953)—of Cree, Stoney, and Chippewyan descent on his mother's side and Icelandic, Scotch-Norman descent on his father's—tells about his prison experiences in *Paper Radio* (1984). His poems, predominantly short, display an amusing conversational style:

ENGLISH LINGUAL ACCOMPLISHMENT
The English lingual accomplishment
is a snarky one
for which a medal should
be given
if one can create a line
sans a mistake
had Radisson and Groseilliers
tried to capture the Bay
in this heathen tongue
we'd all be speaking Swampy Cree
and praising the Bourbon

It has no rules
that I
can see
England created it in fun
to drive poor nigger and métis
to a factory with rubber rooms
believing they're Tom Thumb

The solution to this problem
is as simple as can be
everybody in the world
could learn to speak like me

Several publishing outlets for new native writers—such as *Whetstone*, a literary publication of the Department of English at the University of Lethbridge, which has devoted three issues to native writers, and *The Magazine to Re-establish the Trickster*—have published the poetry, short stories, and essays of writers who have written in the 1980s. Along with such familiar names as Daniel David Moses, Basil Johnston, Lenore Keeshig-Tobias, Drew Taylor, and A.G. Ruffo, there are the new names who have made their appearances in the 1980s: John McLeod, J.B. Joe, Thomas King, Marie Annharte Baker, Joanne Cardinal-Schubert, Harry Robinson, William Merasty, Edna King, and Anne Acco.

Native periodicals and newspapers are continually in flux. Lack of funds causes irregular publication and often demise. A few have survived, such as *Micmac News*, *Akwesasne Notes*, *Saskatchewan Indian*, and *Wawatay News*; but many come and go. Every decade has its chequered lists. In the 1980s a large number of new periodicals have sprung up: *Windspeaker*, published by the Aboriginal Multi-Media Society of Alberta; *Masenayegun*, published by the Winnipeg Friendship Centre; *Tapwe* in Hay River, NWT; *New Breed*, published by the Saskatchewan Native Communications; and *Free Lance* published by the Saskatchewan Writers' Guild. *The Phoenix*, published in Toronto by the Canadian Alliance in Solidarity with Native Peoples, provides new opportunities for native writers such as Beth Cuthand, Marie Annharte Baker, Lee Maracle, Lenore Keeshig-Tobias, Drew Taylor, and Daniel David Moses, who are becoming confident enough to write book reviews and other articles. In fact, Taylor, Tobias, and Moses are writing reviews for such mainstream journals as *Books in Canada* and *Maclean's*.

Leading newspapers are also using native journalists to deal with native issues. Brian Maracle (b. 1947), the well-known Mohawk broadcaster and writer, often appears in the Ontario and Quebec press. His informative and perceptive article on the troubles at the Akwesasne Reserve near Cornwall, Ontario, which appeared in the *Toronto Star* (7 May 1990), maintains the style of the native tradition of protest, appealing always to history as the true and rightful authority, and possessing the paramount gift of conviction:

SOVEREIGNTY IS SOLUTION TO STRIFE AT AKWESASNE

Although roadblocks, beatings and shootings have been occuring for months at Akwesasne and although 'Canadian' Mohawk leaders have been calling for government intervention for weeks, two Mohawks died before Canada and U.S. decided to step in.

More telling, though, is the fact that two young men had to die before the Canadians and Americans would even get together to begin searching for answers to the problems there.

That they have done so without inviting or involving the Mohawk leaders is not so much a telling indictment of their attitude as it is a recipe for failure and continued strife.

The bureaucrats won't find the answers to the problems at Akwesasne in their policies and legislation because their laws create the problem in the first place.

If Canada and the US really want to solve 'the problem' at Akwesasne, they have to begin by understanding exactly what the problem is.

For starters, Mathew Pyke and Arnold Edwards did not die because of the dispute over gambling.

They died, ultimately, because the Canadian and American governments refused to recognize the Mohawk Nation of Akwesasne.

True, they recognize the laws they passed to apply to their portions of the reserve and they recognize the tribal councils they helped create.

But they don't recognize the traditional chiefs and they don't recognize the wish of the Mohawk people of Akwesasne to be treated as one community—one nation.

Akwesasne is a jurisdictional nightmare. The international boundary that divides the reserve has crippled the ability of Mohawk people to respond to major problems.

Because the community is divided, the 'gamblers' were able to use guns and hundreds of low paying jobs to impose their will on the US side of the reserve even though a majority of the Mohawks are said to oppose gambling.

Up to now, the Americans and the Canadians have been reluctant to become involved in the gambling dispute because they say they want the Mohawks to settle their own differences.

Good idea! That's what the Mohawks want, too. So why didn't they involve the Mohawks? By hanging on to their tattered bits of jurisdiction, the Americans and Canadians won't let the Mohawks do what's best for them, for Canada and the US.

The solution to 'the problem' at Akwesasne is simple—erase the international border that divides Akwesasne. Instead of having the border run through the community, have it run around the outside of the Mohawk territory.

Make Akwesasne one independent political unit, Akwesasne would then not be part of either the U.S. or Canada.

Allow the Mohawks there to decide their own form of political representation—one tribal government, not two—one police force to enforce their own laws and keep the peace.

Let the Mohawks, all of them, decide if they want to allow gambling. If they say 'no', then give their police force the resources, money, training and assistance to enforce the people's will. If they say 'yes', then let them control it, regulate it, and benefit from it.

The American and Canadian governments should share the cost of servicing and developing the community. But it won't take that much.

An independent Mohawk Nation could use its unique political status as the key to its economic development. There are already plenty of precedents for this kind of arrangement in Europe—San Marino, Andorra, Lichtenstein, Monaco, and Vatican City.

Like the European models, an independent Mohawk Nation at Akwesasne could generate revenue from tourism, the sale of postage stamps, as a duty-free zone and as a centre for international banking and business.

This arrangement, although unusual in a North American context, can lead to a peaceful and prosperous future at Akwesasne. What's more, it's the only one that makes sense. Anything else will guarantee only continued confrontation.

Canada gives lip service to the idea of Indian self-government. But if there ever was a place to really put self-government to work and to reap the benefits, Akwesasne is it. If this arrangement had been in place, the roadblocks, beatings, shootings and killings would not have occurred.

The sad fact is that violence and confrontation at Akwesasne is not new. The first major flareup over the international boundary occurred 22 years ago, when the Mohawks blockaded the international bridge to Cornwall.

If the Canadian and American governments had only listened to the Mohawks then and acted on their calls for recognition of the Mohawk Nation at Akwesasne, then Matthew Pyke and Arnold Edwards would be alive today.[7]

Brian Maracle attended high school in Niagara-on-the-Lake, Ontario, and Rochester, N.Y. He graduated from Dartmouth College in Fine Arts (1969) and holds a BA degree in journalism from Carleton University (1982).

The most exciting literary development in the 1980s has taken place in drama. According to Tomson Highway, in this decade 'There has been the first emergence on a national scale of a native literary movement, particularly within the realm of theatre. Native voices are being heard on a scale similar to that of the native visual artists of the sixties.[8] This is not surprising, considering that the inclination to theatricality, performance, and participation in a shared event is a legacy inherited from the past. Both the number of playwrights and of plays produced has grown remarkably since the tentative attempts by Duke Redbird, George Kenny, and Nona Benedict in the 1970s. Native performing groups, full- and part-time, have sprung up across the country. Native Earth Performing Arts Co. was founded in 1982 in Toronto. There are also Spirit Song, founded in 1981 in Vancouver, which began as a native youth theatre project and specializes as a threatre-arts training centre; the Sen' Klip Native Theatre Company in Vernon, B.C., which also began as a native-youth Summer Project in 1987—Sen' Klip, which means Coyote, focuses chiefly on the culture and heritage of the Okanagan people in its productions; 4 Winds Theatre of Hobbema, Alberta; the Saskatoon Survival School; Awasikan Theatre Inc. of Winnipeg, which has broadened its mandate as a puppet theatre to include a wider variety of the performing and visual arts; De-Bah-Jeh-Mu-Jig Theatre in West Bay on Manitoulin Island; and Northern Delights Theatre in Sioux Lookout. The Native Theatre School, a project of the Association for Native Development in the Performing and Visual Arts—founded in 1974 and based in Toronto—is the longest continuously run theatre school in Canada.[9]

The actress, playwright, and director Ida Labillois-Williams (Micmac) has been the moving force in English-speaking native theatre in Montreal. Working out of the Montreal Native Friendship Centre, of which she is the executive director, she has worked with children and adult groups. She directed a small amateur theatre group, First People and Friends, in a production of her play *Beads, Feathers and Highrises*, which premièred at the Third Annual Native Cultural Festival in 1985 and toured the reserves in the area. In 1987 she produced her play *I Hear the Same Drums/Le Son du même Tambours*, which she wrote in English but work-shopped half in French. Although both plays treat the problems that plague Indian young people in the cities, *I Hear the Same Drums* focuses on the particular difficulties of the French-speaking Montagnais/Naskapi.

One of the most important activities of the various theatre companies is their work with children and young adults in the drama courses, summer theatre camps, and workshops they conduct. Studies include music, dance, and mime, since in Indian culture music, dance, and ceremony were meshed into an aesthetic unit. Touring to various reserves is another important function. Many new plays are collective works that are performed in the manner of the actors' ancestors, as a sharing of each other's ideas and a blending of each other's rhythm, with many voices speaking louder than one. For example, the 1989 Native Theatre School's production of *Seriwakwaniosta* was a collaborative effort to express the themes, images, and scenes that emerged from a few weeks' exploration of the Mohawk philosophy of respect for the circle of life. Over the years native theatre groups have tried to develop a new form of theatre that restores and recreates their native cultures with non-native theatre to articulate and express a theatrical mode that both informs and entertains. Using theatre as the vehicle for instruction and entertainment, they emphasize community-theatre techniques for native social development in what Cat Cayuga, the first native woman to direct the Toronto Native Theatre School (1985), calls 'Prevention Through Drama'.[10]

In all this activity a few playwrights—notably Tomson Highway in Toronto and Sadie Worn Staff and Margo Kane on the West Coast—have established names for themselves. Daniel David Moses, Val Dudoward, John McLeod, Darrel Wildcat, and Drew Taylor are beginning to become known; while new talents such as Floyd Favel, Evan Adams, Lynn Phelan (b. 1957, Okanagan), and Ruby Alexis (b. 1967, Okanagan) give promise of achievement. Except for Highway's *The Rez Sisters* (1988) and *Dry Lips Oughta Move to Kapuskasing* (1989), Daniel David Moses' *Coyote City* (1990), Linda Griffiths' and Maria Campbell's *Jessica* (1989), and the three plays in *The Land Called Morning* (1986), native dramas have received performance, but have not yet found publishers.

On the whole, their plays are inspired by contemporary social problems facing native Canadians: alcohol and drug abuse, suicide, wife battering, family violence, the racism of the justice system, loneliness, rejection, youth awareness, as well as modern-day environmental issues. The politics of the streets, of the sub-culture, is a recurring theme.

Canada's most celebrated native playwright is Tomson Highway. *The Rez Sisters* won the Dora Mavor Moore award for the best play in 1986/7 and later went on to earn extravagant praise at the Edinburgh Festival; and *Dry Lips Oughta Move to Kapuskasing* swept the Dora Mavor Moore awards for 1988/9 and is slated for production at the Royal Alexandra Theatre, Toronto, in 1991. Highway was born in 1951 on his father's trapline on a remote island on Maria Lake in northwestern Manitoba. The second-youngest of twelve children, he spoke only Cree until he was six, when he was sent to a Roman Catholic boarding school, the Guy Hill Indian Residential School in The Pas, Manitoba. He stayed there until he was fifteen, when he finished Grade 9. He was then sent to Churchill High School in Winnipeg, where he lived in a number of white foster homes and graduated in 1970. He then spent two years at the University of Manitoba Faculty of Music, studying piano. When his teacher went to England on a sabbatical, Highway went with him to continue his studies as a pianist. After one year he returned to the University of Manitoba and then, with his teacher, spent a year at the University of Western Ontario, where he graduated in Honours Music (1975) and English (1977). While at Western, Highway worked with James Reaney on *The Canadian Brothers* and *Wacousta*, for which he supplied the Cree words used in a lacrosse game in the latter play. Highway was especially influenced by Reaney's *Donnelly Trilogy* because of its use of poetic language, imagery, and its mythological overtones. After graduation he worked for a number of native support groups. In 1981, at the age of thirty, he started writing plays. 'Theatre for me gives the oral tradition a three-dimensional context, telling stories by using actors and the visual aspects of the stage.'[11] He set out to combine his 'knowledge of Indian reality in this country with classical structure, artistic language. It amounted to applying sonata form to the spiritual and mental situation of a street drunk . . . that is the first and only way most white people see Indians. . . . that's our national image.'[12] Highway is currently the Artistic Director of the Native Earth Performing Arts Company in Toronto.

Not fluent in English until his mid-teens, Highway writes the first draft of his plays in Cree, a language that has no gender distinctions. Because his culture's dominant mythological figure is a trickster clown who is a very sensual character, the language can be both hilarious and visceral. The possibilities of language are very important to Highway, who has said: 'I love playing with words—the sound and sensuality of syllables, the feeling and images and meaning.'[13]

The Rez Sisters—the first in an intended cycle of seven plays—is a raucous mix of the comic and the tragic, full of life and dreams. It is the story of seven women who live in the imaginary reserve of Wasaychigan Hill on Manitoulin Island. Their boring life on the 'rez'—the reservation—is made bearable by bingo, but even bingo is losing its attraction, since the pots have been getting smaller. When the women hear that the biggest bingo game in the world, with a $500,000 jackpot, is coming to Toronto, they raise the money for the trip and set out for Toronto to try their luck. On their journey they are accompanied by the Ojibway Trickster, Nanabush, disguised in turn as a seagull, a nighthawk, and finally as the Bingo Master himself. He is visible to only two characters in the play: the gentle Marie-Adele Starblanket, who is about to die, and the unfortunate Zhaboonigan Peterson, a retarded spastic young woman who has been sexually abused. The women do not win the jackpot and return to the reserve disappointed, but not completely demoralized.

The play hangs on a thin plot, but it is fast-moving, at times even frenetic. The Rez sisters are vibrantly alive, endowed with titanic energy, and are very funny. Nothing is private or sacred to them; they know each other's sex habits, health problems, family histories, and daily routines. And they insult and ridicule one another relentlessly in a banter that sometimes borders on the puerile and the outrageous.

The characters vary in age and personality, from the twenty-four-year-old Zhaboonigan Peterson to Pelajia Patchnose, who wants to pave all the roads on the rez, and Veronique St Pierre, who dreams of having 'the biggest stove on the reserve'.

I'll cook for all the children on the reserve. I'll adopt all of Marie-Adele Starblanket's 14 children and I will cook for them. I'll even cook for Gazelle Nataway's poor starving babies while she's lolling around like a pig in Big Joey's smelly, sweaty bed. . . . I'll enter competitions. I'll go to Paris and meet what's his name Cordon Bleu! I'll write a cookbook called 'The Joy of Veronique St Pierre's Cooking' and it will sell in the millions! And I will become rich and famous!

Highway's play is informed by insight into, and deep knowledge of, reserve life, and it is both exhilarating and exhausting. One wonders how any reserve community could be boring with such exuberant and resilient women among its members. *The Rez Sisters* was first performed at the Native Canadian Centre, Toronto, in November 1986.

Dry Lips Oughta Move to Kapuskasing is a two-act sequel to *The Rez Sisters* and features the men who are only mentioned in that play—seven eccentric characters who, among other things, argue about their women's plans to form a hockey team and bear such names as Creature Nataways, Spooky Lacroix, Simon Starblanket, and Dickie Bird Halked. Their high-pitched exchanges—not quite as funny as those of the women—are sprinkled with Cree and Ojibway and filled with energy; they are in turn coarse, violent, hilarious, obsessive, desperate, and touching. Overseen on the upper level of the set by Nanabush in the form of a comical sex goddess, the action suddenly explodes in two horrific moments when the Nanabush figure is raped with a crucifix and Simon accidentally kills himself with a shotgun. Into all this, stunning lighting effects inject the spirit world of Nanabush and a sense of magic. (Highway has said: 'We grew up with myths; they're the core of our identity as a people. But I'm urban by choice, so I translate that mythology into contemporary terms. The trickster now takes strolls down Yonge Street and goes into bars.')[14] The play was first performed by Native Earth Performing Arts Inc. at the Theatre Passe Muraille, Toronto, on 21 April 1989.

Highway's *Aria* is a series of 22 monologues that were first performed by Makka Kleist at Toronto's Annex Theatre in 1987. The play
is a loosely structured exploration of native womanhood that draws
on classical and Cree mythology as well as on contemporary reality.
The characterizations include a native woman as grandmother,
mother, and young girl; Zeus's wife, Hera, railing at his infidelities; a
statue of the Blessed Virgin Mary, whose foot rests on a globe ent-
wined by a snake that comes to life; a sex goddess who croons in German; a young wife labouring at an old-fashioned washing machine
retelling a tale about the Windigo; a Cree cannibal that devours the
bodies and souls of all it meets; a smart ruthless executive secretary
who has clawed her way up the business ladder of success; a director
of a native organization bribing board members; and the Cree woman
of the Rolling Head who made love to thousands of snakes and was
beheaded by her husband (the head lives on, however, and roams the
night, lusting after victims).

The Sage, the Dancer and The Fool, performed at the Native Canadian
Centre in February 1989, focuses on a day's experiences of a young
native in downtown Toronto. He is played by three performers sym-
bolizing the mind (the sage), the spirit (the dancer), and physical desires (the fool), each trying to understand the city in his own way.
According to the critic Ray Conlogue, 'the show works. And that,
considering how difficult it is to tell an outsider's story without com-
promising his language, and so resorting to pathos, is a considerable
achievement.'[15]

In *Coyote City* Daniel David Moses has attempted to blend reality
and myth, the lyrical and the colloquial, in combining a story about a
young woman in search of her lover with elements of the Nez Percée
legend of Coyote the trickster who, like Orpheus, descends into the
underworld to retrieve his wife. Lena, living on a reserve north of
Toronto, receives late-night phone calls from Johnny, her dead lover,
begging her to join him at Toronto's Silver Dollar, where he had been
killed in a drunken brawl six months earlier. Accompanied by a minister who is a reformed alcoholic, she leaves for Toronto pursued by
her concerned mother and sister. All the characters—including Clar-
issa, an amusing prostitute—meet in the ghostly bar, which was
swathed in white in the play's first production (May 1988) by Native
Earth Performing Arts, Toronto. The dialogue was weak and sat un-
comfortably with the inexperienced actors. But in spite of the play's
flaws, a certain dramatic force shone through, and the performances,
while wooden, nevertheless achieved many moments that were authentic and convincing.

Moses' sequel to *Coyote City*, *Big Buck City*, was workshopped at
Theatre Passe Muraille the following month.

The Dreaming Beauty—a one-act play by Moses in twelve scenes, published in *Impulse*, vol. 15, no. 3, 1989—is a revision of the Sleeping Beauty fairy tale as a feminist satirical fantasy. After a sleep of almost five hundred years, the dreaming beauty rejects her suitor's kiss and requests her own name. The play can be read to symbolize hope and optimism for Canada's native peoples, expressed in the words of old woman moon: 'Your name is Beauty of our People. Wake up, Beauty of our People. Walk into the world. Wake up young woman. Morning will come to you and everyone.'

Jessica: A Transformation, a two-act play by Linda Griffiths and Maria Campbell, is based on Campbell's *Halfbreed*. The Métis Jessica survives sexual and physical abuse, prostitution, drug addiction, and mental breakdown before she comes to terms with her spirituality and strength as a woman. She is helped on her journey to self-discovery by her spiritual mentor, Vitaline, as well as by the guiding spirits of Bear, Coyote, Crow, Unicorn, and Wolverine, who represent disparate aspects of Jessica and the people in her life. When it was first performed in October 1986—by the Great Canadian Theatre Company at Theatre Passe Muraille, Toronto—its ambitiousness and complexity were recognized, though the movement back and forth between the spiritual and ordinary worlds were hard to follow, and the lessons and discoveries of the stages in Jessica's life did not clearly come across. The play was published in *The Book of Jessica* (1989), two thirds of which is devoted to a series of heated conversations between the co-authors about the ups and downs of their collaboration.

John McLeod's first play, *Diary of a Crazy Boy*—which opened at the Native Canadian Centre on 8 February 1990 and was directed, with many interesting special effects, by Tomson and René Highway—examines the conflict between modern psychiatric and traditional spiritual healing practices. It focuses on an intelligent and sensitive fourteen-year-old Indian boy, Darrel Shallafoe. He is undergoing treatment at a clinic owned by a native psychiatrist, Dr Post, who has given up his roots in order to succeed in the white world and is himself haunted by his neglected family's totemic animal, the lynx. His clinic is having financial problems and its fate somehow hinges on Shallafoe's successful treatment. The troubled teenager, however, relies on the help of his Uncle Bob, the last of a long line of medicine men, and his guardian Ojibway ancestral spirits, who send him an energetic Spirit Boy to guide him.[16] Darrel achieves healing without the help of his doctor, and the viewer is left with the question, 'Who is really crazy?' The play is all the more moving when one considers the statistics of the growing number of Indian patients that are found in Canada's psychiatric hospitals.

John McLeod, part Caughnawaga-Mohawk and part Ojibway, was born in Oakville, Ontario, in 1949 and is a member of the Mississauga Alderville band, though he has never lived on a reserve. He lives in Port Credit and is a visual artist, an oral storyteller, and a writer of short stories. His 'Virgil Executes Big Bertha', 'The Name of the Game', and 'Puttin' on Style' are humorous stories that have a quiet grace, and express an acute and ironical understanding of people, whether Indian or white.

Shadow Warrior is by Sadie Worn Staff (Chirachuo-Apache), who also wrote *The Tribes of Dawn*, a play with an environmental message. *Shadow Warrior* focuses on a young native's struggle with alcohol and cultural awareness. He finally comes to terms with his problems by using his culture's strengths and heritage to fight the shadow that stalks him. The play deals with the shadows of 'shame and pride' within each of us that cause many to seek hiding-places. A former playwright/director with Spirit Song in Vancouver, Sadie Worn Staff is now associated with Sen' Klip in Vernon, B.C.

The Land Called Morning (1986), edited by Caroline Heath, is a collection of three plays that explore the lives of young native people today in the light of traditional native values, Métis history, and the pressures of white society. The title piece, *The Land Called Morning*, written by John Selkirk (Cree) and performed at the 1985 Edmonton Fringe Theatre Event, dramatizes the tensions in the relationships among four young Cree teenagers: one pair, a successful boxer and his dutiful wife, the other, the boxer's introspective sister, who reads Emily Dickinson, and her carefree boyfriend—all of whom are trying to cope with life on the reserve. The sister, who is misunderstood, commits suicide. 'There's more to life than just having fun together. There has to be,' she tells her boyfriend. There is guilt, pain, and anger, but it is too late.

Teach Me the Ways of the Sacred Circle, by Val Dudoward, was performed by Vancouver's Spirit Song Theatre in 1985. In it Matthew Jack, a materialistic, ambitious, urban-oriented, goal-motivated young high-school graduate (the first in his family) is confused because he has not come to grips with his Tsimshian heritage. Through his dream-vision of his grandfather, and the traditional wisdom of his grandmother—who advises 'Don't live in the past, because we cannot do that, we are meant to live life by each moment. But remember your past . . . Fly for yourself'—Matthew is finally able to resolve his predicament. Dudoward explains, in her introduction, that she wrote her play 'with very specific intentions to educate cross-culturally, to entertain with both music and the spoken word, and to connect heritage, youth and the elderly.' The play succeeds well enough, given its carefully specified goals.

Gabrielle, a collective work of the students at Rossignol School in Île-à-la-Crosse, Saskatchewan, was performed in Cree and English in 1985. The play focuses on Gabrielle, a young Métis leader who communicates with the Métis patriot, Louis Riel. Riel teaches the young woman how to establish a local Métis government in order to fight the federal government and an oil development company that threatens to pollute the lakes where her people fish and trap.

All My Relations, by the twenty-four-year-old native playwright Floyd Favel, was premièred at the Catalyst Theatre, Edmonton, on 8 March 1990. It centres on the misfortunes of George, a young Cree who arrives in the big city from the reserve. George frequents the bingo halls, beer parlours, and pawnshops, searching for an appropriate relationship to, and expression of, traditional culture. But every recourse to the old ways makes him an object of laughter to his relatives and friends, who merely find humour in his plight.

In the 1980s a growing number of young natives wrote for radio and television—media whose attractions, considering how the oral arts are at the very core of their culture, are not surprising. For example, Brian Maracle has written for radio, and J. B. Joe, a Nootka from Victoria, B.C., wrote 'Shale', a radio drama based on a Nitinaht legend that was published in *Whetstone* (Spring, 1987). The best-known of these writers is Drew Taylor (b. 1962), an Ojibway from the Curve Lake Reserve, Ontario, who has written for radio, television, film, and the stage. He graduated from Seneca College in Radio and Television Broadcasting and served as playwright in residence (1988-9) for Native Earth Performing Arts, Toronto. Besides his scripts for *Beachcombers* and *Street Legal* for CBC-TV, he has written a number of stage plays that the De-Bah-Jeh-Ma-Jig Theatre group from Manitoulin Island have taken to schools and reserves in Ontario and Quebec. His most successful stage play is *Toronto at Dreamer's Rock*, a fantasy involving three native teenagers from different time periods who meet at Dreamer's Rock, a tourist attraction that was once a sacred site, which native young people used to visit for their vision quests. Taylor's plays are message-centred because he wants to present an accurate portrayal of native people and show their struggle to reconcile their own heritage with the society in which they live. His plays are not overtly didactic, however, because Taylor performs a delicate balancing act between traditional values and new influences. There is also never any anger or bitterness: Taylor writes in a matter-of-fact style, with an ironic wit and quiet grace, and has a special talent for inventing young peoples' dialogue that captures their humour, idioms, and interests. *Toronto at Dreamer's Rock* is being published in 1990 with Taylor's one-act-play *Talking Pictures*, written for young people, about two native teenagers who go in search of magic pictographs.

Children's stories continued to be written in the 1980s. Jeannette Armstrong wrote *Enwhisteetkwa* (1982), in which a young girl named Enwhisteetkwa ('Walk in Water') tells of a romanticized past of plenty, harmony, and spirituality during the course of 'the most exciting year of all [her] life.' In Armstrong's *Neekna and Chemai* (1983), another young girl tells of a similar beautiful world. The dialogue between Neekna and her young friend, however, is stiff.

Bernelda Wheeler—part Cree and Saulteaux, part Scottish and French—was born in the Fort Qu'Appelle Valley, Saskatchewan, in 1937. She has been a journalist and the host, writer, and broadcaster of *Our Native Land* on CBC National Radio. Her three children's books have been well received: *A Friend Called 'Chum'* (1984), illustrated by Andy Stout, *I Can't Have Bannock but the Beaver Has a Dam* (1984), and *Where Did You Get Your Moccasins?* (1986), both illustrated by Herman Bekkering.

In Beatrice Culleton's animal autobiography *Spirit of the White Bison* (1985) the mythological white bison tells, with much historical detail, about the decimination of the buffalo on the Plains.

Murdo's Story: A Legend from Northern Manitoba (1984) by Murdo Scribe (1920-83)—who was born and raised on the reserve at Norway House, Manitoba, an important freighting centre during the York boat era—records stories of summer and winter and how Fisher became the Big Dipper. It is illustrated by Terry Gallagher.

How Food Was Given (1984) and *How Turtle Set the Animals Free* (1984) are picturebook versions of ancient legends told by the Elders of the Okanagan tribe in British Columbia and illustrated by Ken Edwards in a new series published by Theytus Books.

Fifth House published in 1988 two traditional Cree stories for children, translated and edited by Freda Ahenakew, a Cree language teacher who is currently Director of the Saskatchewan Indian Languages Institute in Saskatoon, and illustrated by George Littlechild: *How the Mouse Got Brown Teeth* and *How the Birch Tree Got Its Stripes*. These stories—a few lines of simple text on each page—were first composed by Cree youngsters, and 'the writing has been standardized to represent the sounds of a single variant of Plains Cree'.

In 1989 Pemmican Publications of Winnipeg published *Eagle Feather—An Honour* by Ferguson Plain, an Ojibway from the Sarnia Indian Reserve who also did the illustrations. A young Indian boy tells how his grandfather taught him about traditional customs and values and gave him an Eagle feather. In another Pemmican book,

The Birth of Nanabosho (1988), illustrated by Joe Kirby, Joseph McLellan effectively retells the Nanabosho trickster tale of the Manitoba Ojibway in a contemporary setting.

Native leaders continued to deliver their protest-driven speeches on matters such as their hundreds-of-years-old land claims, and counter-claims, in courts and on the public platform, with the same articulate and forceful style as their predecessors. This extract from testimony given by Chief Gary Potts[17] of the Teme-Augama Anishnabai of northeastern Ontario to the Standing Committee on Resources Development (Second Session, 34th Parliament) on 22 November 1989 deserve attention because of their significant thought and oratorical excellence. Perhaps more than non-natives, Indians have long spoken against pollution and the destruction of the environment, and advocated the conservation of natural resources—for they have always believed in ecological interdependence: in the symbiotic relationship of nature with the rest of creation.

Keep in mind that you are not hearing from the moose that have to live with the results of clear-cutting in our area. Keep in mind that you are not hearing from the dew worms that have to live in land after the forest is cut out. Keep in mind that you are not hearing from loggers 30 years from now who will have no jobs in our area because there is no forest left for them. Keep in mind that you are not hearing from the children who want to live and use our area at least 600 years from now. Keep in mind that you are not hearing from the birds that build nests and live in those forests. Keep in mind that you are not hearing the water speak; the water evaporates after the forest cover is gone; the water-table drops down . . .

The standards that our people have applied to the lands: there is first and foremost the principle of sustained life, and I imagine it has been read to you. I am assuming that it has been read to you. This was something fundamental to our people because our people's natural laws were set out by the four seasons in our area. We did not have a work plan set out that was five days work, two days off. We had the things that were done during certain seasons, and the older people knew what had to be done to make a living, to continue on with life, to ensure continuity of life, and those were done. And that was the way we operated. The life on the land was connected with humans; our humanness was interwoven with that. Each moon was described in a way that heralded some kind of event that was going to take place during that moon. If it is a snow-shoe-break-in moon or the strawberry-picking moon or the fish-spawning moon, these were the ways that our people looked at things.

The patriotism that we feel is hard to put into words, but it is embodied in the stewardship concepts that we have that the main principle of life is that you can use the land in any way you want to use the land, but you cannot use it in a way which prevents future life from using the land as well. That is the responsibility of us as human beings to protect that land for future generations and ourselves because the land is our mother.[18]

Of significance is Tomson Highway's prediction for the nineties: 'I think native people, and particularly native artists, have something to say about what direction we should take to ensure the earth survives for another 2,000 years.'[19]

Conclusion

The literature of Canada's native peoples has always been quintes-sentially political, addressing their persecutions and betrayals and summoning their resources for resistance. The political dimension is an inherent part of their writing because it is an inherent part of their lives. Debasing experiences reflecting the new realities of political and social changes created by changing contact situations—suicide, alcoholism, self-destructive behaviour, poverty, family violence, disintegration of the extended family, and the breach between generations—are real problems in the lives and tragedies of Indians today all across the country. The presentation of these lives in po-etry, short fiction, novel, drama, and memoir constitutes a political comment. Native writers tell what they see, what they have experi-enced or are experiencing. They tell what it is like to live as an Indian in today's society, increasingly caught between tradition and main-stream culture. Already many are able to deal with the culture clash and their own identity not only with perception but with some de-tachment and control, moving beyond the worst excesses of emotion and diction that marred much earlier protest writing.

A resurgence of Indian cultural and religious values has made these writers realize that they are heirs to a wealth of traditional oral literature upon which they can draw for inspiration and direction. Hence themes and predilections associated with pre-contact litera-ture also persist, giving the literature of Canada's native people a his-torical continuity founded on oral sources. Indian writers have learned to draw on their ancient traditions: a biospheric world where humans, plants, animals, rocks, and wind participate in a dynamic cosmic relationship; the significance of ancient ceremonies and rituals; the special role of grandmothers as a source of instruction and healing—the bonding that exists between youth and the elderly; the voice of vision and prophecy; the importance of community life, family closeness, and kinship; the importance of the role of elders as wise counsellors and custodians of cultural and spiritual beliefs and values.

Native writers are also influenced by many of the oral features of their pre-literate culture, even though they are using new literary forms. They tell their stories in a loosely episodic and discursive structure, juxtaposing traditional stories, songs, and fantasy with personal experiences. Although life stories are central, they tend not to be told sequentially. They move backward and forward in time—recounting private history along with communal stories, folklore, the collective advice of generations, and little essays on how to acquire specialized skills like the best beaver-trapping methods—creating a distinctive literary style that weaves story, traditions, beliefs, skills training, and personal experiences into unified works.

Moreover, plot structure as non-natives know it, based on some form of conflict in a rising and falling linear structure, is not compatible to native thought. Native writers also have a predilection for satire and irony, and for humour (an important force in their survival), along with a penchant for didacticism, because any minority literature has a proselytizing bent to it. Until fairly recently they were one-book writers. But all have a deep desire to communicate, to set the record straight in telling non-natives the true details of their past and present. In the course of doing this they have unfolded a moving theme of survival.

The future for young native writers looks bright. Inheritors of a rich history and literature of survival, they will continue to express their own vision, create their own forms, in responding to the fast-changing society they live in. Once the outrage has been exorcised, the self-pity and self-indulgence worked out, and the frictional heat of catharsis has subsided, new subjects and themes will take their place. In drawing upon traditional values to heal their scars, they will become liberated, and the victim syndrome will disappear.

In drama alone the creative energy and imagination of Tomson Highway, Daniel David Moses, and John McLeod—deeply rooted in the real world as well as in a mythological world of dreams and vision that gives easy birth to the surreal—have already produced a new and invigorating literature that is bound to be the harbinger of greater accomplishments, endowing their chosen genre with a whole new range of attributes and qualities.[1]

Canada's native writers have borrowed from Western traditions the forms of autobiography, fiction, drama, and the essay. Their uses, however, judged by Western literary criteria of structure, style, and aesthetics, do not always conform. They are different because form is only the expression of the fabric of experience, and the experience of native writers has been different. Like the archetypal figure, the trickster, native writers easily adopt a multiplicity of styles and forms to suit their purposes, and in so doing they are giving birth to a new literature: a written literature that is finally and gratefully being given to us by the first peoples of our country—enabling us to hear voices most of us have not heard before, bringing to life people, places, experiences, and problems that are uniquely Canadian, yet universal too.[2]

In *The Backwoods of Canada* (1836) Catharine Parr Traill complained that Canada was a 'too matter-of-fact country. . . . Here there are no historical associations, no legendary tales of those that came before us.' This, of course, was not true. Mrs Traill knew nothing about the heroes and spirits and monsters that were part of the imaginative life of the natives who surrounded her. The literature created by Canada's native peoples today echoes with these ghostly, influential, mythological figures, and they are part of our shared heritage. It is time we accepted them, and time too that we accept the literature they have infused, as an integral part of what we call Canadian literature.

Bibliography

ABEL, BEN. *Okanagan Indian Poems and Short Stories*. Cobalt, Ont., Highway Book Shop, 1976.
_____. *Wisdom of Indian Poetry*. Cobalt, Ont., Highway Book Shop, 1976.

Achimoona. Saskatoon, Fifth House, 1985.

ADAMS, HOWARD. *Prison of Grass*. Toronto, New Press, 1975.

AHENAKEW, EDWARD. *Voices of the Plains Cree*. Ed. by Ruth M. Buck. Toronto, McClelland & Stewart, 1973.

AHENAKEW, FREDA. *Stories of the House People*. Winnipeg, University of Manitoba Press, 1980.
_____, ed. *How the Mouse Got Brown Teeth*. Illus. by George Littlechild. Saskatoon, Fifth House, 1988.

ALLEN, PAULA GUNN, ed. *Studies in American Indian Literature*. New York, The Modern Language Association of America, 1983.
_____. *The Sacred Hoop: Recovering the Feminine in American Indian Traditions*. Boston, Beacon Press, 1986.
_____, ed. *Spider Woman's Granddaughters*. Boston, Beacon Press, 1989.

ANAHEREO. *Devil in Deerskins: My Life with Grey Owl*. Toronto, New Press, 1972.

ARMSTRONG, JEANNETTE. *Enwhisteetkwa Walk in Water*. Cloverdale, Man., Friesen Printers, 1982.
_____. *Neekna and Chemai*. Penticton, B.C., Theytus Books, 1984.
_____. *Slash*. Penticton, B.C., Theytus Books, 1985, 1988.

ASSIKINACK, FRANCIS. 'Legends and Traditions of the Odahwah Indians', *Canadian Journal*. New Series, III, 1858, 115-25.
_____. 'Social and Warlike Customs of the Odahwah Indians', *Canadian Journal*. New Series, III, 1858, 297-309.
_____. 'The Odahwah Indian Language', *Canadian Journal*. New Series, 1858, 481-5.

ASTROV, MARGARET, ed. *The Winged Serpent: An Anthology of American Indian Poetry*, 1946; reissued as *American Indian Prose and Poetry*, New York, Capricorn, 1972.

BAKER, MARIE ANNHARTE, *Being on the Moon*. Winlaw, B.C., Polestar Press, 1990.

BARBEAU, MARIUS and GRACE MELVIN. *The Indian Speaks*. Toronto, Macmillan Co. of Canada Ltd., 1943.

BIERHORST, JOHN, ed. *In the Trail of the Wind: American Indian Poems and Ritual Orations*. New York, Farrar, Straus and Giroux, 1976.

BOAS, FRANZ. 'Poetry and Music of Some North American Tribes', *Science*. V. 9, no. 220, April 22, 1887, 383-5.

BOUCHARD, RANDY and DOROTHY KENNEDY, eds. *Shuswap Stories*. Vancouver, Concept Publishing, 1979.

BOULANGER, TOM. *An Indian Remembers: My Life as a Trapper in Northern Manitoba*. Winnipeg, Peguis Publishers, 1971.

BOYLE, DAVID. 'On the Paganism of the Civilized Iroquois of Ontario'. *Annual Archeological Report 1901*. Toronto, 1902, 115-25.

BRANT, BETH, ed. *A Gathering of Spirit: Writing and Art of North American Indian Women*. Toronto, The Women's Press, 1988.
_____. *Mohawk Trail*. Ithaca N.Y., Firebrand Books, 1985.

BRANT-SERO, JOHN OJIJATEKHA. 'The Six Nations Indians in the Province of Ontario'. *Wentworth Historical Society Journal and Transactions*, Vol. 2, 1899, 62-73.
_____. 'Dekanawideh the Law-Giver of the Caniengahakas', *Man*, 1901, 166-70.
_____. 'Indian Rights Association after Government Scalp', *Wilshire's Magazine*, October 1903, 70-5.
_____. 'Views of a Mohawk Indian', *Journal of American Folklore*, 58(1905), 160-162.
_____. 'O-No-Dah', *Journal of American Folklore*, 24 (1911), 251.
_____. 'Some Descendants of Joseph Brant', *Ontario Historical Society Papers and Records*, 1(1989), 113-17.

BRASS, ELEANOR. *Medicine Boy and Other Cree Tales*. Illus. by Henry Nanooch. Calgary, Glenbow-Alberta Institute, 1978.
_____. *I Walk in Two Worlds*. Calgary, Glenbow Museum, 1987.

CAMPBELL, MARIA. *Halfbreed*. Toronto, McClelland & Stewart, 1973.
_____. *People of the Buffalo: How the Plains Indians Lived*. Illus. by Douglas Tait and Shannon Twofeathers. Vancouver, J.J. Douglas, 1976.
_____. *Riel's People: How the Métis Lived*. Illus. by David Maclagan. Vancouver, Douglas & McIntrye, 1978, 1983.
_____. *Little Badger and the Fire Spirit*. Illus. by David Maclagan. Toronto, McClelland & Stewart, 1980.

Canadian Literature, Special Issue, No. 124-125: *Native Writers and Canadian Writing*. Vancouver, University of British Columbia Press, 1990.

CARDINAL, HAROLD. *The Unjust Society: The Tragedy of Canada's Indians*. Edmonton, Hurtig, 1969.
_____. *Rebirth of Canada's Indians*. Edmonton, Hurtig, 1977.

CARPENTER, JOCK. *Fifty Dollar Bride*. Sidney, B.C., Gray's Publishing, 1977.

CHESTER, BRUCE. *Paper Radio: Book of Poetry*. Penticton, B.C., Theytus Books, 1986.

CHAPMAN, ABRAHAM, ed. *Literature of the American Indians: Views and Interpretations*. New York, New American Library, 1975.

CLARKE, PETER DOOYENTATE. *Origin and Traditional History of the Wyandotts, and Sketches of Other Indian Tribes of North America* . . . . Toronto, Hunter, Rose & Co., 1870.

CLUTESI, GEORGE. *Son of Raven, Son of Deer: Fables of the Tse-Shaht People*. Sidney, B.C., Gray's Publishing, 1967, 1975.
————. *Potlatch*. Sidney, B.C., Gray's Publishing, 1969.

COLDEN, CADWALLADER. *The History of the Five Nations of Canada*. London, T. Osborne, 1747. Coles Canadiana Collection, 1972.

COLOMBO, JOHN ROBERT, ed. *Songs of the Indians*. 2 vols. Ottawa, Oberon Press, 1983.

COLTELLI, LAURA, ed. *Native American Literatures*. Pisa, Servizio Editoriale Universitario, 1989.

COPWAY, GEORGE (KAHGEGAGAHBOWH). *The Traditional History and Characteristic Sketches of the Ojibway Nation*. London, Charles Gilpin, 1850.
————. *Organization of a New Indian Territory, East of the Missouri River*. New York, S.W. Benedict, 1850.
————. *The Life, History, and Travels, of Kah-ge-ga-gah-bowh (George Copway), A Young Indian Chief of the Ojibwa Nation, A Convert to the Christian Faith, and a Missionary to his People for Twelve Years*. Philadelphia, 1847. Republished a̓s *Recollections of a Forest Life; or, The Life and Travels of Kah-ge-ga-gah-bowh, or George Copway*. London, Charles Gilpin, 1851.
————. *Running Sketches of Men and Places, in England, France, Germany, Belgium and Scotland*. New York, J.C. Riker, 1851.

CRATE, JOAN. *Breathing Water*. Edmonton, NeWest Publishers, 1989.
————. *Pale as Real Ladies: Poems for Pauline Johnson*. Ilderton, Ont., Brick Books, 1989.

CRONYN, GEORGE W. *American Indian Poetry: An Anthology of Songs and Chants*. New York, Liveright, 1934.

CULLETON, BEATRICE. *In Search of April Raintree*. Winnipeg, Pemmican Publications Inc., 1983.
————. *April Raintree*. Winnipeg, Pemmican, 1984.
————. *Spirit of the White Bison*. Winnipeg, Pemmican, 1985.

CURTIS, NATALIE [Natalie Curtis Burlin], ed. *The Indians' Book: Songs and Legends of the American Indians*. Reprint of 1923 ed., New York, Dover, 1968.

CUTHAND, BETH. *Horse Dance to Emerald Mountain*. Vancouver, Lazara Publications, 1987.
————. *Voices in the Waterfall*. Vancouver, Lazara Press, 1989.

DAVIDSON, FLORENCE ADENSHAW and MARGARET B. BLACKMAN. *During My Time*. Washington, University of Washington Press, 1982.

DAY, A. GOVE, ed. *The Sky Clears: Poetry of the American Indians*. Reprint of 1951 ed., Lincoln, University of Nebraska Press, 1964.

DAY, DAVID and MARILYN BOWERING, eds. *Many Voices: An Anthology of Contemporary Canadian Indian Poetry*. Vancouver, J.J. Douglas, 1977.

DENSMORE, FRANCES. *Chippewa Music*. Minneapolis, Ross & Haines Inc., 1973.

Deskaheh: Iroquois Statesman and Patriot. Six Nations Indian Museum Series, Rooseveltown, N.Y., *Akwesasne Notes*, no year.

DICK, LEONARD G. *Broken Spirit*. Cobalt, Ont., Highway Book Shop, 1978.

DION, JOSEPH F. *My Tribe the Crees*. Calgary, Glenbow, 1979.

DUNN, MARTY. *Red on White: The Biography of Duke Redbird*. Toronto, New Press, 1971.

ERASMUS, PETER. *Buffalo Days and Nights*, as told to Henry Thompson. Calgary, Glenbow-Alberta Institute, 1976.

FINNEGAN, RUTH. *Oral Poetry: Its Nature, Significance, and Social Context*. Cambridge, Cambridge University Press, 1977.

FITZGERALD, JUDITH, ed. *First Person Plural*. Windsor, Black Moss Press, 1988.

FREEMANTLE, ANN. *The Papal Encyclicals in their Historical Context*. New York, The New American Library, 1963.

GEORGE, CHIEF DAN. *My Heart Soars*. Drawings by Helmut Hirnschall. Saanichton, B.C., Hancock House, 1974.

GOODERHAM, KENT, ed. *I Am an Indian*. Toronto, J.M. Dent & Sons, 1969.
————, ed. *Notice, This is an Indian Reserve*. Toronto, Griffin House, 1972.

GRANT, AGNES. *Monogaphs in Education XV: Native Literature in the Curriculum*. Winnipeg, University of Manitoba, 1986.

GREENE, ALMA. *Forbidden Voice: Reflections of a Mohawk Indian*. Don Mills, Ont., Hamlyn, 1971.
————. *Tales of the Mohawks*. Toronto, J.M. Dent & Sons, 1975.

GIFFITHS, LINDA and MARIA CAMPBELL. *The Book of Jessica: A Theatrical Transformation*. Toronto, The Coach House Press, 1989.

GRISDALE, ALEX. *Wild Drums: Tales and Legends of the Plains Indians*. Winnipeg, Peguis Publishers, 1972.

GROS-LOUIS, MAX in collaboration with Marcel Bellier. *First Among the Hurons*. Montreal, Harvest House, 1973.

HALE, HORATIO. *The Iroquois Book of Rites*, Vol. 2. Philadelphia, D.G. Brinton, 1883. Reissued New York, AMS Press, 1969.
_____. 'An Iroquois Condoling Council', *Proceedings and Transactions of the Royal Society of Canada*. Second Series—vol. 1, 1895, 45-65.

HARRIS, KENNETH B. in collaboration with Frances M.P. Robinson. *Visitors Who Never Left: The Origin of the People of Damelahamid*. Vancouver, University of British Columbia Press, 1974.

HENRY, ALEXANDER. *Travels and Adventures in Canada and the Indian Territories Between the Years 1760 and 1776*. Ed. by James Bain. Edmonton, Hurtig Publishers, 1969.

HENRY, GEORGE [MAUNGWUDAUS]. *Remarks Concerning the Ojibway Indians, by One of Themselves Called Maungwudaus, Who Has Been Travelling in England, France, Belgium, Ireland, and Scotland*. Leeds, England, C.A. Wilson, 1847.
_____. *An Account of the Chippewa Indians, Who Have Been Travelling in the United States, England, Ireland, Scotland, France and Belgium; with Very Interesting Incidents in Relation to the General Characteristics of the English, Irish, Scotch, French, and Americans, with Regard to Their Hospitality, Peculiarities, etc.* Published by the author, Boston, 1848.
_____. *An Account of the North American Indians, Written for Maungwudaus, a Chief of the Ojibway Indians Who Has Been Travelling in England, France, Belgium, Ireland, and Scotland*. Leicester, England, T. Cook, 1848.

HIGHWAY, TOMSON. *The Rez Sisters*. Saskatoon, Fifth House, 1988.
_____. *Dry Lips Oughta Move to Kapuskasing*. Saskatoon, Fifth House, 1989.

HUNGRY WOLF, BEVERLY. *The Ways of My Grandmothers*. New York, William Morrow, 1980.

JACKSON, LOUIS. *Our Caughnawagas in Egypt*. Montreal, Drysdale, 1885.

JACOBS, PETER. *Journal of the Reverend Peter Jacobs, Indian Wesleyan Missionary, from Rice Lake to the Hudson's Bay Territory, and Returning, Commencing May 1852, With a Brief Account of his Life, and a Short History of the Wesleyan Mission in that Country*. Published by the author, New York, 1858.

JENNESS, DIAMOND. *The Corn Goddess and Other Tales from Indian Canada*. Bulletin No. 141, Anthropological Series, no. 39, National Parks Branch, 1956.
_____. *The Indians of Canada*. 6th ed. Ottawa, Queen's Printer, 1967.
_____. *The Sekani Indians of British Columbia*. Ottawa, National Museum of Canada Bulletin, no. 84, Anthropological Series, no. 20, 1977.

JOE, RITA. *Poems of Rita Joe*. Halifax, Abanaki Press, 1978.
_____. *Song of Eskasoni: More Poems of Rita Joe*. Charlottetown, Ragweed Press, 1988.

JOHANSON, JIM. *Indian Preacher: The Life and Teachings of Rev. Allen Salt, 1818-1911*. Forest, Ont., Pole Printing, 1985.

JOHNSTON, BASIL H. *Ojibway Heritage*. Toronto, McClelland & Stewart, 1976.
_____. *How the Birds Got Their Colours*. Toronto, Kids Can Press, 1978.
_____. *Moose Meat and Wild Rice*. Toronto, McClelland & Stewart, 1978.
_____. *Ojibway Language Course Outlines*. Ottawa, Department of Indian and Northern Affairs, 1978.
_____. *Ojibway Language Lexicon for Beginners*. Ottawa, Department of Indian and Northern Affairs, 1978.
_____. *Tales the Elders Told: Ojibway Legends*. Toronto, Royal Ontario Museum, 1981.
_____. *Ojibway Ceremonies*. Toronto, McClelland & Stewart, 1982.
_____. *Indian School Days*. Toronto, Key Porter Books, 1988.

JOHNSON, E. PAULINE. *The White Wampum*. London, Bodley Head, 1895.
_____. *Canadian Born*. Toronto, George N. Morang & Co., 1903.
_____. *Legends of Vancouver*. Toronto, McClelland & Stewart, 1911; reissued 1961.
_____. *The Moccasin Maker*. Toronto, William Briggs, 1913.
_____. *The Shagganappi*. Toronto, Ryerson Press, 1913.
_____. *Flint and Feather*. Toronto, Musson, 1913; Don Mills, Ont., General Publishing, 1971.

JOHNSTON, C.M., ed. *The Valley of the Six Nations: A Collection of Documents on the Indian Lands of the Grand River*. Toronto, Champlain Society, 1964.

JOHNSTON, PATRONELLA. *Tales of Nokomis*. Toronto, Musson, 1970.

JONES, CHIEF CHARLES with STEPHEN BOSUSTOW. *Queesto, Pacheenaht Chief by Birthright*. Penticton, B.C., Theytus Books, 1981.

JONES, PETER [KAHKEWAQUONABY]. *Life and Journals of Kah-ke-wa-quo-na-by (Rev. Peter Jones), Wesleyan Missionary*. Published under the direction of the Missionary Committee, Canada Conference. Toronto, by Anson Green at the Wesleyan Printing Establishment, 1860.
_____. *History of the Ojebway Indians: With Especial Reference to Their Conversion to Christianity*. London, A.W. Bennett, 1861; reprinted Freeport, New York, Books for Libraries, 1970.

JOSIE, EDITH. *Here Are the News*. Toronto, Clarke, Irwin, 1966.

KELLER, BETTY. *Pauline: A Biography of Pauline Johnson*. Vancouver, Douglas & McIntyre, 1981.

KENNEDY, DAN [OCHANKUGAHE]. *Recollections of an Assiniboine Chief*. Toronto, McClelland and Stewart, 1972.

KENNY, GEORGE. *Indians Don't Cry*. Toronto, Chimo Publishing, 1977.
_____. *October Stranger*. Toronto, Chimo Publishing, 1978.

KEON, WAYNE. *Sweetgrass: An Anthology of Indian Poetry*. Elliott Lake, Ont., W.O.K. Books, 1972.

_____ and ORVILLE. *Thunderbirds of the Ottawa*. Cobalt, Highway Book Shop, 1977.

KING, THOMAS. 'The Dog I Wish I Had, I Would Call It Helen', *Malahat Review*, Winter 1989.

————. 'One Good Story, That One', *Malahat Review*, Spring 1988.

————, ed. *All My Relations: An Anthology of Contemporary Canadian Native Writing*. Toronto, McLelland & Stewart, 1990

————. *Medicine River*. Toronto, Penguin, 1990.

————, CHERYL CALVER, and HELEN HOY. *The Native in Literature*. Winnipeg, Hignell Printing Ltd, 1987.

KIRKNESS, VERNA. *Indians of the Plains*. Toronto, Grolier, 1984.

KROEBER, KARL, ed. *Traditional Literatures of the American Indian*. Lincoln, University of Nebraska Press, 1981.

The Land Called Morning. Saskatoon, Fifth House, 1986.

LAROQUE, EMMA. *Defeathering the Indian*. Agincourt, Ont., Book Society of Canada Ltd., 1975.

LE CLERCQ, CHRESTIEN. *New Relation of Gaspésia*. Translated and edited by William F. Ganong. The Champlain Society, 1910.

LEE, BOBBI. *Bobbi Lee: Indian Rebel*. Recorded and edited by Don Barnett and Rick Sterling. Richmond, B.C., LSM Information Center, 1975.

LONG, J. *Voyages and Travels of an Indian Interpreter and Trader, 1791*. Coles Canadiana Collection, 1974.

McCLELLAN, CATHARINE. *The Girl Who Married the Bear*. Ottawa, National Museum of Canada Publications in Ethnology No. 2, 1970.

McCUE, HARVEY ed. *The Only Good Indian*. Toronto, New Press, 1970.

MacEWAN, J.B. GRANT. *Portrait from the Plains*. Toronto, McGraw-Hill Ryerson, 1971.

McILWRAITH, T.F. *The Bella Coola Indians*. Toronto, University of Toronto Press, 2 vols, 1948.

MacLEAN, JOHN. *Canadian Savage Folk: The Native Tribes of Canada, 1896*. Coles Canadiana Collection, 1971.

MacLEOD, MARGARET ANNETT. *Songs of Old Manitoba*. Toronto, Ryerson, 1960.

McLELLAN, JOSEPH. *The Birth of Nanabosho*. Winnipeg, Pemmican, 1987.

The Magazine to Re-Establish the Trickster: New Native Writing. Fall, 1988, vol. 1, no. 1; Spring, 1989, vol. 1, no. 2.

MANUEL, GEORGE and MICHAEL POSLUNS. *The Fourth World: An Indian Reality*. Toronto, Collier Macmillan, 1974.

MARACLE, LEE. *I am Woman*. Vancouver, Write-on Press Publishers, 1988.

————. *Seeds*. Vancouver, Write-on Press Publishers, 1990.

————. *Sojourners and Other Stories*. Vancouver, Press Gang, 1990.

————. DAPHNE MARLATT, BETSY WARLAND and SKY LEE. *Telling It: Building Language Across Cultures*. Vancouver, Press Gang, 1990.

MARCHESSAULT, JOVETTE. *Like a Child of the Earth*. Translated by Yvonne M. Klein. Vancouver, Talonbooks, 1988.
————. *Mother of the Grass*. Tr. Y.M. Klein. Vancouver, Talonbooks, 1989.

MAUD, RALPH. *A Guide to B.C. Indian Myth and Legend*. Vancouver, Talonbooks, 1982.

MECHLING, WILLIAM HUBBS. *Malecite Tales*. Ottawa, Government Printing Office (Canada Department of Mines, Geological Survey, Memoir 49; Anthropology Series, no. 4), 1914.

MELANÇON, CLAUDE. *Indian Legends of Canada*. Toronto, Gage, 1974.

MONTOUR, ENOS T. *The Feathered U.E.L.s.* Toronto, Division of Communication, United Church of Canada, 1973.

MOORE, KERMOT A. *Kipawa: Portrait of a People*. Cobalt, Ont., Highway Book Shop, 1982.
————. *The Will to Survive: Native People and the Constitution*. Val d'Or, P.Q., Hyberborea Publishings, 1984.

MORRIS, THE HON. ALEXANDER. *The Treaties of Canada with the Indians of Manitoba and North-West Territories*. Toronto, Belfords, Clarke & Co., 1880.

MORRISEAU, NORVAL and SELWYN DEWDNEY. *Legends of My People, The Great Ojibway*. Toronto, McGraw-Hill Ryerson, 1977.

MOSES, DANIEL DAVID. *Delicate Bodies*. Vancouver, Blewointment Press, 1978.
————. 'The Dreaming Beauty', *Impulse*. Vol. 15, no. 3, 1989, 13-41.
————. *Coyote City*. Stratford, Williams-Wallace Publishers, 1990.

MOUNTAIN HORSE, MIKE. *My People the Bloods*. Calgary, Glenbow-Alberta Institute, 1979.

Native Sons by Ken George Batisse, Richard Bedwash, Ronald Cooper, Pat Jocko, Tona Mason, Roy Nobis Jr, Tom Shearer, Freddy Taylor. Cobalt, Ont., Highway Book Shop, 1977.

NIATUM, DUANE, ed. *Harper's Anthology of Twentieth Century Native American Poetry*. 1988.

NORMAN, HOWARD, ed. *Where the Chill Came From: Cree Windigo Tales and Journeys*. San Francisco, North Point Press, 1982.
————. *The Wishing Bone Cycle: Narrative Poems from the Swampy Cree Indians*. Santa Barbara, Ross-Erikson, 1982.

NOWELL, CHARLES JAMES. *Smoke from Their Fires: The Life of a Kwakiutl Chief*. Hamden, Conn., Anchor Books, 1941; reissued 1968.

ORONHYATEKHA. 'The Mohawk Language', *The Canadian Journal*. New Series, no. XC, April, 1876, 1-2.

_____. *History of the Independent Order of Foresters*. Toronto, Hunter Rose & Co., 1894.

OSBORNE, RALPH, ed. *Who Is the Chairman of This Meeting?* Toronto, Neewin, 1972.

OVERHOLT, THOMAS W. and J. BAIRD CALLICOTT. *Clothed-In-Fur and Other Tales*. New York, University Press of America, 1982.

PELLETIER, WILFRED. *Two Articles*. Toronto, Neewin, 1969.

PELLETIER, WILFRED and D.G. POOLE. *For Every North American Indian Who Begins to Disappear, I also Begin to Disappear; Being a Collection of Essays Concerned with the Quality of Human Relations between the Red and White Peoples of This Continent*. Toronto, Neewin, 1971.

_____ and TED POOLE. *No Foreign Land*. New York, Pantheon, 1973.

PENNIER, HENRY. *Chiefly Indian*. Vancouver, Graydonald Graphics, 1972.

PERREAULT, JEANNE and SYLVIA VANCE. *Writing the Circle: Western Canadian Native Women—An Anthology*. Edmonton, NeWest Publishing, 1990.

PETTIPAS, KATHERINE. *The Diary of the Reverend Henry Budd, 1870-1875*. Winnipeg, Hignell Printing Ltd., 1974.

PETRONE, PENNY, ed. *First People, First Voices*. Toronto, University of Toronto Press, 1983.

The Queen v. Louis Riel. With an Introduction by Desmond Morton. Toronto, University of Toronto Press, 1974.

RADIN, PAUL. *The Trickster: A Study in American Indian Mythology*. New York, Schocken Books, 1973.

RAND, SILAS TERTIUS. *A Short Statement of Facts Relating to the History, Manners, Customs, Language and Literature of the Micmac Tribe of Indians in Nova Scotia and P.E.Island*. Halifax, James Bowes & Son, 1850.
_____. *Legends of the Micmacs*. New York, Longmans, Green and Co., 1894. Reprint, New York, Johnson, 1971.

REDBIRD, DUKE. *We are Métis: A Métis View of the Development of a Native Canadian People*. OMNSIA, 1980.
_____. *Loveshine and Red Wine*. Cutler, Ont., Woodland Studios Publishing, 1981.

REDSKY, JAMES. *Great Leader of the Ojibway: Mis-quona-queb*. Toronto, McClelland & Stewart, 1972.

RICHARDSON, MAJOR JOHN. *War of 1812*. Brockville, Ont., 1842.

ROBINSON, HARRY. *Write It on Your Heart: The Epic World of an Okanagan Storyteller*. Compiled and edited by Wendy Wickwire. Vancouver, Talon Books, 1989.

ROBINSON, WILL. *Men of Medeek.* As told by Walter Wright. Kitimat, B.C., Centennial Museum, 1962.

RUOFF, A. LAVONNE BROWN. 'American Indian Literatures: Introduction and Bibliography', *American Studies International.* October 1986, vol. XXIV, no. 2, 2-52.

SALT, ALLAN. 'A Mississaga Legend of Naniboju', *Journal of American Folk-lore.* V (1892), 291-2.

SANDERS, THOMAS E. and WALTER E. PEEK, eds. *Literature of the American Indian.* Beverly Hills, Benziger, Bruce & Glencoe Inc., 1973.

SCHOOLCRAFT, HENRY ROWE. *Algic Researches: Comprising Inquiries Respecting the Mental Characteristics of the North American Indians.* New York, Harper & Bros., 1839.

_____. *Personal Memoirs of a Residence of Thirty Years on the American Frontiers: With Brief Notices of Passing Events, Facts, and Opinions, A.D. 1812 to A.D. 1842.* Philadelphia, Lippincott, Grambo & Co., 1851.

_____. *Information respecting the History condition and Prospects of the Indian Tribes of the United States.* Philadelphia, J.B. Lippincott, Co., 1855, v. 5.

Schoolcraft: The Literary Voyager or Muzzeniegun. Edited with an introduction by Philip P. Mason. Michigan State University Press, 1962.

SCRIBE, MURDO. *Murdo's Story: A Legend from Northern Manitoba.* Winnipeg, Pemmican, 1985.

SEALEY, D. BRUCE, ed. *The Métis: Canada's Forgotten People.* Winnipeg, Manitoba Métis Federation Press, 1975.

SEALEY, D. BRUCE and VERNA KIRKNESS, eds. *Indians with Tipis.* Agincourt, The Book Society of Canada, 1973.

SEWID, JAMES. *Guests Never Leave Hungry: The Autobiography of a Kwakiutl Indian.* Montreal, McGill University Press, 1972.

SIDNEY, MRS. ANGELA. *Tagish Tlaagu (Tagish Stories).* Recorded by Julie Cruikshank. Whitehorse, Council for Yukon Indians and the Government of Yukon, 1982.

SILMAN, JANET, ed. *Enough Is Enough: Aboriginal Women Speak Out.* Toronto, The Women's Press, 1988.

SLIPPERJACK, RUBY. *Honour the Sun.* Winnipeg, Pemmican Publications, 1987.

SLUMAN, NORMA and JEAN GOODWILL. *John Tootoosis: Biography of a Cree Leader.* Ottawa, Golden Dog Press, 1982.

SMALL, LILLIAN, compiler. *Indian Stories from James Bay.* Cobalt, Ont., Highway Book Shop, 1972.

SMITH, DONALD. 'The Life of George Copway or Kah-ge-ga-gah-bowh

(1818-1869)—and a Review of His Writings'. *Journal of Canadian Studies/Revue d'études Canadiennes*, vol. 23, no. 3. (Autumn 1988), 5-38,
————. *Sacred Feathers: The Reverend Peter Jones (Kahkewaquonoby) and the Mississauga Indians.* Toronto, University of Toronto Press, 1987.

SNOW, CHIEF JOHN. *These Mountains Are Our Sacred Places: The Story of the Stoney People.* Toronto, Samuel Stevens, 1977.

SPEARE, JEAN. *The Days of Augusta.* Vancouver, J.J. Douglas, 1973.

SPECK, FRANK G. *Naskapi: The Savage Hunters of the Labrador Peninsula.* Norman, University of Oklahoma Press, 1935.

STAMP, SARAIN. *There Is My People Sleeping.* Sidney, B.C., Gray's Publishing, 1970.

STANLEY, GEORGE F. *The Collected Works of Louis Riel/Les Écrits Complets de Louis Riel.* Edmonton, University of Alberta Press, 5 vols, 1985.

STEPHENSON, MRS. FREDERICK C. *One Hundred Years of Canadian Methodist Missions, 1824-1904.* Toronto, The Missionary Society of the Methodist Church, 1925.

STEVENS, JAMES, ed. *Sacred Legends of the Sandy Lake Cree.* Toronto, McClelland & Stewart, 1971.
————, ed. *Legends from the Forest.* Moonbeam, Ont., Penumbra Press, 1985.

STREET, ELSIE, recorder. *Sepass Tales: The Songs of Y-Ail-Milith.* Chilliwack, B.C., Sepass Trust, 1963, 1974.

SWANN, BRIAN. *Smoothing the Ground: Essays on Native American Oral Literature.* Berkeley, University of California Press, 1983.

SWANN, BRIAN and ARNOLD KRUPAT. *Recovering the Word: Essays on Native American Literature.* Berkeley, University of California Press, 1987.
————. *I Tell You Now, Autobiographical Essays by Native American Writers.* Lincoln, University of Nebraska Press, 1987.

TETSO, JOHN. *Trapping is My Life.* Toronto, Peter Martin, 1970.

THATCHER, B.B. *Indian Biography; or An Historical Account of Those Individuals Who Have Been Distinguished Among the North American Natives As Orators, Warriors, Statesmen, and Other Remarkable Characters.* 2 vols, New York, J. & J. Harper, 1832.

THOMPSON, CHIEF ALBERT EDWARD. *Chief Peguis and his Descendants.* Winnipeg, Peguis Publishers, 1973.

THWAITES, REUBEN GOLD, ed. *The Jesuit Relations and Allied Documents.* Cleveland, Burrows Brothers (Volumes V, VI, XLI), issued between 1896 and 1901.

TOYE, WILLIAM, ed. *The Oxford Companion to Canadian Literature.* Toronto, Oxford University Press, 1983.

TURNER, PETER JOHN. *The North-West Mounted Police, 1873-1893*. Ottawa, King's Printer, 1950.

TYMAN, JAMES. *Inside Out: The Autobiography of a Native Canadian*. Saskatoon, Fifth House, 1989.

VELIE, ALAN R., ed. *American Indian Literature*. Norman, University of Oklahoma Press, 1982.

Victoria Daily Colonist, 1 April 1896.

WATETCH, ABEL. *Payepot and His People*. Saskatchewan, History and Folklore Society, 1959.

WALLAS, CHIEF JAMES. *Kwakiutl Legends*. As told to Pamela Whitaker. Vancouver, Hancock House, 1981.

WAUBAGESHIG, ed. *The Only Good Indian: Essays by Canadian Indians*. Toronto, New Press, 1970.

We-gyet Wanders on: Legends of the Northwest. Saanichton, B.C., Hancock House, 1977.

Wesleyan Missionary Notices Relating Principally to the Foreign Mission. New Series, vol. IV. For the year 1846. London, Wesleyan Mission House, 1847.

WHEELER, BERNELDA. *A Friend Called 'Chum'*. Illus. by Andy Stout. Winnipeg, Pemmican, 1984.
————. *I Can't Have Bannock But the Beaver Has a Dam*. Illus. by Herman Bekkering. Winnipeg, Pemmican, 1984.
————. *Where Did You Get Your Moccasins?* Illus. by Herman Bekkering. Winnipeg, Pemmican, 1986, 1988.

WHEELER, JORDAN. *Brothers in Arms*. Winnipeg, Pemmican Publications Inc., 1989.

Whetstone. Spring, 1985, *Native Issue*.
————. Spring, 1987, *Native Issue*.
————. Fall 1988, *Native Issue*.

WIGET, ANDREW. *Critical Essays on Native American Literature*. Boston, G.K. Hall & Co., 1985.

WHITE, ELLEN. *Kwulasulwut: Stories from the Coast Salish*. Penticton, B.C., Theytus Books, 1981.

WILLIS, JANE. *Geniesh: An Indian Girlhood*. Toronto, New Press, 1973.

WOLFE, ALEXANDER. *Earth Elder Stories*. Saskatoon, Fifth House, 1988, 1989.

WUTTUNEE, WILLIAM. *Ruffled Feathers: Indians in Canadian Society*. Calgary, Bell Books, 1971.

ZOLLA, ELÉMIRE. *The Writer and the Shaman: A Morphology of the American Indian*. New York, Harcourt Brace Jovanovich, Inc., 1973.

Notes

INTRODUCTION

[1]Anne Freemantle, *The Papal Encyclicals in Their Historical Context* (New York: New American Library, 1963), 80-1.

[2]Diamond Jenness, *Indians of Canada* (Ottawa: Queen's Printer, 1967), 264.

[3]Hartmut Lutz, 'The Circle as Philosophical and Structural Concept in Native American Fiction To-Day' *Native American Literatures* (Pisa: SEU 1909), 90.

[4]Karl Kroeber, ed., *Traditional Literatures of the American Indian* (Lincoln: University of Nebraska Press, 1981), 2, 3. *Recovering the Word: Essays on Native American Literature* (Berkeley: University of California Press, 1987), edited by Brian Swann and Arnold Krupat, contains the most recent scholarly work on Indian oral narratives. It advocates an interdisciplinary approach incorporating anthropology, ethnology, folklore, linguistics, and literature, each enriching the others.

[5]George Cornell, 'The Imposition of Western Definitions of Literature on Indian Oral Traditions', Thomas King, Cheryl Calver, and Helen Hoy, eds, *The Native in Literature* (Winnipeg: Hignell Printing Ltd, 1987), 178.

[6]Paula Gunn Allen, *Spider Woman's Granddaughters* (Boston: Beacon Press, 1989), 4.

[7]Jeffrey F. Huntsman, 'Traditional Native American Literature: The Translation Dilemma', quoted in Brian Swann, *Smoothing the Ground: Essays on Native American Oral Literature* (Berkeley: University of California Press, 1983), 90.

[8]Chrestien Le Clercq, *New Relation of Gaspesia*, ed. William Ganong (Toronto: The Champlain Society, 1910), 241-2.

CHAPTER I: ORAL LITERATURES

[1]George Copway, *The Traditional History and Characteristic Sketches of the Ojibway Nation* (London: Charles Gilpin, 1850), 124.

[2]Margaret Astrov, *American Indian Prose and Poetry* (New York: The John Day Company, 1972), 19.

[3]George Copway, *The Traditional History and Characteristic Sketches of the Ojibway Nation* (London: Charles Gilpin, 1850), 95-7.

[4]Silas Tertius Rand, *A Short Statement of Facts Relating to the History, Manners, Customs, Language and Literature of the Micmac Tribe of Indians in Nova Scotia and P.E.Island* (Halifax: James Bowes & Son, 1850), 29.

[5]*Ibid.*, 18.

[6]Paula Gunn Allen, *Spider Woman's Granddaughters* (Boston: Beacon Press, 1989), 5.

[7]Alexander Wolfe, *Earth Elder Stories* (Saskatoon: Fifth House, 1989), IX.

[8]Catharine McClellan, *The Girl Who Married the Bear* (Ottawa: National Museums of Canada, 1970), 34-5.

[9]*Ibid.*, 46-7.

[10]In Nancy Wigston, 'Nanabush in the City', *Books in Canada* (March 1989), 8.

[11]Daniel David Moses, 'The Trickster Theatre of Tomson Highway, *Canadian Fiction Magazine* (No. 60, 1987), 88.

[12]Barbara Babcock, 'A Tolerated Margin of Mess: The Trickster and His Tales Reconsidered' in Andrew Wiget, *Critical Essays on Native American Literature* (Boston: G.K. Hall & Co., 1985), 154.

[13]*Ibid.*

[14]Chief Kenneth B. Harris, *Visitors Who Never Left* (Vancouver: University of British Columbia Press, 1974), xv.

[15]Henry Rowe Schoolcraft, *Personal Memoirs of a Residence of Thirty Years on the American Frontiers: With Brief Notices of Passing Events, Facts, and Opinions, A.D. 1812 to A.D. 1842* (Philadelphia, Lippincott, Grambo & Co., 1851), 109.

[16]*Ibid.*

[17]Reuben Gold Thwaites, ed., *The Jesuit Relations and Allied Documents . . . 1610-1791* (Cleveland, 1896-1901), Volume VI, 185.

[18]A. Grove Day, *The Sky Clears* (Lincoln: University of Nebraska Press, 1964), 6.

[19]Edward S. Curtis, *The North American Indian* (1916; New York: Johnson Reprint Corporation, 1970), XI, 23.

[20]Chief James Wallas, *Kwakiutl Legends* (Vancouver: Hancock House, 1981), 116.

[21]Frances Densmore, *Chippewa Music* (Minneapolis: Ross & Haines Inc., 1973), 73.

[22]Diamond Jenness, *The Sekani Indians of British Columbia* (Ottawa: National Museum of Canada. Bulletin No. 84, Anthropological Series No. 20, 1937), 77.

[23]David Boyle, 'On the Paganism of the Civilized Iroquois of Ontario', *Annual Archeological Report*, Toronto, 1901, 122.

[24]*Ibid.*

[25]Natalie Curtis, *The Indians' Book* (New York: Dover, 1968), xxvi.

[26]*Ibid.*, xxvii.

[27]*Ibid.*

[28]Frances Densmore, *Chippewa Music*, 150, 151.

[29]Henry Rowe Schoolcraft, *Information Respecting the History, Condition and Prospects of the Indian Tribes of the United States* (Philadelphia: J.B. Lippincott & Co., 1855, v. 5), 559.

[30]Franz Boas, 'Stylistic Aspects of Primitive Literature', *Journal of American Folklore* (XXXVIII, no. 149, July-September, 1925), 331.

[31]George W. Cronyn, *American Indian Poetry* (New York: Liveright, 1962), 7.

[32]Franz Boas, 'Poetry and Music of some North American Tribes', *Science*, IX (1887), 385.

[33]*The Songs of Y-Ail-Mihth*, typescript copy in Queen's University Archives, Glossary, 10.

[34]*Ibid.*, Glossary, 1.

[35]*Ibid.*, Glossary, 1.

[36]*Ibid.*, Glossary, 2.

[37]Horatio Hale, ed., *The Iroquois Book of Rites*, 1883. Reprinted AMS ed. (New York, 1969), 150. It is interesting to note that during the colonial period the rites were considered useful for the 'new and unexpected' ethnological information they contained regarding the Iroquois: 'the love of peace, the sentiment of human brotherhood, the strong social and domestic affections, the respect for law and the reverence for ancestral greatness.'

[38]*Jesuit Relations*, V, 195

[39]George Copway, *The Traditional History and Characteristic Sketches of the Ojibway Nation* (London, 1850; Toronto: Coles Canadiana, 1972), 127.

[40]*Jesuit Relations*, V, 205.

[41]Cadwallader Colden, *The History of the Five Nations of Canada* (London, 1747; Coles Canadiana Collection, 1972), 14.

[42]*Ibid.*

[43]Noted in Roy F. Fleming, 'Indian Chief Set Record for Long Speech', unidentified clipping dated March 1955: Little Current—Nowland Centennial Museum.

[44]Chrestien Le Clercq, *New Relation of Gaspesia*, ed. William Ganong (Toronto: The Champlain Society, 1910), 241-2.

[45]Alexander Henry, *Travels and Adventures in Canada and the Indian Territories, Between the Years 1760 and 1776* (New York, 1809). Edited by James Bain (Edmonton: Hurtig, 1969), 75-6.

[46]*Jesuit Relations*, XLI, 87-9.

[47]B.B. Thatcher, *Indian Biography* (New York: J. & J. Harper and Brothers, 1832), II, 42-4.

[48]Alexander Henry, *Travels and Adventures*, 43-5.

[49]B.B. Thatcher, *Indian Biography*, II, 117-18.

[50]Major John Richardson, *War of 1812* (Brockville: Canada West, 1842), 119-20.

CHAPTER II: 1820-1850

[1]Peter Jones, *History of the Ojebway Indians* (Freeport, 1861, Report 1970), 29.

[2]*Ibid.*, 221-2.

[3]From the 'Letters to Miss Field', Peter Jones Collection, Victoria University Library, University of Toronto.

[4]'Kahkewaquonaby, The Red Indian Chief and Missionary', *The Ladies' Own Journal and Miscellany* for 2 August 1845, n.p.

[5]'Sketch of the Life of Peter Jones', *Buffalo Christian Advocate*, 10 July 1856.

[6]'Kahkewaquonaby, the North American Indian Missionary', *The Witness* (Edinburgh, 26 July 1845).

[7]John MacLean, *Canadian Savage Folk* (1896), 412-13.

[8]Quoted in Sunday's Obituary in the Missionary Notices of the Methodist Church of Canada, 3rd Series, no. 7 (April 1876), 108.

[9]*The Wesleyan Missionary Notices Relating Principally to the Foreign Missions.* New Series, vol. IV. For the year 1846. (London: Wesleyan Mission House, 1847), 7.

[10]From a handwritten sheet in the John Sunday File (Biography File Collection, United Church Archives, Toronto).

[11]In 1851 Copway published an epic poem *The Ojibway Conquest*, but it was not his work. In his Preface to *The Ojibue Conquest: An Indian Episode* (1898), Julius Taylor Clark (1814-1908) explained that he had written the poem about 1845 and had allowed Copway to publish it under his name so that Copway could raise funds to help him 'in his work among his people'. However, the following poem addressed to his wife, which appeared along with the epic, was Copway's work:

TO ELIZA
I have no words to tell the loveliness
Which breathes o'er thy fair form; then how much less
The bright, the pure, the beautiful, the blest,
Which wake their harmony within thy breast.
When after weary wanderings by wood,
And lake, and stream, and mountain wilds, I stood
Upon thy island home, thy guileless heart
A healing welcome gave. When forced to part,
And the frail bark, that o'er the waters bore
Me on my way at last from thy loved shore,
Receded in the distance from thy view,
Thy lovely hand waved a most sweet adieu.
Fair daughter! accept this tribute of a breast,
Rich in thy smiles, hath been so richly blest.

[12]George Copway, *Recollections of a Forest Life* (London, 1851, Canadiana House, 1970), 247. This mixture of styles has been noted by other critics: George Harvey Genzmer, for instance, described it as 'an amalgam of Washington Irving, St Luke, and elements derived from Methodist exhorters'. (*Dictionary of American Biography*, vol. II, 1958, 433.)

[13]George Copway, *Organization of a New Indian Territory, East of the Missouri River* (New York: S.W. Benedict, 1850), 19.

[14]George Copway, *Recollections*, 26.

[15]*Ibid.*, 10-12.

[16]George Copway, *The Traditional History and Characteristic Sketches of the Ojibwa Nation* (London: 1850; Toronto: Coles Canadiana, 1972), v.

[17]*Ibid.*, 108-9.

[18]*Ibid.*, 123.

[19]*Ibid.*, 124-7.

[20]Anna Jameson, *Winter Studies and Summer Rambles in Canada* (London, 1838; Toronto: Coles Canadiana, 1972), 80.

[21]George Copway, *Running Sketches* (New York: J.C. Riker, 1851), 18.

[22]*Ibid.*, 17, 18.

[23]In his autobiography (1847) Copway stated that 'it would be presumptuous in one, who has but recently been brought out of a wild and savage state; and who has since received but three years' schooling, to undertake without any assistance, to publish to the world a work of any kind' (vii). According to

Donald B. Smith, it is probable that Elizabeth helped her husband—suggesting, for example, the quotations from Shakespeare and Pope that are in his *History* (1850) as well as the German and French words and the lengthy passage from Byron in *Running Sketches* (1851).

[24]George Henry, letter dated 10 March 1837 quoted in the *Christian Guardian* (29 March 1837), 82.

[25]Quoted in Donald B. Smith, 'Maungwudaus Goes Abroad', *The Beaver* (Autumn, 1976), 5.

[26]George Henry, *An Account of the Chippewa Indians* (Boston: published by the author, 1848), 3-8.

[27]Peter Jacobs, *Journal* (New York: 1853), 9-10.

[28]*The Wesleyan Missionary Notices Relating Principally to the Foreign Missions* (June and July 1851), 110.

[29]*Ibid.*, 111, 112.

[30]*The Wesleyan Missionary Notices Relating Principally to the Foreign Missions* (April 1850), 59-60.

[31]Jim Johanson, *Indian Preacher* (Forest, Ont.: Pole Printing), n.p.

[32]*Ibid.*, n.p.

[33]*Forty-sixth Annual Report of the Missionary Society of the Wesleyan Methodist Church in Canada from June 1870 to June 1871* (Toronto: Printed for the Wesleyan Missionary Society, 1871), xxvii-xxviii, quoted in Johanson.

[34]*Christian Guardian* (10 May 1854), 120.

[35]From the first issue of *The Literary Voyager*, December 1826, quoted in *Schoolcraft: The Literary Voyager or Muzzeniegun* edited and with an Introduction by Philip P. Mason (Michigan State University Press, 1962), 8.

[36]Katherine Pettipas, *The Diary of the Reverend Henry Budd, 1870-1875* (Winnipeg: Hignell, 1974), 172.

[37]Peter Jones Collection, Victoria University Library, University of Toronto.

[38]*Ibid.*

[39]*Ontario Indian*, III, 12 (December 1980), 25.

[40]From the Catherine S. Sutton file in the County of Grey Owen Sound Museum.

[41]Peter Jones, *History of the Ojebway Indians* (Freeport, 1861, Rpt, 1970), 196.

[42]*Ibid.*, 29.

[43]In *I Tell You Now. Autobiographical Essays by Native American Writers*, its editors, Brian Swann and Arnold Krupat, state that 'Although the tribes, like people the world over, kept material as well as mental records of collective and personal experience, the notion of telling the whole of any one individual's life or taking merely personal experience as of particular significance was, in the most literal way, foreign to them, if not also repugnant.'

CHAPTER III: 1850-1914

[1]Peter Dooyentate Clark, *Origin and Traditional History of the Wyandotts* (Toronto, 1870), iii.

[2]*Ibid.*, 46-7.

[3]Louis Jackson, *Our Caughnawagas in Egypt* (Montreal: Wm. Drysdale & Co., 1885), 25-6.

[4]Francis Assikinack, 'Social and Warlike Customs of the Odahwah Indians', *Canadian Journal* (New Series, III, 1858), 300-1.
[5]Letter quoted in the *Citizen*, Ottawa, on 17 January 1901, taken from *The Times* of London (2 January 1901). Clipping in Ontario Archives.
[6]Quoted in an unidentified newspaper clipping in the Hamilton Library file (Canada—Biography).
[7]Quoted in a promotional brochure (p. 6) in the William Kirby Papers, Ontario Archives.
[8]Pauline Johnson, *Flint and Feather* (Toronto: Musson, 1931), 94. This poem was first published in *Canadian Born* (1903).
[9]*Ibid.*, 3-5. This poem was first published in *The White Wampum* (1894).
[10]Letter in the Queen's University Archives.
[11]Pauline Johnson, *The Moccasin Maker* (Toronto: William Briggs, 1913), 9-10.
[12]Pauline Johnson, *The Shagganappi* (Toronto: Ryerson, 1913), 8.
[13]*Sessional papers #16, Dominion of Canada Council Report of the Department of Indian Affairs for the year ended 31 December 1889* (Ottawa: Queen's Printer, 1889).
[14]Letter in the William Kirby Papers, Ontario Archives.
[15]Alexander Morris, *The Treaties of Canada with the Indians, 1880* (Toronto: Coles Canadiana, 1971), 272.
[16]*The Queen v. Louis Riel* (Toronto: University of Toronto Press, 1974), 312-13.
[17]John Peter Turner, *The North-West Mounted Police, 1873-1893* (Ottawa: King's Printer, 1950), II, 244.
[18]Morris, *The Treaties of Canada with the Indians, 1880*, 174.
[19]J.W. Grant MacEwan, *Portraits from the Plains* (Toronto: McGraw-Hill Ryerson, 1971), 111-12.
[20]*Victoria Daily Colonist* (1 April 1896), 6.

CHAPTER IV: 1914-1969

[1]Grey Owl, *Tales of an Empty Cabin* (Toronto: Macmillan, 1936), 91-5.
[2]Norma Sluman and Jean Goodwill, *John Tootoosis: Biography of a Cree Leader* (Ottawa, Golden Dog Press, 1982), 86.
[3]National Archives of Canada, RG10, vol. 3211, File 527787, pt. 1.
[4]Norma Sluman and Jean Goodwill, *John Tootoosis*, 133.
[5]*Deskaheh: Iroquois Statesman and Patriot* (Rooseveltown, N.Y.: Askwesasne Notes, no year), 13-19.
[6]*Special Joint Committee of the Senate and the House of Commons Appointed to Examine and Consider the Indian Act* (Ottawa: Edmund Cloutier, 1946), 420-1.

CHAPTER V: 1970-1979

[1]Mike Mountain Horse, *My People the Bloods* (Calgary: Glenbow-Alberta Institute, 1979), x.
[2]Lenore Keeshig-Tobias, 'Stop Stealing Native Stories', *Globe and Mail*, 26 January 1990.
[3]Basil H. Johnston, *Moosemeat and Wild Rice* (Toronto: McClelland & Stewart, 1978), 73.
[4]*Ibid.*, 7.
[5]*Ibid.*, 174-5.

[6]*Ibid.*, 9.

[7]Jon C. Stott, 'A Conversation with Maria Campbell', *Canadian Children's Literature* (No. 31/32, 1983), 19.

[8]Marty Dunn, *Red on White: The Biography of Duke Redbird* (Toronto: New Press, 1971), 38.

[9]D. Bruce Sealey and Verna J. Kirkness, *Indians Without Tepees* (Agincourt: Book Society, 1974), ix.

[10]Duke Redbird, *Loveshine and Red Wine* (Cutler, Ont.: Woodland Studios Publishing, 1981).

[11]George Kenny, *Indians Don't Cry* (Toronto: Chimo, 1977), 18.

[12]Rita Joe, *Poems of Rita Joe* (Halifax: Abanaki, 1978), 9:I.

[13]Chief Dan George, *My Heart Soars* (Saanichton, B.C.: Hancock House, 1974), 78.

[14]Ben Abel, *Wisdom of Indian Poetry* (Cobalt: Highway Book Shop, 1976), 53.

[15]Daniel David Moses, *Delicate Bodies* (Vancouver, blewointment Press, 1978).

CHAPTER VI: 1980-1989

[1]This statement by Paula Gunn Allen is interesting: 'Traditional tribal narratives possess a circular structure, incorporating event within event, piling meaning upon meaning, until the accretion results in a story. The structure of tribal narratives . . . is quite unlike that of western fiction; it is not tied to any particular time line, main character, or event.' *The Sacred Hoop* (Boston: Beacon Press, 1986), 79.

[2]Three books by Lee Maracle will appear in 1990: *Seeds*, a collection of poetry, published by Write-On Press; *Sojourner's Truth and Other Stories*, published by Press Gang; and a collaborative work with Daphne Marlatt, Betsy Warland, and Sky Lee, *Telling It: Building Language Across Cultures*, also published by Press Gang.

[3]A number of other oral histories have been published: *Speaking Together: Canada's Native Women*, published in 1975 by the Secretary of State to commemorate International Women's Year, includes such women activists as Kahn Tineta Horn, Alanis Obamsawin, Eleanor Brass, and Jane Willis. *In Our Own Words: Northern Saskatchewan Métis Women Speak Out* (1986), edited by Dolores T. Poelzer and Irene A. Poelzer from taped conversations, was published by Lindenblatt and Hamonic Publishing, Saskatoon. In 1987 Pemmican Publications published *Ste. Madeleine: Community Without a Town: Métis Elders in Interview*, edited by Ken and Victoria Zeilig.

[4]Thomas King, 'The Voice and the Performance of the Storyteller', *Globe and Mail* (10 February 1990), C-7.

[5]Redbird wrote a commemorative poem entitled 'The Canadian Museum of Civilization' on the occasion of the opening of that museum in Hull in June 1989. It was published in *Soirée Asticiou*, 22 June 1989.

[6]In Nancy Wigston, 'Nanabush in the City', *Books in Canada* (March 1989), 9.

[7]In his 1925 radio address Deskaheh also advocated sovereignty for the Mohawk nation. See pages 102-5.

[8]Liam Lacey and Deborra Schug, 'Trends of the Eighties and What to Expect Next Decade', *Globe and Mail* (1 January 1990), C-7.

[9]The Association for Native Development in the Performing and Visual Arts was founded by the late Jim Buller, who believed that theatre lent power to the self-image of native communities. The Native Theatre School has evolved as one of its most successful programs.

[10]The Native Drug and Alcohol Program utilizes this form of instruction and treatment.

[11]In Jon Kaplan, 'Translating the Spoken Word to Native Theatre Writing', Now (27 November-3 December 1986), 31.

[12]In Nancy Wigston, 'Nanabush in the City', Books in Canada (March 1989), 8.

[13]In Jon Kaplan, 'Translating the Spoken Word . . .', 31.

[14]Ibid.

[15]Ray Conlogue, 'Another Triumph for Highway', Globe and Mail (10 February 1989), A-18.

[16]According to Kennetch Charlette, who played Darrel Shallafoe in the play, 'This mythological world has almost been forgotten . . . and it's up to this generation to bring it back to life. I'm happy and proud to be part of the generation that's helping the circle to come around again.' Quoted in 'Play Gives New Life to Ojibway Myths' by Jon Kaplan in Now (8-14 February 1990).

[17]The proposed extension of logging of white-pine stands in the Temagami area has caused conflict among loggers, environmentalists, the provincial government, and native people. Potts led the blockade of the Red Squirrel Road (1989) to prevent logging until the Band's land-claims were settled, and insists that logging techniques must be compatible with native hunting and trapping in order to ensure the regeneration of the forest.

[18]Quoted in Hansard, 'Official Reports of Debates Legislative Assembly of Ontario Standing Committee on Resources Development, Temagami District Resources, R-1555-2, R-1600-1'. In May 1990 the Ontario government decided to allow native bands to help decide the fate of Temagami forests.

[19]Quoted in 'Trends of the Eighties, and What to Expect Next Decade' by Liam Lacey and Deborra Schug, in the Globe and Mail (1 January 1990), C-7.

CONCLUSION

[1]'The truth is the most important thing we have to offer the world,' Paula Gunn Allen said in an interview with Susan Cole, Now (24-30 May 1990), 22.

[2]According to Brian Richmond of Theatre Passe Muraille, 'Canadian theatre has been too narrow for too long. The voices we let in have traditionally been white voices that mirror only a portion of our society. The native authors are an invigorating blast of fresh air.' Quoted in Imperial Oil Review (Winter 1989), 23.

Index

NATIVE LITERATURE IN CANADA

From the Oral Tradition to the Present

PENNY PETRONE

This is the first critical study of the literature of Canada's native peoples, which at long last is commanding the attention it deserves. Focusing on the work of Indians and Métis, and beginning with an examination of the oral tradition from which their literature grew, and that continues today, it discusses both works generically classified as literature, and forms such as speeches that are significant for their eloquent expression of protest and alienation. Indeed, it is impossible to describe and quote from much of this material without conveying more than three centuries of political and social dissatisfaction.

Orations, sermons, petitions, letters, journals, autobiographies, historical and travel writings, and journalism are considered, as well as short stories, novels, poetry, drama, traditional tales, and essays. The Indian sensibility and imagination—reflected in modes of literary expression, figurative language and symbols, spiritual and religious concepts, the visionary element—are seen to have given birth to a rich literature and a unique aesthetic that are evident in the many quotations.

Ranging from the seventeenth century to the recent publications of Maria Campbell, Beatrice Culleton, Ruby Slipperjack, Basil H. Johnston, Daniel David Moses, Tomson Highway, and Thomas King, among many others, this is an illuminating and timely survey that will greatly interest, and inform, natives and non-natives alike.

PENNY PETRONE, Professor Emeritus of Lakehead University, edited *First People, First Voices* and *Northern Voices: Inuit Writing in English*. She is an honorary chief of the Gull Lake Ojibway.

ISBN 0-19-540796-2

OXFORD UNIVERSITY PRESS

9 780195 407969

7 404TF 950
91 24 BR P 4147